As I moved from room to room, finding fresh disorder and damage at every turn, and fighting my revulsion at the smell of smoke, I had the feeling there was something ugly, something evil all around me—a presence I could almost touch. And I saw again, with sudden shock, those long, black strands of canvas, the charred remnants of the awning, casting elongated, dark shadows in the morning sunlight. That was the last party I ever gave in the house on the crooked street.

Vari-Vue International, Inc., Mt. Vernon, New York, has produced this cover, designed to visually entice the reader with the drama and excitement contained in the book.

Vari-Vue®, the registered trade name for the first mass-produced printed Lenticular products, requires very specialized camera work, precise printing register, and forming of the overlay lens that projects the image to your two eyes, adding a dimension not present in conventional printing.

THE
INTRUDERS

Pat Montandon

A FAWCETT CREST BOOK

Fawcett Publications, Inc., Greenwich, Connecticut

THE INTRUDERS

THIS BOOK CONTAINS THE COMPLETE TEXT OF THE
ORIGINAL HARDCOVER EDITION

A Fawcett Crest Book reprinted by arrangement with Coward,
McCann & Geoghegan, Inc.

ISBN: 0-449-22963-7

Library of Congress Catalog Card Number: 74-16638

Selection of the Universe Book Club

Printed in the United States of America

First printing: September 1976

1 2 3 4 5 6 7 8 9 10

Contents

*To Alfred Wilsey, who saved my life
and then made it worth living,
and Sean,
an added dividend of Love*

In Memory
of
Mary Lou Ward
Vera Scott
and
Carolyn

Preface

Almost five years have passed since the events recorded in these pages, events which affected not only me personally, but the lives of a number of people to whom I was tied by close bonds of affection. The distress, the anguish I suffered over a relatively short period of years made me reluctant to reopen old wounds. For a long time I shut off all recollection.

The lingering doubts that remained in my subconscious about the cause of those events, and the tragedies which developed from them, have been pressing in on me, now that I can look at them in a calmer frame of mind. And although I have felt an increasing compulsion to go back in time and dig deeply for causes and reasons for the inexplicable happenings, I held back for a while, as some of my researches began to suggest psychic, supranormal explanations, too farfetched, too bizarre for me to pursue, still less to share with others. I have never been a devotee of the supernatural, and yet it seemed some of the threads of my enquiries were leading irresistibly in that direction.

My nagging doubts about the final tragedy were eventually resolved on rereading a certain coroner's report, which raised such extraordinary speculations in my mind, I began to feel the need not only to research, but to write down an account of what I discovered. There is always a risk of ridicule in relating a series of events that do not seem to have a rational, scientific explanation. At least I can vouch that they happened as I describe them in the chapters that follow. The only concessions or modifications I have made have been to alter or omit a few names and incidents in order to protect the innocent and save the guilty from embarrassment.

San Francisco, 1974   PAT MONTANDON

1

The House on the
Crooked Street

Looking back, I feel that those were happy times, the days I spent during the mid-sixties in the house on Lombard Street—at any rate, at first. And perhaps the house had something to do with it. It was an old house, as San Francisco houses go in that part of town called Russian Hill, for it must have been built in the year of the earthquake. I have looked into the records since, in search of anything that might shed some light on what happened later, and they have given some precise details, although whether they have any significant bearing on what concerned me so closely, I have yet to uncover. I did learn that early in the nineteenth century the area had been used as a cemetery for Russian soldiers, since their orthodox countrymen had not been allowed to bury them in the Catholic Mission Dolores; additionally, I discovered that the same site had been used as a place for public hangings. At least I know that the house itself began as a family home, on three floors arranged with that charming disregard of symmetry or even logic that often characterizes an edifice adapted to the contours of a steep hill. And certainly, the irregular course of that block of Lombard Street, careening down its erratic length, might lead any imaginative architect to lose his head a little, and echo in his building the headlong convolutions, twists and bends that still make the unwary motorist wish he had started more slowly or knew in advance what was ahead around the next bend in the road and over those innocent-looking hydrangeas.

Since the house was on the switchback course, it was always a little safer to reach it by tripping down the path from the summit, closest to the cable car stop; for the slope was, so to speak, lying in wait for occasional catastrophes, when automobiles out of control from brake failure or simple miscalculation, roared out into the street below, and cannonaded into the parked cars on either side of the roadway.

The sound of rending metal was an integral part of living on the famous crooked street, as were the sounds of the foghorns booming through the nights, or even in the daytime when the mist was thick. And there was a certain comforting quality even in their mournful hooting.

Yes, they were happy, those days I spent in the house. It is true I had only an apartment there, but it seemed to be all mine; and at times in some ways it was. I was happy in all aspects of my life at once. Every side of it seemed touched with success. I enjoyed the friendship and affection of many people, famous and obscure; work as a television performer for KGO, an affiliate of the American Broadcasting Company, was a pleasure, and brought more strands of association to color my life. And a certain gift for entertaining had made my parties widely and flatteringly publicized. The poverty and tragedies of my childhood as seventh child of an Oklahoma Nazarene minister were far behind, and I seemed to move on a buoyant current of popularity and fulfillment, all the more welcome to me, and even unexpected, after the trauma of a divorce, and the daily drudgery of my earlier life as a sales girl.

And at the end of each day, there was the house, a welcoming haven, wonderfully separated from the rest of the world. A pair of ten-foot black gates opened the way. As one ascended the steps, a little Dutch garden with formal beds led off to the left, with some standard roses setting the scale, and trees bending down branches to form shady places—including the gnarled old magnolia that erupted into blossom in the spring and canopied over the garden table and chairs.

Up the first flight of stairs, around another corner, and up a further ascent past an eighteenth-century garden figure on a plinth, suddenly one encountered the front door. Once across the threshold, one could see that the building had originally been interconnected. A large stained-glass window cast colorful shadows on the right wall, and beyond it, a graceful staircase led to an upper floor. My apartment opened off this entrance hall, in what was thought to have been the living room of the family of the first owners, and above me was another apartment, which I was sure started life as a ballroom.

My front door opened into a living room, white walled and bright, although it faced north. Large windows on that side framed a view across San Francisco Bay, overlooking Fisherman's Wharf and the Bay Bridge. A long couch, following the line of the windows, let me sit and watch the passing sea traffic, and the yachts dancing in the sunlight, or mysteriously wreathed in the fog which stole across the Bay; its soft veil descended at almost predictable intervals in the summer months, and with disconcerting and erratic suddenness throughout the rest of the year.

Sometimes, even now, when I come back home after dark, in the winter months, swathed in the damp coldness of the fog, I can relive those moments when the aureole of angel's hair around the streetlights would give me a lift of spirit that bore me up the stairs, around the twisted walks, until I reached the security of my own door, and my own familiar rooms, to be greeted by Dog, my white Lhasa apso, with a torrent of joyful barking. And in the rooms were all the brightness of my favorite colors, harmonies of the cheerful oranges and pinks I also loved to wear.

Nowadays I can look down on those canyons of buildings, to where the house still stands, on the crooked street, and questions cross my mind. How can a house change a person's life? Or was it the people I knew? Or again, some inexplicable forces or powers that escape our knowledge?

In those crowded days I felt secure and confident, and everything I did seemed to turn toward success.

My television program was billed as *Pat's Prize Movie.* When I first started the show, I merely introduced the picture; usually oldies like Jeanette MacDonald and Clark Gable, together in *San Francisco,* or one of the endless Betty Grable musicals. But as I became more at ease on television, I was given "talk time" that eventually encompassed a full twenty-minute spread over a two-hour interval, wedged between commercials for Aileen Feather's reducing methods and Mrs. Olson's coffee.

As a novice TV performer, I pulled a number of ridiculous boners like calling Joan Fontaine Olivia De Havilland and announcing in what I hoped were mellow tones at the end of my show: "Now stay tuned for Safeway Sweepstakes," which was news to Safeway. And the sponsor for Supermarket Sweeps was not too happy either.

By the time I had relaxed into the format, I found I loved communicating with my audience. The camera was very much alive for me and I always felt as if I were talking to one person—a person who was attentive, attractive, and receptive. I used my talk time to read poetry, discuss the philosophy of that day's film, or talk about makeup. (I once had the nerve to go on barefaced and do a step-by-step makeup demonstration. I blanch at the thought of such a thing now.)

Whatever I was doing, I must have been doing it right, because the ratings soared and the mail poured in, sometimes as many as seventy-five to a hundred letters a day, until I realized I couldn't cope with it. Papers were strewn everywhere, spilling off chairs and tables, stacked on every available surface. It was clearly time I had some help, so I advertised for a secretary. Well, perhaps not quite a secretary—something more, something less. My ad read: "Help wanted. Girl Friday. Friend, secretary, flexible hours, flexible salary—to meet the challenge of the moment!"

It was January, 1968, and I did not count on much response, for the Bay Area was unexpectedly hit by a newspaper strike. It was disappointing all the same—five replies. Only one sounded possible: Mary Louise Ward. I called her the next day, and was daunted by a loud background blast of rock and roll. "This is a hopeless waste of time," I thought, "I'll get it over with as quickly as possible," and set a time for us to meet the following morning.

Promptly at eleven the doorbell rang and I found myself facing a lovely, slender woman of about forty-three, wearing a bright yellow coat. There was a light, happy quality about her, a radiance that reminded me of someone I knew—Virginia Brown—and by a strange coincidence, it turned out they were friends. After the final tragedy, Virginia planted a memorial tree on a hillside in the Napa Valley.

I shall have to move backward and forward in speaking of Mary Lou (that was the name that soon fell into place instead of Mary Louise, just as I was Patsy Lou to her) for she became my dearest friend, as I believe I was hers—each dependent on, and equally needing the other.

When she told me her husband had died only the previous year, her face clouded: She looked away. They had walked out of their house one bright, sunny day, and suddenly he collapsed from a heart attack and was gone. She had treasured her marriage and, even though they had been married for twelve years, they were like newlyweds. They had been intensely in love, and he had been a warm and conscientious father to their children—two girls, Jeannie and Robin, by a first marriage, and a son, Jimmy, from the second.

I did not hear all these details at once, nor did I find out until later that the happy surface she showed me that first day had sadness beneath it. Although she had the three children, she felt they no longer needed her. And yet she needed to look after someone. Luckily for me, I was able to fill one small gap—someone to be helped, someone whose problems presented a challenge—and she tore into my letters the very next day. Not only did she answer my mail, she kept my engagements straight and went with me on lecture tours. She would face every crisis with a demure, "I'm just Meeting the Challenge of the Moment," and we, and the crisis, would both dissolve in laughter.

That, of course, belongs to a later time. By the end of that first interview—an interview that turned into a friendly visit—I had forgotton all about the cacophony on the telephone that seemed so entirely out of key with the chic, sensitive personality, for whom I had felt an instant sympathy. I might have guessed. It was her twelve-year-old son who had been responsible for the racket. I also knew there was no need to look further for help.

It was an informal arrangement. Mary Lou came when she could and always when I needed her. I never think of her as motionless, a figure remembered in a still photograph. She was always quick; she darted.

Once, when I was about to give a talk to a group of some five hundred women, I spilled something on my long evening gown. Mary Lou immediately rose to the occasion; she whipped off her own dress and helped me change into it. Then, entirely unruffled, she put on a coat and we proceeded as though nothing had happened. My audience, eagerly waiting to welcome advice on good taste and haute couture, must have wondered why I was wearing evening sandals with a houndstooth check—if challenged I suppose I could have said I was simply setting a trend.

We were really rather alike, both unpredictable. I remember coming home one morning to find, surprisingly, that I was hostess to an unexpected assortment of guests in the garden, none of whom I knew, with the exception of one elderly gentleman whom Mary Lou invited to everything because she felt he was so lonely. We had dubbed him "The Boy Friend." Mary Lou had decided the day was too glorious to waste, so she had invited anyone who passed by on the crooked street to have a bit of lunch.

An important part of Mary Lou's job became "finding solutions to insoluble problems." Faced with these, she had an undeflectable tenacity. No dust was left in the crack, she was a thorough investigator, and she set about the pursuit with a bubbling gaiety and cheerfulness, however much work or trouble it entailed. The television correspondence continually turned up challenges—requests for all sorts of unlikely material—and of course, every inquiry had to be answered as best we could.

One letter especially took Mary Lou's fancy: an unmarried woman's request for a love potion. She took it upon herself to satisfy the poor lonely spinster's wish with all the ardor of a crusade. And, inevitably, one of San Francisco's well-known characters was a self-professed suzerain of a devil worship cult, a man devoted to the black arts, witchcraft, demonology and other hermetic mysteries—the chosen representative of Satan himself—Anton Szander La Vey. He, if anyone, said Mary Lou, would know how to brew a love potion—such a brew, perhaps, as Madame de Montespan obtained from the widow Voisin to give to Louis XIV. Mary Lou's eyes sparkled at the thought, and she badgered me to call and request a recipe. Against my better judgment, I did so, and he readily agreed to supply a "guaranteed" aphrodisiac, if I went to his house.

I have never been drawn to the occult, still less wished to meddle with the more sinister preoccupations of Satanism and I was supremely reluctant to involve myself in what I foresaw as a possibly embarrassing experience. My objections were overruled by Mary Lou's enthusiasm, and I found myself one evening approaching the threshold of the Master's house. It was certainly sinister enough—painted entirely in black, and showing no sign of light or life. I was already prepared to retreat, but Mary Lou was adamant, and I knocked at the front door. No answer, and I turned to leave, sighing in relief. Mary Lou urged me to try again. This time the door swung slowly open, and a tall, broad-shouldered, bald-headed figure dressed in black trousers, boots, and a scarlet satin shirt open at the throat, stood in the doorway. The Master Himself. His face was surprisingly kind in spite of his black Fu Manchu mustache and pointed devil's beard.

"I hope we're not disturbing you," I stammered, feeling the conventional remark sounded idiotic under the circumstances. But to my chagrin, he passed over my protestations with a wave of the hand and graciously invited us in.

Down a long hallway he ushered us past several unlit rooms into a small dark chamber, in which we could dimly perceive skulls, and other equally disquieting objects ranged on shelves and tables. I was at first slightly reassured to find myself sitting in front of a coffee table until I slowly registered that it was an upended tombstone. The black-robed figure disappeared as silently as he had materialized, and returned shortly with two liqueur glasses filled with layers of pink and purple fluid, which he offered us.

I more than a little suspected that the drink might be one of several versions of the beverage whose recipe we sought, which may have been doing Mr. La Vey an injustice. At any rate, I summoned my best manners, held the glass in my hand, and made as if to sip from it, admiring the colors. Its aroma was overpowering and I quickly placed it on the tombstone coffee table in front of me. Mary Lou downed hers, obviously enjoying herself enormously.

"I'm very fond of animals," said La Vey, fondling a stuffed wolf, whose head peered menacingly out from under a tall armoire with a skull standing on top. As my eyes became accustomed to the dim lighting, I could see the other creatures which inhabited it. An owl glared down at us from its wall perch and I soon discerned, thankfully, that it was not alive; two ravens and a gigantic stuffed rat skulked atop a bookcase. I felt even more uncomfortable remembering the newspaper accounts of La Vey's mascot, or rather, "familiar," a full-grown lion named Togare, which I knew lived in the backyard. I kept listening nervously for a roar.

"Would you like to see more of the house?" he asked politely.

"Yes," said Mary Lou eagerly.

I hesitated until his steely eyes fastened on me. I quickly stammered, "Sure . . . yes . . . sure." He led us down a narrow hall into another room, dominated by a glass case. I was no longer startled to see it housed a skeleton.

"Lovely, don't you think? Notice the massive eruptions on the bones, the abnormally extended rib cage, the toes as long as most people's fingers."

"Is it human?" Mary Lou asked.

"In life," continued La Vey, "this person resembled a monster."

I edged toward the door flexing my own fingers and wishing we were in northern Siberia.

"What are you doing?" Mary Lou asked. I followed her gaze to the fireplace. I saw La Vey tug at the mantel and to my horrified astonishment the entire section of wall swung outward, revealing a cavern and shadowy stonework.

"There's a secret passage in every room in the house," he said, closing the space. As he talked, he slowly rubbed the skull hanging on a chain round his neck.

"How about another liqueur?" he asked.

I was feeling increasingly discomfited and blurted out, "We've got to go," inventing a mythical appointment. La Vey vanished again into the blackness and reemerged smiling—Satanically? I asked myself—and holding aloft a small piece of red paper, which he handed me with a slight bow. We thanked him profusely and were ushered once more into a shadowy foyer, where our host pointed out yet another small, eerie, intimidating room, which he explained was a classroom for his witches' school.

Once out of the house on California Street (he has since moved his Church of Satan to southern California) and into the comparative safety of a car, Mary Lou burst into peals of laughter and continued alternately roaring and giggling over the episode all the way home. And the nearer we got to Lombard Street, the funnier we found it.

As we drove the crooked street, Mary Lou read the love potion ingredients aloud.

"*Lovey Sauce. One two ounce jar instant coffee.*"

"What brand?" I asked.

"Doesn't say," she replied.

"*One fifth vodka.*

"*One vanilla bean.*

"*One-half ounce mandrake root (whole).*"

"Where can we get that?" I wondered. "And what is it?"

"*One-half cup sugar.*"

"Got that."

"One cup water."

"Got that too."

"Dissolve coffee, sugar in hot water. Add this to vodka which has been poured into crock or jug of ample size to contain all ingredients. Drop vanilla bean and mandrake into jug. Allow to set, stirring occasionally for one month."

"What if she's in a hurry?" I said.

"Too bad," Mary Lou replied.

"Serve in one-ounce portions as after dinner drink or over ice cream. CAUTION: Do not give love object too much or it will act as a laxative."

We were momentarily speechless.

Later I challenged Mary Lou to try the love potion on "The Boy Friend"—but alas, we couldn't locate the mandrake root. Whether the lonely lady of the letter was more successful, we unfortunately never heard.

After Mary Lou had been working with me for some time, I said, "M.L., it's time to give a party!" After all, I was in the middle of writing a book on party-giving, which had been accepted for publication by McGraw-Hill. I was thrilled at the prospect of having a book in print. I couldn't believe it really to be mine, as I had never actually learned to spell.

We were also busy sending out biographies to the cities the publisher wanted me to tour, as part of a national publicity campaign. The publishers had been most encouraging. They had told me they had already made plans for a second printing, based on their conviction my book would be one of their major releases of the coming season. My spirits danced; I was enthralled at the prospect.

Mary Lou, knowing I had no savings, worried over my future, and she murmured anxiously to me many times, "When your book comes out, you'll be able to put some money away. You know, Patsy Lou, you've got to think of the day when your glamour runs out and makeup won't help." She knew there were no rich parents in the background—quite the opposite. And in spite of making a good salary, I was spending it on clothes and entertaining. It was all a part of promoting my image, and although I often appeared to possess limitless funds, I had little or nothing in the bank. Everything I was doing then was part of a building process, one that involved spending money to make money—a dangerous gamble but the only way I could then see to make progress.

Nor did I have a special man in my life. Although I was dating a number of men, they could hardly be classified as romances. One, Bernt Lindström, was a design engineer and, among other things, had built a novelty car that included blue flowered upholstery, magazine racks, hair spray and perfume, a hair dryer, and a horn that played "A Pretty Girl Is Like a Melody."

And there was Robert Cohn, who lived in Los Angeles and produced movies. He was always exceptionally thoughtful and introduced me to fascinating people like Ernest K. Gann. In fact, at Ernie's insistence, we went out on the bay in a heavy fog at about eleven o'clock one evening in a small fishing boat. Ernie wanted to be sure Bob knew what the huge foghorn under the Golden Gate Bridge sounded like, because that was the sound he wanted reproduced in the film version of his novel *Of Good and Evil*. Unfortunately, the only sound Bob heard on that trip was me, begging to be taken back to shore before we were run down by a freighter.

I also dated Arthur Alarcon, a Superior Court Judge from Los Angeles, who had been in a near-fatal automobile accident near San Francisco. Since I was one of only three people he knew in the area, I had spent many hours at his bedside trying to cheer him. As a result, we had become good friends, but that was the extent of it.

There didn't seem to be anyone in San Francisco for me to build a life with—no one I could wholly rely on, although, goodness knows, I knew enough people. I had only myself. I had to be completely self-sufficient.

So I gave parties—even with nothing in reserve—and all my friends pitched in. Parties were like theater to me, and the preparation, weaving all the strands together in their proper sequence, was always more important to me than the event itself. I suppose in some way I felt a sense of self, of identity, in being known as a creative party-giver—an identity I hadn't achieved in any other way: The play was almost more real than the audience.

This was the moment, then, with the dizzying prospect of a best seller on my hands, that Mary Lou agreed was the proper time to give another party. "After all," she said, "how can they call you 'the Perle Mesta of the West,' when you haven't tossed a bash for almost a year?"

We turned over dozens of ideas, toying with this and rejecting that. Finally, we decided it would be fun to have an Astrology party, with crystal gazers and a palmist, and all sorts of cabalistic decorations. Astrology was very much the fad, and while I didn't believe a word of it, it was undeniably topical. The idea wasn't exactly new, as I had given a similar party several years before and it had been such an overwhelming success I thought it bore repeating.

Once the motif caught hold, various embellishments suggested themselves. Someone knew a man who could tell fortunes simply by casting shadows on a wall; there was that eerie mechanical doll at Playland at the beach that laughed and wheezed out, "I will tell your fortune." Perhaps I could borrow that. And with all those empty rooms upstairs, I could invite absolutely everyone! All was suddenly a ferment of preparation; invitations went out asking the guest to respond with his or her birth date. I planned to have a huge round panel hanging by the entrance, with the signs of the Zodiac on it, and everyone would have a birth sign pinned on. There would be a lot of easy ice-breaking as each guest tried to find a partner with the same sign. And welding all together would be an "occult" orchestra, strategically placed on the deck outside the library.

It promised to be a marvelous success, innocent fun. And yet, that is perhaps the moment when it all started to go wrong. I have been trying since to follow up all the clues and will endeavor to present them in some sort of order, though I have not yet been able to make up my own mind about them. And I suspect the reader will form his own conclusions. If I had to pinpoint a time, was it then that all the trouble started? And what was it that really happened? I know, at least, that I had no premonition of what was to follow.

2

Curses Not Loud, But Deep

The whole house was alive with movement. Although the invitations read nine o'clock, the guests arrived exceptionally early; some even at eight thirty, which was most unusual for San Francisco. They gathered in groups in front of the orange-, green-, and pink-felt panels hanging in the foyer, peering over each other's shoulder and excitedly identifying their birth signs.

I was completely occupied in moving from greeting newcomers to seeing that those who had already arrived were supplied food and drink, and the sort of company they liked; although I noticed they were entirely absorbed in the idea of having their fortunes told. The buzz of talk was a good sign, and the ripple of movement through the house, up stairs lit by rows of candles, and down again into the bedrooms below (which I had stripped of furniture and hung with tents in colorful striped felt), augured well. Somehow, with no press coverage because of the newspaper strike, I felt more relaxed than usual about the party's happy outcome. I had moved almost all the furniture out to allow guests to circulate freely. The door to my apartment, leading off the hall, had been taken off its hinges, and I had borrowed every potted palm I could find to cast mysterious shadows in each room. There was a fascinated group around the crystal-gazer. Another animated circle in a pool of light, surrounded the palmist, and delighted shivers of laughter were coming from a bunch clustered around the interpreter of shadows. Immersed as I was in seeing that all was running smoothly, I did not have time to have my own fortune told, and perhaps that was better.

I was worried about one thing. The Tarot card reader hadn't arrived. I knew nothing about him except that one of my friends had suggested him as a novelty—and now he was late. Mary Lou slipped quietly up to me at one point and asked what had happened. I shrugged and we returned to our preoccupation with the party.

When I had almost forgotten the Tarot man was expected, he swept into the sitting room and made his way to me. He was wearing a curious costume in green velvet, with a great pouf of feathers, and had brought an ill-assorted entourage of three or four people along with him. Additionally, he had a beard which, because of its fierce, red color, made him an unusual sight in any crowd. I concealed my annoyance at his late arrival and the uninvited guests and settled him down to his appointed place at the dining room table. I now discovered his name and that he regarded his presence as an immense favor to me. He was singularly imperious for one so small—but there he was, so I made the best of him.

He proceeded to read the cards, dropping each one on the table and peering at what the shuffle had brought. The hum of talk was increasing; drinks were being passed around as I moved from one group to another, exchanging a word here and there, separating incompatibles, escaping the clinging vines, and presenting what I hoped was a calm, poised profile to the world. As I moved through the steady chatter in a haze of cigarette smoke, I could see that Aubrey, leaning against a doorjamb, was deep in talk of horses with Stephanie; Paul was laying down the law, as usual, to a respectful circle; and from time to time, as our paths crossed, Mary Lou and I would exchange telegraphic signals, whenever I saw a trouble spot developing.

As I went near the Tarot reader's table, he suddenly stood up and demanded a drink. I said I would be happy to bring him one and started toward the bar. I was interrupted at every step—a word here and there, a quick smile for a friend—and in the bustle and swell of people and talk, I forgot the errand I had set out on. A further distraction came when I saw new arrivals at the door. I went to greet them—a slight acquaintance who had brought a complete stranger with him. One of the unvoiced hopes of the unattached hostess is always that she will meet an attractive male, and I paused long enough to note the stranger was fair, stocky, and intelligent-looking, and named Earl Raymond. Several of the single girls immediately moved in on him, and I thought, *Well, there goes the only attractive new face in town.*

Half an hour later I was back by the Tarot reader's table, and I could see at once he was in a towering rage, the absurd feathers trembling in his headdress, and wisps of hair emerging from beneath it. He almost spat at me: "You forgot my drink!" I felt embarrassed and apologetic.

"I'm sorry. I'll get you one—" But he didn't allow me to finish. He bolted to his feet, with his curious retinue following suit, and explaining loudly that he'd never been so insulted in his life. Quivering with rage, he directed a stream of abuse at me: He had never been treated so rudely . . . I was an insufferable, ungracious hostess . . . he was leaving, but not before he made certain I would never have any happy moments in that house again. He fixed me with a glare, his face puffed and distorted.

"I lay a curse upon you and this house. I do not forget, and I do not forgive. Remember that!" And sweeping up his cards into a satchel, he marched out of the house, followed by his uninviting and uninvited familiars.

I stared after him in shocked horror. Mary Lou, attracted by the commotion, came running over. She had heard only the last few words.

"What on earth provoked that?" she whispered anxiously.

"I don't know. . . . The woman who recommended him didn't prepare me for a scene, but she did say he went in for voodoo. I suppose that's one of the side effects."

The scene that had blown up so suddenly, had as suddenly vanished, and I was relieved only a few people had noticed. Fortunately, on all sides, I could see my guests were enjoying themselves. The cheerful hubbub was deafening, and conversations were broken into strands and fragments. The lovely colors of dresses were dappled with shadows as they passed beneath the palm fronds; deep voices, high voices, shrill voices, melded and mingled.

Snatches of conversation floated past: *"What d'you suppose she's meant to be! . . . Darling, she's not supposed to be anything, she always looks like that . . . I'm kept together with safety pins . . . Not Scotch tape? Scotch and safety pins . . . Have you had your palm read? The palmist is divine . . . If she weren't wearing quite so much jewelry, one might suppose some of it was real . . . You're a Leo? I always felt Virgo was more you. . . ."*

My observations were interrupted by a voice over my shoulder. It was the fair-haired man, Earl Raymond, whom I had welcomed earlier. We plunged into conversation, and I learned he was an architect, with one office in the San Francisco area and one in the East Bay. I felt flattered he had singled me out, considering the bevy of beauties who had surrounded him. I found him amusing and witty, though his sarcastic references to the Tarot reader's curse showed he had not missed the incident, and even seemed to dwell on it. It was with a tinge of regret that I was torn away from him by the demands of the party, but not before he had promised to call me soon.

One never relaxes, of course, until the last guest has left, the maids and the barmen thanked, paid, and dismissed. But the reluctant departures, the effusive farewells, the extra trouble each guest seemed to take to say something appreciative on leaving, told me the party had been a brilliant success.

The house, of course, as after every festivity, looked as though a cyclone had struck. Empty of furniture, every room had an abandoned look. There were the usual trails from drinks accidentally spilled, cigarette ash in gray daubs on carpets, cutlery and plates higgledy-piggledy in the kitchen. Still, I saw all the sparkling company again, moving in a colorful tide. I was exhausted but happy, and sleep came easily.

The party ended, but my woes were just beginning. The Tarot card man had been true to his curse. I had many friends at the newspapers at that time, and, in the quiet hours during the strike, they called to tell me of an anonymous man who had telephoned them and criticized me sharply for the way, he alleged, I had treated him. Nor did that satisfy him. His next move was to call me, with fresh insults, new threats. "I've cursed your place," he hissed. "You're going to have a very unhappy life there. I'll never allow you a moment's peace or happiness." More followed in the same vein. I am giving the gist of what he said—the exact words I cannot recall, but the venom in his voice I shall never forget.

It was upsetting momentarily, but set against my busy and enjoyable life, it did not seem important, and life went on happily. I regarded the incident as one of the hazards of party-giving and of accepting the unfortunate advice of an acquaintance. I dismissed it from my mind—that is, until some two weeks later. . . .

I had been shopping downtown with Warren Arnold, a doctor friend of mine, early one Saturday afternoon, expecting to be home before dark. The afternoon progressed into early evening and we decided to go to a movie. When we got back to the house it was dark, and I had a feeling as I started up the stairs that something strange was in the air.

The front door opening into the foyer was unlocked, although it was always closed by a dead bolt, and my own front door, which gave access to the living room, was ajar. After the initial shock, Warren said half kiddingly. "You go inside and see what's wrong. I'll go across the street and phone the police." I took no notice of this, and on pure impulse I ran into the living room, seized the telephone, that was on a long cord, took it out into the foyer and called the police.

When the officers finally arrived, we found the apartment had been ransacked. Some jewelry, a mink jacket, a television set and a rather mangy tiger skin rug were missing. Headlines in the local papers the next day announced, PAT'S TIGER STOLEN! It was a help to have a little laugh after a shaky experience, and again, I was soon engrossed in my everyday routine. I collected some insurance and installed some more deadbolt locks. Even so, I felt a little insecure—an alien feeling for me

Of course I am not suggesting a physical connection between the break-in and the Tarot man's threats. That would have been too obvious, and I certainly did not associate them at the time. But imperceptibly, a series of happenings, some actual, others less tangible, began to shake my confidence.

I do remember one thing, though, that particularly disturbed me just then. After the burglary, there was a penetrating chill about the house. Try as I might, I could not get warm. I would turn the heat up, and even *with* the heat I would still feel cold. Friends who came to see me would often ask why I had turned the thermostat up to ninety, and I would have no easy explanation—although later on, I would notice they, too, would shiver and make some remark about my living room facing north. It was inexplicable, as though the cold emanated from the very walls and was proof against the sun's rays or man-made furnace.

The apartment was heated by a series of radiators. Two in the living room were installed under the wide windows overlooking the Bay. My white sofa hid one of the unsightly-looking things from view and the other was obscured by a round table covered by an off-white linen skirt draped to the floor, and serving as a lamp stand. There was another in the small hall opposite my miniature closet bar and immediately outside my bedroom door. Another was housed in the foyer in a niche next to the stained-glass window and its incessant hissing was a constant irritation to me.

My living room fireplace was a beauty, with a straw-colored marble hearth and mantel. It was constructed on a jog in the wall, and as a result I had heat from one side as well as the front. I learned to burn cannel coal in it for its long-lasting properties, and as the house grew colder, I kept a fire in it most of the time. Later, when I would awaken almost every night to pace the floor, it was reassuring to see the glow from the fireplace. And by adding a newspaper and a few chunks of coal, I could temporarily warm myself from the flame. Often I would bend into pretzel shape to test the radiators in back of the sofa and, finding them quite warm to the touch, would wonder aloud why, then, it was so cold in the room.

My landlord really became exasperated with me when I asked him for the third time to check the boiler in the basement as I was sure it was malfunctioning. He repeatedly assured me it was in perfect working order and would give me a half-hour dissertation on how much it cost to heat the building and how expensive service calls were. Finally, I would give up and merely push the thermostat still higher and hope it would help.

There is something evil about cold; fire is frightening, but a coldness that comes without warning, bringing with it a pervasive sense of gloom and depression, has a more insidious effect. And that others had noticed it did not add to my comfort.

Two nights after the break-in, I woke suddenly from a deep sleep without any apparent reason. My bedside alarm showed it was two in the morning, a time that was to have an increasing significance. I found myself shivering—the damp, dull coldness invaded the room. Then, I heard an unfamiliar whimpering and, throwing on a wrap, went into the living room. I realized at once that Dog, my Lhasa apso, who slept on the enclosed back porch, was whining desperately and scratching to be let in at the kitchen door.

I could not understand why, as he was normally the most peaceable of dogs, everybody's friend, and there was nobody to disturb him in the rooms above or the apartment below. The whole house was empty. The ballroom apartment had been vacant for several months and Evelyn Walker, the woman who rented the little one below, was in Europe on one of her frequent trips.

Dog's behavior became even stranger in succeeding days, and particularly in the dead of night, at about the same hour, at two o'clock, when he began to whimper frenziedly. He became so disturbed that he began to gnaw and worry his fur until he had chewed bare patches into sores.

Mary Lou suggested I take him to a vet to see if there was something physically wrong. The vet treated his symptoms, but he could offer no explanation of Dog's singular behavior. And his nightly agitation, distressing to witness, continued.

I had taken to going to bed very early to try to get

a good night's rest, as I had to get up at six to face the television cameras at eight o'clock. Turning off the telephone ensured I would not be disturbed. Nervous exhaustion would at first bring deep sleep, but in the early hours Dog would start his whining and scratching at the kitchen door, forcing me to get up. He began barking fiercely when he saw me, as though he wanted to tell me something, or warn me in his own way, and I noticed he was always shivering. I calmed him and carried him back to the bedroom, but natural sleep was over for the rest of the night, and I reluctantly took a sleeping pill. Soon I felt perpetually tired, and even if Dog did not wake me, which was exceptional, I fell into a pattern of arousing every night as the clock struck two.

Even in the daytime all the cheerfulness had gone. My home had become a dreary place despite its bright colors and the sunlight streaming into the front rooms. My footsteps dragged more and more slowly as I came nearer the house on my way from work, and when I stopped at the gate, I would look up at the gray-colored building high above me, torn with nameless dread of what waited for me within.

There was reason enough to wonder. There had been another strange incident that I did not discover until the night after that first disturbance. I woke up again in the middle of the night, at about two thirty, with the odd sensation of hearing footsteps outside. They appeared to ascend the stairs, come to the first landing, and pause; then go on to the second, followed by silence. I waited, with constricted throat and heart throbbing; I peeped through the draperies, but could see no one. The moonlight only cast deep formless shadows. I stood on my balcony for half an hour, then, finally, curiosity overcoming anxiety and caution, I stole out into the foyer and peered through the glass panes of the front door. All I could detect was the shadow of something, something that did not move, resting against the door.

I opened it cautiously, and a wreath of baling wire covered in dead flowers fell into the room. I stared at the obscene object, not wanting to go near or touch it, wondering who could have done such a thing. Then, impulsively I picked it up, flung it outside and bolted the door. I rushed back to my bedroom, feeling sick and breathless, and torn by questions. I lay on my bed reviewing all that had happened, tormented by self-doubt. What *was* happening? Why was my dog suddenly so obviously disturbed? Who could have done this thing tonight? And why the cold, eerie feeling about the house? What was happening to my life? Question on question turned over in my brain as hour after hour passed, and even the first light of day did nothing to dispel the encompassing blackness of my thoughts, or bring any answers. It was as though the house had a chill of darkness about it that made itself felt even in the daytime, and that shadowed the brightest electric light when dusk fell.

The next morning I tried to analyze the happening of the night before as rationally as I could, but it was still disturbing. Could the dead flowers have been a joke—a silly, tasteless one perhaps, but still a joke? If so, someone would eventually reveal himself. But there was a psychopathic senselessness to it, and I could not believe any of my friends, however misguided, would have devised it. And a second nagging thought occurred to me. Although I had heard those steps climb the stairs, pause, then climb the second flight, I had never heard them retreating down again. Whoever it was who left the wreath against the door—had he been standing watching me in the shadows? All the sick terror of the previous night came back as that thought sank into my consciousness and returned nightly to haunt me. No explanation of the incident ever came, and although the dead blooms were thrown away as hastily as possible, they appeared continually before my inner eye, and I could not get their evil immanence out of my mind.

Mary Lou became concerned about me; she saw how drawn I was looking, and she had already noticed the peculiar way Dog was behaving. She tried to lighten my schedule, growing more demanding all the time, by standing in for me on a number of occasions so I could have an early dinner, relax over television, and retire by nine. But I was to have no peace. Busy as I might be during the day, there was always the silent, echoing house to come back to in the evening—such a big house for one girl and one dog to occupy—some fifteen or sixteen rooms and a basement, and all empty but mine. In the past, when people asked me whether I was anxious at living in such an enormous place by myself, I would laugh, as I had never been afraid in my life, and in fact, enjoyed occasional solitude. It afforded a chance to read, or write, or just be, and I was intolerant of friends who were afraid of being alone.

Now they began to worry about me and to feel uncomfortable in the apartment. No one could explain why. There was an underlying sense of unpleasantness to the place; and they urged me, too, at least to find a roommate to prevent my being alone. I had long enjoyed my privacy and was reluctant to share my living quarters with a stranger. But when my landlord told me he had rented the upstairs ballroom apartment, I was delighted. In a few months I should at last have company in the house.

3

Of Good and Evil

I come from a large family: three brothers and four sisters, and the age gaps are wide. Eighteen years separate me from my eldest brother, and I have another who is eight years younger. Such wide differences do not make for close relationships. The one common bond was the strict, fundamentalist faith in which we had been brought up. Our life centered on the church, and the members of the congregation were our family. One consequence was that we were, as our father repeatedly told us, always expected to set an example. Looking perpetually over our shoulder were Big Brother and Big Sister, to ensure we were paragons of good behavior. As a result, we never experimented as other children normally do with worldly, sophisticated pleasures. For instance when one of my brothers came back late one night from a basketball game my mother threw him out of the house and he was forced to sleep in the garage. The smell of cigarette smoke detected on his jacket was enough to ensure his exile.

My mother was as strict with herself as she was with us. If we were not allowed to have playing cards in the house, neither did she ever wear jewelry—not even a wedding band. She knew, with complete faith and conviction, that personal adornment was sinful. We were taught to believe in the power of God and the reality of evil—dramatically reinforced by appropriate Biblical texts.

I do not want to suggest that either of my parents was harsh or cruel. Certainly we had a great feeling of love for each other, but the path of virtue was narrow, and we were expected to follow it. Our Sunday regimen was inflexible, endless. At the three services, my mother played the piano, my brothers and sisters sang, and I had to learn and recite reams of edifying poetry or long quotations from the Bible. I once tried to get away with the shortest one I could find—"Jesus wept"—but my mother would have none of it and made me learn two long passages as penance.

For all their strict attitude in bringing us up, my father and mother always set an example of Christian charity in dealing with others. Our home was open to any strangers who needed help, and the path to our door was marked by hobos with the secret signs that can be read by members of their fraternity and indicate a place of welcome. My mother had a huge pot of vegetable soup perpetually simmering on the back burner, and I sometimes felt we were feeding the multitude when we didn't have enough to fill our own bellies.

As I grew older and moved away from home, I had less contact with my family, as our paths had gone in different directions and my brothers and sisters lived at a considerable distance from me, with the exception of one brother, Carlos Montandon, in Hillsborough. There was no rupture between us, only a gently widening gap of activities, interests, and attitudes, and unfortunately it would no more have occurred to me to refer any of my problems to them than I should have expected to hear of theirs. They had their own concerns, and we kept such things to ourselves.

In spite of this, my early upbringing has always colored my later attitudes to people and events, and although I have broadened my outlook, I am inclined to apply stricter standards to, and make moral judgments about, myself in a way many people might find old-fashioned.

My father had died when I was fourteen; now, in 1968, my mother was in her middle seventies, living alone, in a small frame house in Fresno. She was as independent as ever, with her delightful sense of humor and wit undimmed.

It was with amusement that she read of my activities in the newspaper and descriptions of me as the "Jet-Set queen." And like Mother, in my naïveté, I thought others could see through the ridiculous title and appreciate the joke with me. It never occurred to me that anyone would take it seriously, especially since I rarely had the leisure or money to "jet" anywhere. In time the joke wore thin and the label became odious as the newspapers made consistent reference to me as the "glamorous Jet-Set queen."

When, later on, I was in the midst of my troubles, my mother spent many hours on her knees praying for help to avert the evil influences which surrounded me. Still, in San Francisco I was a long way from my origins in Oklahoma, and I was consequently surprised when my cousin Carolyn got in touch to ask if she could stay with me awhile.

Much as I valued my independence, I was secretly relieved to have someone with me in the house after the recent disturbances, and delighted to have Carolyn move into the library-cum-office room. Mary Lou merely moved her desk over a few paces, piled papers a little higher, and put in an extra filing cabinet which we needed anyway, as the papers stacked neatly on the sofa bed had to have a new home so Carolyn could have a bed of her own.

Admittedly, it wasn't the best of arrangements for Carolyn, but it worked well enough in the long run. She was then twenty-three: a tall, attractive girl, with softly curling brown hair, enormous cornflower-blue eyes, and the clear, unblemished complexion usually encountered only in novels. But her major asset was an outgoing personality which expressed itself in a radiating happiness and sparkle; and her ready willingness to help dovetailed beautifully with our busy program. She moved in with her few pieces of luggage, hung her clothes in the cramped closet quarters, and settled in as cousin, friend and occasional secretary.

I didn't expect Carolyn would stay with me for long, but it was comforting having her there, especially until the new upstairs tenants moved in. I was surprised to find that my natural reluctance to share my living quarters soon disappeared, although Carolyn, after all, was hardly a stranger: She was flesh-and-blood kin.

Late one evening, not long after her arrival, I was awakened by the sound of music. It was oddly insistent and annoying. I lay in my bed, listening to the repeated ornamentation of a long-forgotten tune. It wasn't particularly loud, but its persistence was unnerving. Eventually, not being able to sleep because of it, I stumbled out of bed and into the living room, intent on finding its source. I was dismayed to see all the lights on, and Carolyn prowling about, also bent on discovering where the annoying music was coming from.

"You sure do have inconsiderate neighbors," she said.

"Nothing like this has ever happened before. I can't imagine what's going on."

I peered down from my kitchen toward Evelyn's windows, as she was the only possible source of the sound. And then, in dawning alarm, I remembered she was away on a businesss trip.

I didn't want to frighten Carolyn. Should I say anything?

The music went on and on, like a record player with no reject, and it repeated endlessly the same tune—out of some dim memory I recalled its name, "Mocking Bird Hill"—a funny old song. Perhaps it was coming to us from a neighboring house, echoing or ricocheting from a strategically angled wall. Rather unlikely—but I was willing to discard logic.

Carolyn appeared distraught as she looked at me and said, uncertainly, "Pat, there's something weird about this apartment."

I could see she was scared and I was feeling far from happy myself. I put my arms around her and led her back to bed, reassuring her all the while, and mentally resolving I would discover what had gone wrong in that house. Because I knew, however much I tried to explain it away, that the sounds were coming from my very own walls. The music died out about two hours later, and it wasn't until 1974 that I discovered a valid connection between it and the building.

I didn't know where to turn for help, reluctant to approach any of my friends and not just for fear of ridicule. Neuroticism had never been my style; word would quickly get around that I was hearing things, and I didn't fancy the prospect. What had been happening to me clearly must have some rational explanation. Mary Lou was understanding, of course, but she was apt to shrug things off with a joke. Feeling not a little foolish, I went to the library to see if I could unearth some information there. I didn't know what to look for, or even precisely where to begin. At length I tracked down and explored some books—Hans Holzer's *Windows into the Past* which describes exploring history through ESP, and *This Baffling World*, by John Godwin, a study of unexplained natural phenomena. I even discovered a book on scientific psychic research in the Soviet Union. I found enough to realize that thoughtful, responsible people around the world gave credence to many strange aspects of psychic phenomena which cannot be explained by the normal processes of scientific logic. But this did not help in my own particular situation. I wanted advice as well as explanations.

The only person I knew connected even remotely with the paranormal or occult was the astrology woman I had gotten for the horoscope party—Fritzi Armstrong. She had been highly recommended by a number of friends, who said she had an extraordinary gift for charting horoscopes. She had been a big hit that evening, and she was pleasant in the bargain. I was at wit's end: Perhaps she could offer some counsel. I looked up her number and called her at the Metaphysical Town-Hall Book Shop.

After I identified myself, she drew in her breath sharply, and said, "Oh, Pat, dear, I hadn't wanted to tell you, but I have had an awful time since your party. I fell down the steps when I was leaving, hurrying to get to my cab. My leg is badly injured. In fact the driver had to practically carry me to his cab and then up to my flat." (Years later I learned she had lived through intense pain for a year. Two doctors had told her she must reconcile herself to permanent disability, and in desperation she had sought the help of a friend, a masseuse, who eventually succeeded in healing her.)

I was disturbed by what she said, and at the curious association of her accident with the very evening of the Tarot reader's curse.

"Fritzi, the strangest things have been happening over here in this apartment."

"What do you mean?"

"It's been a whole combination of things . . . difficult to explain . . . the house is always so cold—although I've had the heaters checked. Then there was a burglary . . . and I've heard footsteps, but I haven't seen anybody. What's shaken me most, though, is that last night I heard music, coming from inside the house . . . and there's nobody in it but my cousin Carolyn and me . . . and she heard it too."

"Well, my dear, these little things do happen sometimes. You must try not to worry about it. In my field, I'm constantly hearing such stories . . . It's a matter of getting the proper perspective."

"Isn't there anything I can do about it?"

"Well, maybe if I do your horoscope, it will help guide you, and you'll look at these little disturbances in a calmer frame of mind."

"Fritzi—I don't want to hurt your feelings, but I don't really believe in astrology, and—"

"That's all right, dear, many people don't, and again, many do. And I've found people have often been helped by the insights it's given them into their problems."

"Well, I guess I don't have anything to lose!"

"That's right. This will be my little present to you . . . I won't charge. Well, dear, I need to know your birth date, and the exact time, if you know it—the exact moment when you were born. And when did you move into the house—at what time of day?"

"I moved here in 1960—December twenty-seventh—about seven in the evening."

She went on to ask for additional details, always cautioning me to make them as precise as possible in order to arrive at my chart. Then she said firmly,

"Fine, Pat dear. That's all I need. And don't worry: You're a strong person. I'm sure you can handle whatever it is. Give me a little time to work all this out and I'll send you the results as soon as possible."

When we hung up, I felt relieved that I had found somebody sympathetic. I needed that, I thought, more than any occult advice, which was not a subject I had ever found particularly interesting before. In fact, I wasn't at all sure *what* I was getting into, but I was glad I'd done what I did. It was a relief to unburden myself. Whatever Mrs. Armstrong determined from the stars, or whatever she might discover about the menace of the house would be, I thought, an interesting and entertaining dividend. I hadn't even considered taking such things seriously yet.

If I had been more introspective, or prescient, I might have wondered why everything I touched at that time seemed to go awry. My personal life was fast becoming a shambles, and as far as I could see, for no logical reason. My last beau, Warren Arnold, and I had not seen nearly as much of one another since an unfortunate incident outside the house. It was really one in a succession of episodes, that may be said to have begun one afternoon when I was sitting in the living room. There was a tremendous crash and I thought immediately, *"Someone has had an accident."* I looked out the windows on the Bay side, but there was nothing discernible. A few minutes later, however, a neighbor came over from across the street to tell me, "Your car has been demolished." It turned out that some men had come down the twisted street in a car out of control and had wrapped themselves around a telegraph pole at the bottom, and my car en route.

No sooner had I had the car repaired than I emerged from the house one morning with minutes to spare on my way to the studio, only to find the windshield shattered; someone had thrown a brick through it. A few weeks later, on leaving the house to go downtown shopping, I looked for my car in its customary parking place. It had vanished. The police were notified, and they traced it shortly afterward, abandoned a few blocks away. Nothing had been taken from it. There was no explanation—no culprits were ever discovered.

Warren Arnold had not been exempt from similar mishaps. He had an English sports car, which he naturally parked outside the house when he called for me. After he had left the apartment one day, I was surprised to hear him hurrying back up the steps, to reappear at the front door, in a fury. His sports car had been lavishly coated in catsup and mustard. On a subsequent date he found jumper cables in his car, all his medical papers stolen, and the air let out of the tires.

The effect on Warren was naturally cumulative, and when he came out of the apartment one day to discover that his car had been carefully pushed downhill and rammed into four other automobiles, his romantic ardor diminished. While we remained friends, the emotional temperature of our relationship plummeted sharply.

After this episode, nothing romantic happened to me for some time, so I was cheered to have a telephone call from Earl Raymond, suggesting we meet for lunch. There had been quite an interim since the astrology party and I had been a little mystified, even piqued, that he had neglected me after promising to phone, so I was pleased to hear from him, and we finally settled on dinner the following evening.

I can't remember now where we went, although I do recall pondering, without pursuing the thought, why Earl was so impressed by the importance of his clientele, which appeared to consist exclusively of retired executives in planning their opulent sunset years retreat in Palm Springs.

Soon I began to notice little eccentricities. Sometimes he would stop by my apartment, pace back and forth touching the living room walls with his hands, then collapse on the sofa and immediately fall asleep. In spite of my most valiant efforts to rouse him and send him on his way, he would refuse to budge, and instead would start muttering some lines of a weird chant. Or again, in the middle of an impassioned speech, he would suddenly drop off into a stupor. I began to find these scenes boring, and I didn't feel the gap in my life was quite worth suffering the obvious gap in his. I began to feel uneasy around him.

Also, new things were happening in the apartment to make me feel uncomfortable. I told Earl about them, but he merely laughed. Carolyn and I, however, would often discuss them. We were no longer troubled by the elusive music, but the doorjamb on the front door had been split open at some point—we didn't know when. One day, we just discovered the wood splintered and the jamb pulled away from the frame, although the locks apparently still held. I had it repaired as soon as I could and in the pressure of proofreading my forthcoming book, *Party Girl,* I managed to push it to the back of my mind.

I still felt unaccountably tired and went out less and less, but with the prospect of the book and my television show, I was, after all, classified as a public personality. And in order to give the book proper exposure and to continue to qualify as an authority on entertaining, I felt I had an obligation to be seen on occasion. Therefore, though I was more than a little reluctant to see Earl again, I found myself agreeing to let him escort me to a dinner party given by a distinguished San Francisco host, who always entertained lavishly in his beautiful Pacific Heights home. His was certainly the reverse of my own entertaining, achieved by the grace of good friends and a nonexistent budget.

Ten round tables, eight people to each, were resplendent with silver and crystal, and branched silver candelabra at the center gave a soft, flattering light. Thomasser, the leading San Francisco caterer, presided over an enormous buffet, and a twelve-piece orchestra played as we consumed caviar, squab, and pears in wine. The champagne and wine flowed freely, as I observed the scene, enjoying it at first, when I became acutely aware that Earl was rapping his glass for attention. All eyes turned expectantly to him, and rising, Earl said mockingly, "I would like to propose a toast to Pat Montandon. Pat has been hearing voices lately and I think we can help her. I'm going to perform an exorcism." With that, he whipped out a small black notebook, read a few senseless lines, and then, before I could assimilate what was happening, dipped his fingers into a glass of red wine and made a cross on my forehead. There were murmurs of embarrassed laughter and I quickly wiped at the liquid running in rivulets down my face and dripping onto the bodice of my dress.

I could hardly suppress the tears, and sensing my discomfort, the man on my right asked me to dance. Once around the floor was enough, as my partner wanted to know about my "voices." I walked back to the table and told Earl I wanted to go home at once.

His answer was an incoherent invitation to dance. I have always hated scenes and in the past would go to lengths to avoid one. Against my better judgment, and certainly against my inclination, I danced with him. I was furious that he had exposed me to such ridicule: that evening I had hoped to escape from the unease I felt in the house, only to find it following me everywhere. Only a woman who has lived alone, without a husband or a man she can depend on, can empathize with me: helpless in the face of the convention that she must be "escorted," and dependent on her partner's whims and vagaries for the evening. And Earl seemed completely unperturbed by anything I said, his behavior becoming steadily more erratic.

He abandoned me in mid-dance floor, walked over to a guest, planted both feet in the middle of a white upholstered chair, and announced how devoutly he wished to take her to bed. This was really too much. I asked a friend if he could possibly take me home; the evening had soured, and I was being disgraced by my escort.

As we walked to the door, Earl caught up with us, insulted the man with me, and insisted he would take me home. As I started out the door, a hard rain driven by a freezing wind whipped my blue silk evening dress against my body. I lifted my skirt and hurried to Earl's car, thinking it didn't matter. I just wanted to get home.

When we got into the car he was all smiles. We took off

in a roar and a spray of raindrops. By then it was late, the streets deserted. I said nothing, and this seemed to infuriate him. His car was entirely automated—you pushed a button on the driver's side and all the doors locked. When I heard the click, I felt a shiver of apprehension.

The next thing I knew, he had pulled over to the curb on a dark street, and begun screaming at me at the top of his voice—entirely out of control.

He was by turns all fire and passion, then all jeers and sarcasm about my anxieties and fears.

"You're crazy! All that nonsense about doors broken down, noises in the night. I bet you're doing it yourself. . . . I've heard of women like you!"

I looked at him incredulously and wondered aloud how alcohol can often affect the brain, as it had apparently affected his although I knew he hadn't been drinking much. He became progressively more infuriated and informed me he was taking me to Squaw Valley, where he had a cabin, whether I liked it or not. "I'll fix you," he said. At first I didn't believe him, but as we headed for the Bay Bridge, across Broadway with its neon signs, I realized he was entirely serious.

There was a feeling of evil in the car, like that in the house—that pervasive evil with which I was now so familiar. And there was even an elusive smell I suddenly identified as the same indefinable odor I had noticed in my living room for the past two weeks. I became terribly frightened. I was literally in the hands of a madman, locked in his car and helpless as the lights of the bridge approach loomed closer. I knew I *had* to *do* something. I forced myself to slide over on the seat of his car—to sit close to him—and putting my hand on his thigh, I said in the softest voice I could muster, "Oh, Earl, I love you. Of course I'll go with you. But I've got to go home and change my clothes. I can't go to the snow in an evening dress."

Earl looked at me skeptically at first, and then, his ego

coming to the fore, seemed convinced that what I was saying was true; just before we reached the bridge approach, he turned right and headed back toward Lombard Street.

I must have looked visibly relieved, for he shot me a suspicious glance and turned the car once again in the direction of the bridge. I searched my mind for some way out. I thought of jumping out of the car even though he was driving at high speed—an accident was the least of my worries—but I knew I couldn't unlock the door.

Feeling the approach of panic, I tried again to marshal my acting talents and told Earl in a shaky voice how much I admired him. "Please take me home, Earl," I pleaded again, "so I can get some warm clothes and pack a suitcase, and then we can go to Squaw Valley together."

I looked at him in the glow from the dashboard, as the windshield wipers swept back and forth in the heavy downpour, his features oddly distorted by some trick of light. One could barely see the oncoming traffic. After a pause, he turned away from the bridge. The tension was unbearable. I had forced myself to put my hand on the back of his head and massage his neck, and this seemed to calm him a little. At least he appeared to believe me.

My only thought was the safety of my own front door. I knew Carolyn was home. Whatever happened when I got there, another person would be on hand to help.

Earl pulled up at the curb. I looked out and saw the lights along the crooked street, and the ones from my own apartment, so unbearably welcome at that moment. "I want you to hurry," he said. "I'll come with you. You get your clothes . . . I'm taking you away."

The most beautiful sound in the world to me was the snap of the locks being released. I jumped out quickly, slammed the door, and thinking I was already safe, made the mistake of yelling, "I wouldn't go across the street with you, you irresponsible bastard!"

For a rather large, heavyset person, Earl was out of

the car in a flash. Before I could race to my front door, he had grabbed me and pinned me against the side of his Jaguar. I am strong, but not as strong as Earl. He was screaming at me, but in my own agitation and the torrential downpour, I couldn't distinguish the words. I tried to scream, but his hand pressed against my mouth. My back was beginning to hurt, as he forced me against the edge of the fender. I could feel the metal of some sharp knob digging into my hips.

Earl suddenly took his hand away from my mouth and put both his hands around my throat. I was struggling and pleading. *This is it,* I thought. *He really is going to kill me.* I dimly recalled something I had heard once. Although it was difficult in the long dress I was wearing, I brought my knee up sharply and in a spurt of energy kicked him hard in the groin. He crumpled slightly and I managed to scramble to the gates of my own entrance-way. I had just reached the steps when Earl caught up with me, but to my surprise, instead of trying to get me back to the car, I realized he was impelling me forward and up the steps to my apartment.

Somehow I found the key. Miraculously, my evening bag was still hooked over my arm, with the door keys pinned safely to its lining. I fumbled with the lock and hurried in. For the first time in months I found those chilly rooms a welcome refuge until Earl's sudden savage laughter seemed to join and mingle with other echoes. *My God,* I thought, *is he possessed?* I ran quickly toward my bedroom, with Earl close on my heels, but I managed to slam the door and lock it before he could follow. I felt bone-weary. My head was pounding; I was shivering as much from fear as cold, and was as wet as I had ever been in my life. Slowly and deliberately, I took off my dress—that sodden, mud-splashed evening gown—and let it drop to the floor, found my old terrycloth bathrobe, put it on and went to the telephone.

Earl had started knocking at the door, a senseless,

rhythmic pounding. "Earl," I said, "if you don't leave, I'm going to call the police." *Knock, knock, knock.* . . ."I don't want to call the police, but I will. . . ." *Knock, knock, knock.* "Earl, I've picked up the telephone; I'm dialing the police. . . . Please don't make it more embarrassing or difficult than it is already. . . ."

When the police answered, I explained that my date had been drinking and I couldn't get him to leave. I was afraid the truth would attract unwanted publicity. How I wished the explanation could have been so simple: There now seemed to be a chilling connection between Earl and the apartment that I couldn't explain and didn't want to face. I didn't think it would serve any useful purpose to tell the police the whole story. Ironically, they'd probably classify me simply as one more neurotic career woman— after my own careful quest to find a convincing explanation for what was happening to me. The officer said they would be right over and would handle the situation tactfully.

During this exchange, the knocking continued. It occurred to me that I should be in my evening dress, wet though it was, rather than in a bathrobe. I picked up the clammy garment distastefully, put it on, and waited impatiently, shivering.

When I saw the police car pull up, I opened the door and walked out, and Earl fell into the room. He had been leaning so hard on the door that my sudden exit had taken him by surprise; but he recovered quickly enough to click the lock and shut me out of my own bedroom.

I was resigned by now to playing out the whole stupid affair. I went out into the foyer to greet the police, and as I waited there, I heard another click. Someone or something had now locked me out of my own house.

I was trembling as I explained to the policemen what had happened and we went around to the sliding plate glass door of the library to rouse Carolyn. This turned out to be unnecessary, as she'd already been awakened by the strange laughter and Earl's knocking. In her drowsy state, she hadn't understood what was going on, and had done nothing except listen. I hurriedly brought her up to date as she let us in; once inside, we realized Earl was still locked in the bedroom.

One of the policemen knocked and said, "Open up, please."

"No, I won't," came the reply. "Who asked you to come here?"

"Miss Montandon asked us."

"Well, go away or I'll call my lawyer."

"Mr. Raymond, open this door!"

"No!"

Earle hadn't put up the chain or turned the dead bolt. He had used only the pushbutton lock on the doorknob, so the police were able to take a plastic card and flip it and the door was open. If it hadn't been so traumatic for me at the time, the sight that met us would have struck me as funny.

My unwelcome guest had completely stripped my bed down to the sheets and was sitting imperiously in the middle of it, in his soaked shoes and tuxedo, pretending to watch the late, late movie on television.

The policemen looked at each other and shrugged. I had no reactions left; I was exhausted. The law could carry on the struggle for me. Earl looked up impatiently. "I demand you get out of here this minute."

"Mr. Raymond, you are to leave this lady's apartment right now."

"No one's asked me to—besides, she's crazy."

I broke in to say, "Earl, if I haven't asked you before, then I am asking you now, in the presence of witnesses, to leave my house and never come back." He completely disregarded my interruption and said, "I'm going to call my lawyer, and I'll get all of you for this."

The policemen retorted, "You do that, buddy—you just do that."

The discussion seemed to be getting nowhere, so I walked away and left them to it. Earl finally deigned to remove his muddy shoes from my once clean sheets and stalked out the front door into the teeming rain. But not before he ran his hands along the living room wall and turned to stare hatefully at me and curse me in words almost identical to the Tarot reader.

The policemen stared after him, incredulous, then shrugged their shoulders and turned their attention to me. They were sympathetic and understanding and said they would stay for a while. By that time I was in a lot of pain. My throat was turning black and blue and I could hardly speak. I made a pot of coffee and Carolyn and I and the two officers sat and drank it, shivering in the cold of the apartment, as we watched Earl steer a course down the crooked street six times before he gave up.

I dragged myself wearily in to go to bed and while I was changing the muddy sheets, I noticed the corner of something white sticking out from under the bed. I picked it up and saw it was a photograph of me which had been scored across and stabbed by a ballpoint pen. I was almost too tired to react. I just wanted the night to be over, and climbing into bed, fell into a deep sleep. Two days later, I developed pneumonia from the bone chill and exposure, and my only thought was recovery. *To hell with romance,* I thought, *I'll concentrate on my career.*

The next day, a thick blue envelope from the Metaphysical Town-Hall Bookshop arrived. I tore it open and read:

"THE STARS INCLINE—THEY DO NOT COMPEL"
Major Epic Ray

Pat dear, you have some serious vibrations of which I do not like to speak, but of which I feel you should know. Because you are definitely A Practical and Farseeing Individual, I think you will take this material and use it wisely. You are now in the midst of a vibration which we might say . . . IS EXACT. This vibration is nothing new in your life. It is rather a fulfillment of Old Conditions which is now in Full Bloom. I am going into this move of yours, and as far as I can discern—the conditions of the house you moved into and THE WHY. You moved into that house under vibrations of deep confusion and the promise of many heartaches and deceptions, intrigue—with possible and probable "witchery," let's call it, strongly in evidence in the moving-in Chart . . . Suicides are strongly indicated due to the fact that the Planet NEPTUNE is very strongly involved. In fact the whole move and the period under which you made it is closely bound up with involvements and entrapments as possible conditions. Even vandalism and cruelty are involved. AND TOO—deep and sudden heartaches are a very powerful part of all this. . . . There is constant tension having to do with your home and even with your business life. Mystery and The Double Cross and The Unsolvable seems to predominate all the while. It is as though you are at the mercy of others . . . ALL THE TIME.

THE UNCANNY—THE PSYCHIC—THE UNKNOWN REALMS —seem to be tapped into your home and into your affairs and into yourself all the while. While a certain element of The Psychic Clear White Light, as it is called, is pulsating through you, you are also enmeshed in the deep, dark psychic entities, too. The entire horoscope seems to indicate just this.

But—Understand it is your own Natal Perseverance plus the run of the planets of this Chart for moving which will enable you to defy these dark entities to absorb you and yours. Probably these are Lower World entities.

The Planet Uranus, too, is very strongly in evidence through this period. Uranus brings . . . THE UNPREDICTABLE. Whatever occurs under this vibration in an adverse way will come like a streak of lightning over your skies. For the most part, Uranus is badly aspected. Its associations with other planets are adverse. Therefore—these two Planets—the Ray of Uranus and the strong, strong configuration of NEPTUNE—put you into The Depths and make you a Potential Victim.

Even for someone so long skeptical about the psychic, the occult and the paranormal, the relevance of this reading, in its often cryptic language, to the events of the last several months was deeply disturbing.

4

The Last Party

During my convalescence, a matter of several weeks, I had many talks with Carolyn, who was obsessed by a love affair with a married man, and although not in the most empathetic frame of mind, I tried to give her helpful advice. I encouraged her to go away for a while to think things over away from the immediate presence of the man, which seemed the only wise thing to do. She was happy enough to be moving out of the house, and started to make plans. She decided to go to Hawaii, and Mary Lou and I saw her off, hoping she would find other, happier relationships there to give her a fresh viewpoint and a mature and happy future. She was young, sweet-natured, and lovely; surely fate would be kind to her.

I found I missed Carolyn's company more than I expected, and became acutely conscious of being again alone in the house, and of the encircling depression it spread about me. I searched around for distraction and found, I thought, something that would help.

Whenever I have felt low, discouraged, out of spirits, I have always felt I would get better if I gave a party. I suppose it provides me a new purpose, a shift of interest, and as it had always helped me out of a temporary depression before, I decided the time had come for another.

An important consideration, which particularly influenced me, was that the new tenants would soon be moving in upstairs, and I would no longer be able to use the ballroom unless I hurried. Also, I felt the need to have people around, from some obscure conviction that they would serve as barrier against the problems hemming me in from every side.

I had tucked the foreboding horoscope away in a drawer, and although I never looked at it again after the first reading, I could still recall some of the passages. I didn't believe in it, yet I couldn't shake it off. It troubled me, and I looked to the party to take my thoughts in an entirely different direction. Although I now had a great underlying fear of the house, I was not prepared to surrender to it—friends reinforced my conviction. I would give the party to thumb my nose at the devil.

Once again Mary Lou and I discussed, rejected, pondered over various motifs, until I hit upon a maharishi party. Eastern mysticism, gurus, meditation were in the air. The theme had interesting possibilities.

I had by this time acquired a second assistant, a plump, jolly girl named Vera Scott, to cope with my ever-expanding program of television, talks, and personal appearances and the mountain of letters that were beginning to intimidate even Mary Lou. And Vera, naturally, was also swept into the party preparations. Vera had just moved into the house and had taken over Carolyn's room in the library. She was able to make a valuable contribution of her own —the music. When the subject came up, she waxed enthusiastic about a close friend of hers who had formed a rock group, and there, ready-made, was the dance band for the evening. As rock hardly suited the mood of the party, I planned to have concealed music from a record player in between: mysterious Indian sitar music, with its endless, repetitive ornamentations and strange modal intervals. Thin wisps of blue smoke would rise from exotically perfumed incense: sandalwood, musk, and frangipani—a refreshing change from that unpleasant unidentifiable odor.

The upstairs ballroom could be brought into play once more, hung with those brightly colored Indian cottons, covered with twisted tendrils and strange flowers. And with a little persuasion, I hoped my friend Sushil Kakar, who knew intimately all the regional cuisines of India, would provide exotic delicacies to tempt the guests.

Somehow I managed to collect my scattered thoughts long enough to send out invitations, Mary Lou helping me, as always; and with the aid of the usual battery of friends, the party began to take shape. Finding all the necessary props and provisions, did not absorb me as it always had in the past. I was deeply troubled, without consciously pinpointing the reason, and I could not give the arrangements my usual care or attention. Yet somehow the plans were made; the guests invited.

My woman's instinct, at least, had not been totally extinguished by the snowballing incidents of recent weeks. I wanted a pretty dress. But how to find something suitable? After some abortive attempts to find a vaguely Indian garment, Rhoda Kakar produced a superb sari in black, heavily interwoven with designs in gold thread; and she even provided exquisite Indian jewelry to match. My hairdresser plaited my long fair hair into a braid that hung down over one shoulder, interspersed with sweet-scented jasmine blossoms. The same generous source furnished Mary Lou with a sari in a deep shade of midnight blue, woven with gold, and a profusion of silver rings and bracelets. I outfitted Vera in a black and white silk caftan and had my hairdresser give her an elaborate hairdo. She looked quite beautiful.

The evening arrived. The guests appeared to be in cheerful mood, a brilliant throng, all dressed in colorful saris, turbans, and caftans, or making some concession to the theme with a display of beads. Glamorously dressed nautch girls came partnered with maharajas; soberly garbed babus contrasted with much whiskered and bearded Sikhs. The clusters of people continually juxtaposed changing harmonies and discords of color, like flights of exotic birds. Some guests began eating immediately, or made for the bar; others drifted up the stairs, drawn by the compelling rock rhythm of the group in the ballroom.

My parties had acquired a reputation for the unusual, and the Press often asked to be invited. Indeed, several members had become close personal friends; and on this particular evening quite a number had turned up. They were soon busy among the guests. I had invited some personalities fairly prominent on the political and television scenes, and they, of course, are often news.

I had arranged for the maharishi himself to be ensconced in the ballroom upstairs, where he took up a commanding position, seated cross-legged on a pile of cushions. The East Indian atmosphere was suggested by shaded lights and votive candles that cast flickering shadows on the brilliantly colored hangings. Masses of flowers, heaped-up mounds of fruits, oranges, mangoes, lemons, and pomegranates, perfumed the air. The house looked brighter than it had for some time.

The stairs from the front entrance foyer led up into a wide atrium, from which the ballroom opened to the left, up six marble steps, so that it was placed approximately over my library at the front of the house; and a large kitchen had been added over my bedroom. A deck, with beautifully proportioned columns, led off the ballroom. In the other direction, to the right of the front door upstairs, and leading to a back door and a fire escape, was a large storage closet. A bathroom and a bedroom at the end of a passage made up the sum of the apartment.

Upstairs, in the ballroom, the maharishi was putting on a splendid performance, intoning in a mysterious undertone: *"Om, Om, Om Mani Padme Hum . . ."* Many of the guests were completely taken in by his convincing impersonation. He was a local businessman who had thrown himself totally into the spirit of the party. Beturbaned and berobed, transcendental and imposing, he was more of a maharishi than any maharishi could ever be.

For light relief, Mary Lou's young boy, Jimmy, was enthroned in the dark recesses of the storage closet as a novice maharishi, equally resplendent, and whiling away the time reading comic books between meditation sessions with the amused onlookers.

From the beginning of the evening I sensed disaster in the air; there was a strange discordant feeling all around. I had no conscious premonitions, only a gnawing unease. I tried to shake off my anxiety—greeting latecomers, passing from one group to another, watching danger spots, racking my brain for the right remarks, summoning the last ounce of energy to give an outward impression, at least, of the cheerful, imperturbable hostess—hoping against hope to get through the evening successfully. And yet, as I scanned the sea of apparently friendly faces, I could not help wondering whether that one—that unknown one who had laid the dead flowers against my door—was there.

All those faces: smiling, laughing, serious, quizzical, coy, began to assume for me the appearance of masks. Which one concealed an enemy? Or, was there more than one? To free myself from these stifling suspicions, and from a mounting sense of claustrophobia, I hurried out through the ballroom colonnade and drew in a deep breath of fresh air on the deck. Stars hung above, reflected in the Bay; the intermittent yellow glow from the lighthouse on Alcatraz comforted like an old friend; and on the far shore the lights of Oakland glimmered and sparkled like strands of jewels.

It took quite an effort to return to the crowded ballroom and thread a way through the brilliantly hued kaleidoscope of dancers, down the stairs to the rooms below, greeting people mechanically in passing; searching faces, masks, suffocated by the crowding mass of humanity, oppressed by the sensuous incense.

The first sign of trouble came when a friend who had promised to run the bar decided to leave—a disruptive touch. That meant Mary Lou had to step into the breach, and all our carefully laid plans had to be altered to cope with this emergency. Yet the party went on, with music to cover any minor mishaps. From upstairs came the lively sound of Vera's rock group, which in an inspired moment I had christened "the Gurus," for the occasion. Even in this, seeds of disaster were hidden. Vera was deeply and emotionally involved with one member of the band, and perhaps something of her future was stirring in the air that evening. I knew, at least, my own misgivings, and that as I moved among the guests, I was beginning to realize that giving this party, or indeed, any party, was no solution to what was happening in that house.

I escaped back into the sitting room to find that there were more late arrivals, among them Senator Edward Kennedy, who had been cornered in the entrance doorway by a crowd of admirers. I did not see how I could rescue him. A buzz of conversation centered on him, and I could hear snatches. "Why, isn't that Ted Kennedy? I didn't know Pat knew Ted Kennedy!" As a matter of record, I didn't. He had been brought by "Red" and Anita Fay, a former Undersecretary of the Navy and his wife, and I had no credit in the matter.

There was also the beautiful blond Pia Lindstrom, wearing a pale blue silk sari. She had a new show on KGO and was successfully creating a career for herself. Seldom was she now referred to only as Ingrid Bergman's daughter. The Willard Watermans were also present. He, of course, was known as the Great Gildersleeve, and was currently appearing in the San Francisco production of *Mame*.

In spite of such interesting guests, I found that, try as I might, I could not relax.

The party had been in progress for perhaps two hours when I suddenly heard the word "Fire!" In an instant, the steady pulse of talk and laughter became jangled and out of phase; the escapist fantasy of the evening came to a halt. I rushed to the doorway of the library, to see flames shooting up from the awning on the balcony outside, and tongues of flame already beginning to lick at the wooden trim of the building.

One part of my brain heard the Gurus, playing a rock number in the ballroom upstairs—where the main party was—while I took in the situation below. I did not panic, although I felt a terrible constriction in my chest as I ran breathlessly up the stairs, shouting to someone as I went, to get out the garden hose.

My first thought was to clear the ballroom, where at least fifty people were dancing, and from which there was only one narrow stairway down. I had no idea where the fire would spread, or if it could be controlled. The people below had seen the flames and were rushing outside to safety, but upstairs no one knew what had happened. Once on the upper floor, I ran down the passage to lower the fire escape, then rushed back to the ballroom. In the ballroom, I yelled above the music and dancers to tell the Gurus to stop playing.

Faces turned to me astonished. Could I be complaining about the music? The band was good, the chief success of the evening so far. What on earth was the matter?

The music stopped. Dancers stood huddled in groups, staring at me. "Please," I gasped, "the house is on fire . . . there is no danger . . . only please leave immediately, down the fire escape."

Nobody moved. Faces looked at me blankly. Perhaps some of them thought it was all part of a surprise, a novelty in the evening's festivities, and no one stirred. How could I convince them their dance could all too easily turn into a dance of death? Everything was happening in a moment of time; yet to me, with my breath short and my heart pumping, it all seemed to pass in slow motion—a nightmare in which time itself was horribly extended. The horoscope with its forecast of horror, flashed across my mind.

I had to take some of my guests by the arm and push them toward the fire escape. They began to drift in the direction of safety with appalling slowness, though the ballroom was beginning to fill with choking fumes, and they gathered in little groups to watch the fire curiously, from a safe distance outside. With alarm I remembered Jimmy, shut in the upstairs closet in the smoke-filled ballroom, and as I ran there, I collided with Mary Lou, bent on the same mission.

Meantime, friends had manned the garden hose, and another had fetched a fire extinguisher from his car (somehow, in the confusion, no one had called the fire department), and eventually someone doused the flames.

Of course, that was the end of the party. I was left to contemplate the wreckage. Alone, I could envision the flames catching those yards and yards of Indian fabric, aided and abetted by the sputtering wax of the votive candles and the tinderlike flammability of the treillage. And outside, the tattered and blackened shreds of the awning hung down over the sundeck like so many threatening fingers. Vera had decided to spend the night away from the house because her "bedroom" was a shambles of broken glass. As she told me later, she now had the excuse she had been hoping for, to get out of that "strange" place.

Mary Lou offered to stay behind and help clear up the mess, but I insisted she go home with Jimmy; and like

Scarlett O'Hara, I said, "I'll think about that tomorrow!" We said goodnight and I went back into the house. Debris lay all around. An acrid smell of smoke pervaded the entire house, blotting out the usual sour odor and clinging obstinately to cushions and hangings. The grime and confusion were more than I could have believed possible. There wasn't any point in dwelling on it further, I thought, as I sank wearily into bed.

One always expects a certain amount of disorder after a party, but what faced me the next morning, when I explored the full extent of the wreckage, was beyond belief. Cigarette butts were ground into carpets; food and drink spilled on furniture and cushions; everything movable in disarray. And straying jets of water had added a finishing touch, smearing dirty trails wherever they had penetrated. The total picture suggested the work of malignant and deliberate sabotage, rather than the natural outcome of an evening's entertaining.

I felt none of my usual willingness to clear up the chaos; instead I experienced an utter weariness of spirit and a consciousness of failure. I was back once more, imprisoned in the sinister influence of the house, searching desperately in the reaches of my mind for a rational explanation of a frighteningly irrational sequence of events, and the unrelenting fate that seemed to be pursuing me.

As I moved from room to room, finding fresh disorder and damage at every turn, and fighting my revulsion at the smell of smoke, I had the feeling there was something ugly, something evil all around me—a presence I could almost touch. And I saw again, with sudden shock, those long, black strands of canvas, the charred remnants of the awning, casting elongated, dark shadows in the morning sunlight. That was the last party I ever gave in the house on the crooked street.

the trenches ever came, and although the dead bodies
were thrown away as hastily as possible, they appeared

5

The Changing of the Guard

To come back to an empty echoing house every day after the accumulation of pressures of the last few weeks was no help to my general depression. Mary Lou and Vera, of course, helped and distracted me during their part-time working hours, but Dog no longer welcomed me with cheerful barks. He would come up to me with ears back and tail between his legs, cowed and miserable. And in the evenings I sought company by telephone, calling up friends to cover my loneliness of spirit.

My thoughts took a different turn shortly afterward, when I saw from the balcony a car draw up; two stringy-haired, unkempt-looking men got out. They made their way up the steps and into the house, and I was disconcerted to realize they must be the new tenants of Apartment 3. They were followed by a rusty van that discharged some odd but expensive-looking furniture onto the sidewalk, and from there it was carried into the house by equally scruffy-looking characters. When the first two men reappeared, I made a point of leaning over from my balcony and welcoming them. They responded shortly and didn't appear particularly friendly, but this didn't bother me, as I wasn't anxious to have nosy neighbors. Of course, I was being nosy myself and watched all day, sizing them up; their furniture, their clothes, their general behavior. And while they weren't at all attractive, their taste in furniture suggested they were reasonably affluent and presumably responsible.

Finally, they were settled in, complete with two curious-looking dogs—or at least, strange to me—smooth and reddish of coat, which I later discovered were the barkless African breed called Basenji. Dog became absolutely frenzied on their arrival and by their mysterious silent approach as though he suspected them of knowing something he did not. Normally everybody's friend, Dog hated the newcomers and their animals alike, which added to my difficulties and my recurrent sleeplessness, the outcome of the burglary, pressure of work, and my general malaise.

Almost imperceptibly, I began to notice other changes. The hallway came to look strangely neglected and dirty, even though a janitor cleaned it every Saturday. Cigarette butts and what looked suspiciously like spittle started to leave traces in the entrance foyer, and I was acutely aware that the doorbell for the upstairs tenants now bore eight names—first names, like John and Buzz and Bob. Little by little I also became conscious that a steady stream of disheveled figures were coming to the house: not at all the sort of people associated with that part of town.

I felt there was something so peculiar going on that I decided to call the landlord. He treated the matter lightly, assuring me there were only two people living upstairs, two brothers, and he couldn't object to their having visitors. There must be some mistake about the doorbell; and as for their respectability, he could assure me they were responsible, because when he told them the rent, one of them pulled out a wad of one-hundred-dollar bills "that would choke a horse" and paid in advance. I protested at this. "I don't see that's any evidence of their respectability. If anything, I would have thought that was suspect." But money was good enough for the landlord, so for the time being I had to be content. The only small crumb of compromise I received was that he would ask them to take the extra names off by the bell.

Now other noises began to interrupt the night. Heavy footsteps constantly tramped overhead, apparently coming from near the kitchen sink, immediately above my bedroom. Sleep was more and more difficult. I would take a sleeping pill, start to drop off only to be awakened by the footsteps above. Then I started to hear discordant chanting, interspersed with raucous music, so loud it made my windows rattle, followed by a regular sequence of footsteps, which, in my agitated state, seemed to advance then halt outside my front door, This became a pattern to be repeated over and over again—and the cumulative effect of noises and sleeplessness began to reduce me almost to a state of hysteria.

One night, about five nights after all this began, in a moment of complete outrage, I threw on a bathrobe, unbolted all the locks barring my way—which by now took some doing—ran up the stairs and knocked furiously at the door. I was ready to tell the tenants there had to be an end to this nonsense: that I was completely exhausted, and they must be more considerate neighbors.

At the sound of my knocking, all the noise suddenly stopped. I knocked again. There was complete silence. Again, a knock—nothing; again, even louder. This time I could hear footsteps shuffling towards the door. It opened a crack. I could see chains and locks—and behind the chains a sallow-faced man of about twenty-eight. His hair was disheveled, he had a growth of beard, and he looked hostilely out at me. I said. "I'm the woman who lives downstairs. You've got to be more quiet. You're keeping me awake. I can't sleep for all the noise, night after night.

If you don't stop this, I'm going to call the police— please be more considerate."

The man continued to stare at me in silence. Then he opened the door wider, put his hands on his hips, and smirking, made an obscene gesture. He then closed the door sharply and locked it. I stood there entirely unnerved.

All the pieces suddenly fitted together—dope! I walked quickly down the stairs and hurried into my own apartment, making sure the dead bolt lock on my front door was securely fastened. The chains were engaged in their sockets and I double-checked the back door to make sure the dead bolt was firmly fastened there as well. All the windows now had locks on them and were in position. I went into my bedroom and tried once again to go to sleep, but sleep would not come. I had read enough about the irrational behavior of dope pushers to be terrified by the thought that they might now be living under my very own roof.

I found, much to my surprise, that all the noise overhead had ceased. It was as if the apartment had become vacant once more, although I knew it was densely inhabited. After the disturbances before, the silence was uncanny. Toward morning I fell into a fitful sleep to awake a few hours later, far from refreshed.

As I dressed slowly for work, putting my television makeup on—with extra white under my eyes to hide the dark circles—I realized I was weak from tension.

When I was ready to leave, I unbolted the locks, stepped into the foyer, and was brought up short, at what I saw. It was completely littered with cigarette butts, and the walls were smeared with obscene drawings and cryptic symbols. I shuddered and ran out the front door.

I realized, as I bolted down the stairs, that someone was sitting on the landing, in the corner against a column. I hurried past, taking in a glimpse of a seedy-looking man and woman, and went on through the garden and got quickly into my car. I called Mary Lou as soon as I arrived at the studio and asked her to call the landlord and tell him what was going on.

I have no idea how my TV show went that morning. My mind was seething with troublesome questions, and I cannot possibly have given any concentrated attention to what was going on. After my show I checked by phone with Mary Lou, who said the landlord was away.

Each day found me more apprehensive, and Mary Lou, sharing my anxieties, was feeling great reluctance to come to the house to work. She would come into the apartment quickly and lock all the doors after her, but not before she had looked all around to make sure there was no one inside. We both now had the feeling—even when we knew full well there couldn't be anyone there—that there was someone, or something, in the apartment with us.

Neither of us—two practical career women, firmly based in the daily realities of friendships and work—was prepared to admit, even to ourselves, that there could be anything paranormal about the sensations we experienced. But even Vera, who had moved out after the fire, and was now working for me part-time, had developed a great fear, not only of the people upstairs, but of the apartment as well. Her normally happy attitude toward life had altered noticeably.

I could not leave matters as they were and I called the landlord once more. He was an amiable garrulous old man who still spoke with a deep accent and loved nothing more than to recount the history of his family and how he came to America. I hesitated a little about talking to him on the telephone because we always talked too long. Still, I had to confront him about the tenants upstairs and I dialed the number. I listened dismayed as he told me someone else had taken over the management of the building: He owned it but he had no power any longer, and he told me whom to get in touch with.

I called the new manager at the first opportunity, and encountered a surly individual who told me that if I didn't like what was happening in the building, I could buy out my lease and move. There were plenty of people who wanted my apartment . . . he couldn't be bothered with complaints.

I did, of course, consider moving, but eventually rejected the idea for many reasons. Apartments like mine were virtually impossible to find. The rooms were spacious: I had a lovely garden, a view, and a fireplace. I was exactly twelve minutes from work, and most important, the rent was precisely what I could afford and much less than the apartment was worth. I certainly couldn't buy out my lease, which still had two and a half years to run. And now, face to face with all the problems involved, an inborn streak of stubbornness rose to the surface. I wasn't going to let anything run me out of my own home. And as for the house, I had somehow wrestled with it till now, and was determined not to be defeated by it.

It was obvious the new manager wasn't interested in getting the upstairs tenants out. I couldn't understand it. However, one thing became plain to me as the traffic increased. I was probably right about there being drugs upstairs. The cigarette butts in the foyer, the crude drawings, the filth, the odd figures sitting on the stairs, and even perched on the curb across the street—these signs, taken together, could have only one meaning.

I remember trying to make a joke of it and saying to Mary Lou, "Well, Mary Lou, I'm sure the neighbors must be thinking I'm giving a wild costume party." But it was a hollow joke and we felt far from humorous about the whole situation.

Obviously, there was only one thing left to do. I called the police. I called them, in all, five or six times. They would come to the apartment, talk to me, but say they could do nothing more than accuse my neighbors of dis-

turbing the peace; there was insufficient corroboration
for any stronger move. I felt completely frustrated, especially as each time I called I noticed less interest. In
desperation, I even called Los Angeles for my friend,
Judge Arthur Alarcon. He had served on the Narcotics
Commission for Governor Pat Brown at one time, and
surely would know what to do. He reassured me, and got
in touch with Police Chief Nelder, who said he would put
extra patrols on—but whether that was done or not, I
never knew.

Between calls to the police, I telephoned innumerable
times to both landlord and manager, asking them whether
they couldn't do something about the tenants upstairs,
who by this time, were quite flagrant in their behavior.
My neighbors did not bother to see that the front door was
locked; on the contrary, they propped it open so anyone
could come in at any hour of the day or night. Many of
these unexplained visitors were now knocking at my door,
mistaking it, I suppose, for the one upstairs. My doorbell
would ring piercingly throughout the night, and I would
find myself literally cowering in my bedroom for fear
someone would break in, with a host of grim imaginings
to follow.

My days at work were terribly strained. The tension was
beginning to tell on Mary Lou as well, and Dog had long
ago given up and was a shivering bundle of fur. I finally
took him to the vet and boarded him out there. When
I visited him, he was once again the happy little dog he
had been. I would take him home and as we approached
the gate, I would have a sense of foreboding, which
seemed to affect Dog equally intensely. Within a day or
two, he would be back at the vet's again, quivering and
trembling and being treated for a persistent sore.

Fears like these—fears of the unknown—are cumulative in their effect, and returning to the house began
to unnerve me sufficiently that Mary Lou and I now
had a code ring for the doorbell. I would ring four times

with one short ring at the end and Mary Lou would let me in. I would run quickly through the filthy hall and into the comparative safety of my own rooms.

We had long since had all the locks on the front door changed, yet I felt there must be something defective about them, as I was finding them constantly unlocked. I had new ones added and my bedroom became a prison it was so thoroughly barred, bolted, and barricaded.

In order to escape during the daytime, we would often have lunch in the green peace of Washington Square Park, having picked up a sourdough French roll, salami, cheese, and a small bottle of wine from the corner grocery store. And as we lunched, Mary Lou and I continually returned to one subject: the strange atmosphere in the house, whether it was the people upstairs who were responsible, and if so, what we could do about them. Even the man I was seeing most of at that time got into the act at my insistence, knowing that a man's voice often carries more weight than a "hysterical" woman's. He was persuaded to call the manager to protest the fact that he was not doing anything about the destruction of property, if nothing else. And we pointed out that he certainly had an obligation to the landlord. The poor man was terribly frustrated by the situation, but the inescapable fact that he had indeed turned over the management of the building to another left him helpless. All our efforts were to no avail.

My bedroom became my retreat. It was the only place in the house where I felt fairly safe. And even there, I didn't feel wholly comfortable. I had had slide bolts installed on the bedroom door, as well as locks everywhere else in the house. I had a chain lock on the outer door too. I had slide bolts put at the top, middle, and bottom of the French doors opening out onto the balcony off my bedroom. Finally, there were bolt locks on the two windows in the bedroom itself: I was a prisoner in my own house but somehow it seemed imperative that I lock myself in, in this manner, even though I wasn't sure whether

I was locking myself in, or someone, or something, out.

There was such a strange—I hesitate to say "unnatural" —feeling throughout the house that no precautions could have been too many for me. Mary Lou and I would often look out and see a motley group sitting on the stairs. A figure would detach itself and move into the house under our very eyes. But even more than these tangible figures, it was increasingly the unseen that was haunting my life. These people frightened me half to death, but I did not feel they were the prime cause of what was happening! I felt increasingly that they were part of the attraction of evil, and had been drawn to the building because of something I did not understand that lay within it. Perhaps there really was a malediction on the house, which had given it power to harm.

One evening I went into my bedroom, locked myself in, and collapsed on my pink tufted bed, listening to the noises upstairs and the silences, too, which were even more ominous.

Suddenly there was a different sound: a choking scream, off-key and desperate, followed by sobs that gradually died away, until there was once more that unnatural silence.

As I lay there, wondering what to do, I looked up at the ceiling and noticed the beginning of a blood-colored stain, and even as I watched, it spread, growing larger and larger. This was too much for me. I slipped to my knees at the side of the bed, praying softly for help. I didn't know what else to do and as with most people, I resort to prayer when I feel there isn't any other recourse. Tears were running down my cheeks as I prayed, and through the blur I could see rust-colored drops stain my bedspread as they dripped from the ceiling. This drove me to instant action. I went directly to the telephone and once again called the police. As I telephoned, I heard the muffled sounds of running feet and a thud on my back porch.

Eventually, two policemen were at my door. I explained for the seventh time the problem upstairs. One of the pair was most sympathetic, and put his arm on my shoulder to steady me, as he could see I was thoroughly unnerved. He said, "Pat, we'll take care of this." And I watched as they went up the stairs.

I waited downstairs, tense, expectant. I heard them knock at the upstairs door: then, silence. I waited and waited. At last, one of the policemen came back and said he would like to use the telephone. I heard him call for a paddy wagon, and then I noticed the second policeman coming down the stairs with two slovenly, squalid-looking men and one bedraggled but defiant girl in tow. After telephoning, the other policeman went up again and brought down the silent dogs, straining on two ropes and looking right and left.

I had Dog back home at the time, and he was barking and shivering in the doorway as the two Basenjis made their silent way down the winding pathway to the SPCA wagon outside.

After the paddy wagon had arrived and carried away its cargo, the policeman asked me whether I would like to see the upstairs apartment. I remembered it so well, of course, from the various parties I had held there. I could see again the bright colors of the maharishi party and hear the sitar music; or the mod party, when I had used fluorescent lights and colorful drawings. I remembered the candlelight flickering between the columns leading from the ballroom to the balcony; and a Christmas party with a cheery fire, sparkling and crackling in the grate, and a huge green tree, laden with decorations.

The contrast, when I was taken upstairs, was as if I had stepped into another world. The furniture I had seen delivered the day the two men had moved in was completely destroyed. It was piled in heaps on the sundeck and had been burned in what appeared to be a ritualistic way. Worse, the toilets were overflowing, the mattresses had been stripped off all the beds, and the stuffing was strewn about the floor in a filthy disorder. Food was scattered round about and marked the walls. Obscenities, graffiti were everywhere. I soon learned the source of the stain on my bedroom ceiling, for the sink in the kitchen was stopped and overflowing: the floor was awash with bloody-looking water, which had made its way through the kitchen tiles and seeped through to the floor below. The police had no explanation for it. They had, however, found quite a cache of dope: not only marijuana, but also speed, hash, heroin, cocaine, and other drugs with names completely unknown to me, as well as razor blades, knives, and hypodermic needles.

The police also told me that the men who had rented the apartment had somehow evaded them. We discovered that the metal fire escape from the upstairs back bedroom had been lowered onto my back porch and had been used for the getaway: and there appeared to be smears of blood on the fire escape as well as on my porch. After putting the fire escape back in place, the policemen left.

It had all been horrible, but at least I breathed a sigh of relief that it was over. I deluded myself into thinking that as soon as the mess upstairs was cleaned away, I could relax and feel at home in my house.

It was a pitch-black night, and already after midnight, when I finally settled down after the officers left. I was once again the only human being in the entire building.

All at once I heard the shrill, penetrating sound of the doorbell, and my entire body tensed in an immediate reflex. I walked cautiously out into the foyer and then stepped back hurriedly into my own recessed doorway. There was an all-too-familiar disreputable face pressed against the glass window on the entry door. I knew instinctively it was one of "them," and I felt the perspiration run down my body although it was chillingly cold. With trembling fingers I made doubly sure the locks were securely fastened on the inside of my door and stood rigidly, straining to hear the sound of retreating footsteps. I then heard an unfamiliar noise coming from the back of the house, which consisted for the most part of glass windows and a glass door opening onto the back porch.

I turned off the lights so that I could not be seen, and held Dog in my arms, cajoling him out of his deep defensive growls. I could make out the silhouettes of two figures coming toward my back entrance, formerly the tradesmen's entrance, but seldom used anymore. They appeared to be two men, and the creaking of the wooden stairs betrayed them as they stealthily made their way up.

I didn't know what to do. I waited mesmerized, to see what would develop, knowing I was entirely alone.

The men came on and on, until they reached the landing of the back porch. I knew that even if I screamed no one would hear me; and worst of all, I knew that in spite of all the locks and chains, all they had to do was to break the glass of the door and they would be inside. Calling the police would be futile as I knew from experience it would easily take them half an hour or longer to respond.

I began plotting my escape, and figured the only way out was down the balcony that led off my bedroom, although the distance was something like a drop of twelve feet and I didn't relish the idea of a broken leg.

As these thoughts were running through my mind, I realized that one of the men had a flashlight; and I could see its narrow beam playing on the now-raised fire escape, which had previously been resting on my back porch. There was a pause, as if they were uncertain, then they came toward my back door. I stood frozen with horror as they fumbled with the knob. Their faces, lit by the reflection from the flashlight, were white, shapeless blobs as they peered through into the kitchen. Apparently some noise from the street must have disturbed them, because they ducked down, hiding, for a few minutes, and then whispering together, they turned and to my vast relief started again stealthily down the moss-covered steps.

I was trembling as I went back into my bedroom and once again locked myself in. I quickly got on the telephone and called the police; they promised to patrol my area throughout the rest of the night. I was cautioned to stay put and not venture out of my bedroom. It was a very long night.

As early as possible the next morning, I called the Burns Detective Agency and asked them to provide me with a guard. I explained what had happened, and they agreed to supply a twenty-four-hour guard at a hundred dollars a day. My funds would hardly cover such an expenditure for any length of time, although I felt it to be absolutely essential.

When the guard arrived, he turned out to be a nice, elderly gentleman, who looked the situation over and just shook his head. He told me not to be concerned: He would take care of me. I looked at his shaky hands and wondered how he could possibly take care of himself, much less me, but I felt comforted just to have someone present. It served to distract me from the omnipresent stench from the upstairs apartment, which had penetrated mine, as though in some obscure way contaminating it.

We now established what I referred to as "the changing of the guard." As one man left, another would take his place, to guard me throughout the night.

The guard would sit in the foyer, on a tiny—probably uncomfortable—sofa, and I would give him the telephone from the living room, which had a twenty-five-foot cord. The cord snaked out from under my own living room door; but even with the guard on watch, I still made sure that all other doors and windows were securely locked.

But how can one be guarded against an unseen presence? One that I now knew to be as real as any of flesh and blood? I had disconnected the doorbell, as its constant shrilling day and night had become nerve racking, and as I was walking out the foyer door the second morning after the raid, I was taken aback to run head-first into a disreputable-looking character who had just arrived outside the front door and apparently rung the bell, not knowing, naturally, that it had been disconnected. And, of course, I didn't have the warning of that ring either. The man looked at me contemptuously as I shrank back, looking over my shoulder for the guard, and said, "Listen, sister, we know you're the one who called the cops. We'll get you." He didn't have to tell me twice. I turned and bolted back into the house completely forgetting whatever I had started out to do.

It took me some time to recover from this disturbing episode, but in the usual course of events, it slowly began to erase itself as work and engagements came to the fore to preoccupy my waking hours.

We expected some relief—Mary Lou and I—from knowing the "dopey ones" (as we started calling them) were finally out of the building, and life could hopefully return to normal.

The landlord was busy getting the upstairs repaired. Cleaning it turned out to be a huge task. Painters, carpenters, plumbers were constantly coming and going, and it took time, work, and money to restore it to some semblance of order.

My own life, however, did not return to normal. It was as though there remained in the house a "residue" of what had gone before. However, I refused to take notice of a recurring incident which I have since reflected on and wondered about. The fire escape which was attached to the upstairs bedroom (it was one of those you roll by hand) which came down on my back porch had been hoisted back up where it belonged immediately after the raid. But I would look out from the kitchen in the morning—on many mornings—to find it back down on the porch. I would inform one of the workmen upstairs; he would wind it back up, and a few days later I would find it was down once again. We couldn't understand this, as we had it checked and found it to be in perfect working order. But I gave it no more than a passing thought because I was far too busy with my own projects.

The coldness in the apartment continued and became even more intense. We took to wearing heavy sweaters around the house, and on occasion I would even don my fur coat.

Many of my former acquaintances, for one reason or another, were no longer a part of my life—and those few friends one always counts on would tell me they didn't really like to come to the house. They couldn't explain it, but they didn't feel comfortable there, and in consequence I was left more and more alone.

way, by now quite accustomed to this sort of behavior, when the bombshell exploded.

6

No Hiding Place

With the upstairs tenants removed and the disorder and filth cleaned away, Mary Lou and I hoped we could settle down once again and get back to work. My book, *How to Be a Party Girl,* was coming out in mid-September, 1968, only a couple of months away. Time was running short. The publishers had been in touch with me, as they had decided they wanted to have a big kick-off in San Francisco, in advance of the national publication date. There was excitement in the air.

Mary Lou once or twice tried to interest me in books on psychic phenomena, paranormal experiences, and the like, but I always brushed them aside. I didn't want to admit I had already looked at some books on these subjects. I was determined not to give substance to my fears and had firmly closed a door on them in my mind. I remembered something I had read somewhere: "If you give energy to evil, it will feed on it and grow."

"Oh, Mary Lou, that's all nonsense. The book we've

got to concentrate on is *my* book—*the* book!"

The book became our lives. In retrospect, I realize I was trying to evade the series of catastrophes, major and minor, which had assailed me ever since the astrology party, with its sequences of burglary, fire, the inexplicable incident of the dead flowers, Dog's irrational behavior, and the devastating consequences of the arrival of the tenants upstairs. Even my traumatic experience with Earl Raymond fitted naturally, or perhaps one should say unnaturally, into the same scheme—and most disturbing of all, the strange coldness of the house, with power, it seemed, to open doors and windows, like some malignant energy determined to harm me.

All this I now resolutely ignored. I could not conceive that the book, could have any connection with what had happened, or might fit just as precisely as the rest into the ominous jigsaw.

Vera Scott had decided to go with her boyfriend to Las Vegas; consequently, I no longer had her to help. Carolyn, of course, was well ensconced in Hawaii, and obviously had no intention of coming back; and although the publishers were handling public relations for the book nationally, there was still a lot to be done, as we were to make all the local arrangements.

"Why don't we ask around and see if we can find just the right person to handle, say, a two-week period of prepublication publicity work, just in San Francisco!" Mary Lou said.

This seemed a good idea to me.

"I'll leave it to you, Mary Lou. You know we don't want anyone who's flamboyant or abrasive."

A few days later, Mary Lou told me she had talked with a woman who sounded as though she could handle the job perfectly. A time and place was set, and with mixed feelings of curiosity and expectation, Mary Lou and I joined Claire Harrison at Enrico's. Enrico's is, I suppose, the nearest San Francisco equivalent to the Deux

Magots in Paris; it has the same slightly raffish artistic and literary habitués, and a stream of beatniks—now replaced by hippies—flows by. Yet it remains, in spite of everything, a pleasant island in a sea of San Francisco topless "palaces." It was the right place, I thought, to meet halfway, to talk about books.

Claire Harrison turned out to be an attractive woman, dark-haired and dark-eyed, and delicately made, with a pleasant personality. I remember her saying, "This will be an easy job. You're known in the area, and that's always a head start. I can get in touch with people easily. . . ."

I left Enrico's, glad I had the matter settled, and Mary Lou said she felt exactly the same way, as she had so much to do. Now, surely, we were going in the right direction.

We also got in touch with two of my fan club members, Mary Ann Gigulito and Michael Gricus. My fan club may need a little explanation. One afternoon, just after my television show had gone off the air for the day, and a short time before the troubles in the house started, one of the studio secretaries came up to me and said, "Your fan club is here."

"What d'you mean? I don't have a fan club!"

"Well, you have one now."

And sure enough, waiting for me in the lobby were three bright-eyed teenagers, Mary Ann and Michael, who I found out were cousins, and a third, Ann Marie.

"*We're* your fan club," they announced in chorus, "and we wanted to see you."

The three were soon recruiting more members; they had twelve when I first met them, which soon grew to fifty, and finally the group numbered in the hundreds. Mary Ann and Michael remained the prime movers and opened my eyes to the needs of teen-agers, their want of direction and guidance, and their uncertainty of their own identity. I had begun with Mary Ann, whom Mary Lou and I had helped to gain confidence in order to express herself to others; and from this start grew the idea of a Teen Seminar. I felt a responsibility to these young people that had to be expressed in action.

The fan club members, in return, turned up to cheer me on at many of my public appearances, waving banners bearing the legend WE LOVE PAT MONTANDON, and wearing buttons with my picture on them. Their loyalty was touching and I naturally turned to Mary Ann and Michael to assist me with the party plans for the book. They were wonderfully helpful. The kick-off was to be in Ghirardelli Square, an attractive group of buildings in old red brick, which used to be a chocolate factory, and has now been pleasantly landscaped with gardens, fountains, plazas and terraces overlooking the Bay.

A great deal of work had to be done and we got on with it, in spite of the distracting moods of the house. I didn't want to talk about it, except with Mary Lou, as I was conscious people would think I was unstable if I had ever said to them, as often occurred to me, "The house is really mad at me today." But for all that, I was becoming increasingly conscious that it had an independent personality. In spite of the complete refurbishing I had undertaken at the same time as the upstairs apartment had been repaired, the negative aspect of the house continued to express itself in changing moods. It was as though one day it would be sullen, or morose; another, ugly and inimical; or again, glowering at me in restrained fury, as if to express a bottled-up rage that could only find an outlet in ill-wishing toward me.

How did this reveal itself? By a door suddenly slamming behind me? Or a draft of wind through the house when all the windows were closed? It was not so simply rationalized as that: It was a feeling, a presence, I could not put into words. And in frustration I would turn my back on it, saying to myself I was becoming paranoid. I would not allow such feelings to influence me. Such things could not be.

It was shortly after our first meeting that Claire Harrison got in touch with me, with a long list of contacts for personal appearances: radio, television and newspaper interviews, one of which was Channel 2 in Oakland, across the Bay from San Francisco, for the *Pat Michaels Show*.

I always had to submit the list of shows proposed to me to David Sacks, my boss at KGO-TV, for his approval. On this occasion, David called me unexpectedly at home, and said, "Pat, I don't want you to do the *Pat Michaels Show*."

I said, "Why?"

David said, "It's just this. You have a very high rating on television—much higher than his—I'm afraid he's using you without your benefiting from it at all, and I don't want to see that happen to you."

I said, "All right, David, you're the boss. If you think I shouldn't, I won't."

I got back to Claire and told her the gist of the conversation with David. She was upset about it, and said, "Well, we'll see what happens. I'll have to call the people at the station and tell them. They were pleased you were going to be on—and it's embarrassing. . . ."

It was obviously awkward for her, and I could certainly sympathize. She called me back soon afterward.

"Pat, they are *really* upset over at Channel 2. They've gotten so much publicity out on you—good publicity— and it's going to be a real blow for them if you can't do the show. They've been so nice and cooperative and they're quite insistent. They have even sent out press releases and they're announcing on the air . . . that you're coming in to do the show. . . . Can't you reconsider? Please call David Sacks and see if he'll do something about it."

When I reached David and told him what had happened, he said, "Okay, Pat, in view of all the advance publicity they've released, go ahead and do the show."

When I called her back she said, "I'm so glad. It gets me off the hook . . . I'm caught in the middle when something like this happens."

I went on with my work as well as making appearances on the *Owen Spann Show,* Jim Dunbar's *A.M. Show*—innumerable local shows—on television and radio. I was to tape the *Pat Michaels Show* on a Thursday, and it was to be aired on Friday, September 13, 1968. I was at home in my bedroom on that Tuesday. I still felt fearful and always locked myself in as I had before, and I only intermittently had the company of Dog, when he was well enough to bring back home from the vet's. At night, I was still waking at two, conscious of the dreary atmosphere in the house, which was quite inexplicable, as my life seemed at last to be straightening out.

On this particular day I had gone home early and was going over papers, working on a project for another book, and research material littered the bed. I was absorbed in plans and details for the new book and the schedule for the current one when the phone rang. It was late afternoon, the eleventh of September, 1968. I recognized the voice at once. It was a friend of mine, Diane Childjen, who worked at Channel 44.

"Pat, how are you?"

"Fine, Diane."

A pause, an awkward silence, then she began again. "Pat, I don't know how to tell you—" Her voice broke off.

I asked, "Diane, what is it?" I detected something hidden in her voice, an undercurrent of tension, and I became alarmed.

"Have you seen *TV Guide*?" she asked.

"No, I don't take it. What are you talking about?"

"Are you supposed to do the *Pat Michaels Show*?"

"Yes, as a matter of fact, I'm going to tape it tomorrow."

Diane began again, "I don't know what to tell you."

And I said, my voice rising, "Tell me what? *What is it*?"

Another voice cut in on an extension, a man's voice. He said, "Pat, we're so sorry."

I sat up on the side of the bed, shivering. *"TELL me what it is!"*

She said, "Well, I'll read it to you."

And then while I listened with growing disbelief, she read me a listing from *TV Guide: "Channel 2: Pat Montandon—From Party Girl to Call Girl!"* The anxious voices broke in again. "Pat, you'll be ruined. . . . They're saying you're a call girl!"

When I could collect myself, I tried to reach someone at Channel 2 for an explanation, but it was early evening. Everybody had left the station except the operator, and I left word with him to tell the producer of the show that I was canceling my appearance and to get in touch with me immediately.

I then dialed Mary Lou. I seemed to turn to her when there was a problem and lately I was never free of one. Just as her phone was ringing, I remembered she had gone to a symphony concert that night. I felt utterly frustrated. I must have called ten people. No one was at home.

Finally, I called my sister, Faye Antrim, who lived in Fresno, and told her what had happened. She was heartsick for me and said she would go immediately to talk to my mother and try to break the news as gently as possible. I particularly dreaded this. Since we had all been reared in such a deeply religious atmosphere the idea that anyone in our family circle could even be thought of in the same breath with a call girl was entirely out of the question.

I knew this kind of innuendo in print would appear an accusation; it was horrible for me but it could be devastating to my mother. Having steeled myself to accomplish that chore, I called Frances Moffat, a close friend of mine, and a reporter for the San Francisco

Chronicle. I asked her to come over and stay with me awhile.

At this point, of course, I hadn't seen the article myself, as it had only just come out. I told Frances about it and asked her to please try to find a copy for me. I didn't feel like even venturing into my living room—much less unlocking all the locks and going out to try to find a copy on my own. I felt shaken and sick, and could only lie on my bed and think about what all this could possibly mean.

My doorbell shrilled loudly, breaking into my disconnected thoughts and making me jump, until I realized it was probably Frances. As had become my habit, I peeked through the bedroom curtain to see for sure who was there. I never opened the door now without being sure.

When Frances walked in, she looked strained and ill at ease. I could see she had *TV Guide* open at the place where the article was. I read it with a sinking heart, and realized that everything Diane had said was true. I was being referred to as a call girl.

I said very little to Frances—not trusting my voice—as we sat on the sofa and made small talk. Frances busied herself for a moment in the kitchen and came back with some hot tea, and we tried unsuccessfully to talk of other things. It was rather like trying to ignore a death in the family.

She made an attempt to convince me it would all blow over . . . and she ended up with, "Pat, don't worry. It's nothing." But I knew by her very manner that she didn't believe what she said.

After Frances left, I relocked all the doors and went to bed. It was a futile gesture—as far as sleeping was concerned. I would drift off into a doze and have nightmares filled with loud derisive laughter and wake up gasping for breath, with my heart racing. And at one point I awoke and froze in terror as I heard footsteps leave my bedroom door and disappear into the kitchen. Ignoring caution, I raced to the door, flung it open, and ran across the living room, down the two steps to the dining room and into the kitchen. But there was nothing there—only a slight breeze that blew my hair across my face. I wondered what strange trick of sound had deceived me, and I went back to bed puzzled, thinking perhaps I had had another nightmare.

As I dressed automatically the next morning, I thought of what the nighttime had brought; and I wondered if, perhaps, it was only night terrors that had made the whole *TV Guide* incident loom larger than life. I reassured myself I had made too much of the whole thing. Feeling better after a warm shower and a splash of perfume, I carefully put on my makeup, did my hair, and headed for work. The television cameras and that second hand which makes performers know what one second actually means are hard taskmasters. As the elevator crept slowly to the third floor where my studio was, I had precious little time as usual. I sprinted down the long, wide hall to my dressing room, found the key, opened the door, and stopped, staring in disbelief.

Huge bold letters stood out in bright red lipstick on my dressing room mirror: CALL GIRL! CALL GIRL! CALL GIRL! Before I could fully absorb the shock, I saw in a confusion of spilled face powder and broken lipstick a copy of *TV Guide* with that hateful article circled in red—the same red lipstick that had been used on the mirror.

I hardly had time to reflect on this whole sordid scene before the floor manager was knocking on my door, telling me I had one minute till air time. I quickly took a Kleenex and wiped at the offending words reducing the letters to a red smear and wishing I could erase them as easily from the magazine. The camera crew was unaccustomedly silent; and during commercial breaks I tried to figure out who had access to my dressing room, who at the studio might be an enemy. It was a vicious circle, coming to no conclusion. I had always had many friends and acquaintances and prided myself on being able to get along with almost everyone. I couldn't understand how I could have made an enemy and not know about it, but obviously I had, and it was apparent that person had a key or at least some means of entry to my dressing room. On reflection I realized there were far too many people who fell into this category; many people over the years had been given keys, and the door was often even left unlocked.

By the end of that two hour stint, I felt totally drained, but I had to rush home to prepare for my first book lecture. slated for that afternoon. I still hadn't talked to Mary Lou and I was anxious to see her and find out what her opinion was of the whole demeaning situation. I needed her to talk to.

As I opened the apartment door, I could hear her call out to me, "Hey, Patsy Lou, the kooks are really out in force. The phone hasn't stopped ringing." And then as I came around the front door, "We really have had some strange ones. Several women called. One had a high shrill voice and demanded to speak to you. 'Is this the residence of Miss Montandon, the famous call girl?' And then she hung up," she continued in one breath. "Then someone else called—another woman—and said you should be ridden out of town. . . ." Mary Lou paused, and now looked at me for the first time since I had come in, and could see at once that something was dreadfully wrong. I could hardly speak. A wave of nausea rolled over me.

I headed for the bathroom, grabbed a wet towel, pressed it against my face, and in a halting voice, while leaning over the sink, told Mary Lou what had happened. She reacted with a sense of outrage that mirrored my own, but we both felt equally helpless.

I went into my bedroom and lay face down on the bed, with a cold washcloth on my neck, trying to pull myself together. Two o'clock was creeping closer, and in spite of it all, I had to put on a happy face and address three hundred people, who would be waiting to hear me give a talk on how to be a gracious hostess.

As I entered the auditorium, my staunch Midwestern upbringing came to the rescue. I remembered the time my father had to report to the deacons of the church, who were infuriated with him for admitting blacks to the services. His example then became my model now. I put my chin up, my shoulders back, and with a smile on my face walked to the lectern. The audience seemed friendly, and I managed temporarily to forget the unfortunate listing. I got through my address in fairly good style. With an inaudible sigh of relief, I then asked if anyone had any questions.

The first had to do with ideas for imaginative birthday parties. I answered, asked for a second, and was totally unprepared when the woman asked in a matter of fact way, "Is it true what they say about you in *TV Guide*? Are you a call girl?" I don't know how I looked to the audience, but I would have been happy had the stage opened up and swallowed me whole.

I answered quietly, "No," concluded my lecture abruptly, and left.

The trip back to the city seemed an eternity. I dragged myself up the stairs to the apartment and collapsed in tears on the bed. Mary Lou came in, put her arms around me, and said, "It's okay, honey . . . at least I was able to track down how all this got started."

She told me that Channel 2 had sent out a release to the press, stating, "From Party Girl to Call Girl: How Far Can a Party Girl Go Before She Becomes a Call Girl?" According to the wording, I was to appear with a masked, anonymous prostitute.

"My God, Mary Lou," I asked, "how can people do such things?"

"I don't know . . . I don't understand anything that's been happening around here lately."

We finally decided to try to forget the whole episode,

as I didn't want to become paranoid, and I could see it would be easy to become obsessed by it.

Mary Lou had saved a huge stack of mail which we decided we would go over together. I thoroughly enjoyed reading it and always did so when I had the time. Knowing this, Mary Lou had made a point of saving more than usual, thinking it would cheer me.

I made a pot of herb tea, and as we drank our tea and opened the mail, I would read aloud from various letters and Mary Lou would jot down notes if they required answering. I was quite unprepared then, when upon opening a thick envelope, a horrible, filthy object fell into my lap. It was a used sanitary napkin! I screamed as I leaped up and the offensive thing fell to the floor.

Mary Lou grabbed a Kleenex, gingerly took it out the back door and dumped it into the garbage can. We both washed our hands thoroughly, and looked at the envelope, trying to get some clue to what deranged mind could have sent it. There was no hint—only the address written in a shaky hand, and it had come to my home, not the studio. And then I saw on the inside flap a further obscenity. We finally took the envelope and burned it over the kitchen sink, watching its curling edges turn to black ash, hoping, I suppose, to rid ourselves of it completely. I was sickened, and indeed I had reason to be wary. More horrible objects cropped up before we were through with that stack. Some were photographs of couples in various "erotic" poses, as well as numerous contraceptive devices. I couldn't face it any longer and left the future mail to Mary Lou. She would only hint occasionally that there had been an unsavory piece of mail that day.

In the meantime, while I was waiting for the nightmare to pass, I was becoming progressively more affected by it. I had become, without realizing it, very sick indeed. I called Warren Arnold. He prescribed medication to calm me down, but it was about as effective as a glass of water. And that night, as on so many others, I paced the floor from two o'clock, until at last, at about four in the morning, I collapsed in a sort of fitful half-sleep.

During the day, after these broken nights, I forced myself to continue with my schedule. One of my duties at KGO was to cover certain news events, and that September I had been asked to report on the opening of the Opera. Knowing my general reluctance to face people, Mary Lou suggested she take my pass and leave before I did to meet the cameraman, Buck Jones, so I would not have to rush. This seemed a fine idea to me, and when I arrived about an hour later, I found she had already conducted some interviews. I said hello to Buck, picked up the microphone, and walked around the outer circle by the carriage entrance where a large group of spectators had gathered to watch the city's beautiful people arrive in their limousines.

I thought it might be interesting to get some reactions from some of the non-operagoers. I started toward the crowd, and as I walked up to a group of three men, one of them turned to me and called out, "Hey, Pat, how much do you charge?" followed by a murmur of laughter. I flinched and responded automatically by walking swiftly back to the Opera House, where I did a brief descriptive piece, handed the microphone back to Buck Jones, and left.

I went home to the crooked street and divested myself of my opera finery, a golden brocade full-length cloak lined in pale blue silk, with a matching blue gown. I had felt so elegant when I put it on, and now it was just another dress, an ensemble that had lost its color and meaning—something I would hate ever to wear again.

I got into bed, turned the electric blanket up to high, and feeling restless and in search of any distraction to take my mind off the evening's humiliating incident, I turned on the eleven o'clock news. There, to my amazement, was Mary Lou, on film, direct from outside the Opera House.

The camera zoomed in on her, as with tears streaming down her face, she handed my opera pass to a little old lady in tennis shoes who had just been expressing, with much histrionic pathos, her great love of the opera, but who couldn't afford to get in. I smiled to myself; and the next day I teased Mary Lou with trying to take my job away from me. I was thankful I still had a sense of humor. But even that soon evaporated.

It had been arranged for me to autograph copies of *Party Girl* at the Emporium, a large San Francisco store. I was sitting at a table on a slightly raised platform, separated by red velvet ropes from the crowd of people waiting for their books to be signed. A stack was piled high on my left, and I was equipped with a battery of felt-tipped pens. The department manager spoke a few words of greeting over a microphone, and I settled down to sign. I warmed to my task, cheered by the kindness of the people who came up, some bringing flowers from their own garden; others, bottles of cologne or perfume. I was beginning to feel so alienated from everyone that these gestures from total strangers were most touching.

I looked up, smiling expectantly at the next candidate for my signature, a tall, gangling, pimply-faced young man, and was totally unprepared when he lowered his voice to a sly whisper and said, "I only wanted to see what a hooker looked like" and went on quickly through the line. I continued autographing books, but everything was a blur. I could hardly see to write my name.

These were only a few, a sampling, of the unpleasantnesses I had to face every day; and after reviewing all that had happened with Mary Lou, I felt I had no alternative but to file a lawsuit (against *TV Guide,* Channel 2, and Pat Michaels). I had hoped it could be handled quietly, but this proved impossible. Headlines the next day observed PAT'S IN A SNIT. It was all treated like a joke, a field day for journalists. It was an additional humiliation. More than three years passed before the suit came to court, and all that while it was a continuous source of pain.

Two nights after filing the lawsuit, I was awakened at two thirty by a nightmare and the same loud, derisive, mocking laughter. The house felt even colder than usual. I could feel a draft, although all the doors and windows in the bedroom were closed. I got up, unlocked my bedroom door, and realized a freezing current of air was sweeping through the living room.

The two casement side windows looking out toward the Bay were wide open and the wind was whistling through the house. It had even scattered all the papers off the tables; and a vase of yellow daisies had been blown over, dripping water onto the carpet; the flowers were strewn over the table and the floor.

I quickly latched the windows securely and went to the kitchen where I heated some milk. This had become almost a nightly ritual. I took the milk back to the bedroom with me, locked myself in, drank it, and drifted off to sleep.

I was awakened again at about half past six. There was an intangible something in the house. I got up, cautiously unlocked the door, and looked into the living room. I stared blankly at the windows I had fastened during the night. They were once again wide open, and the wind was blowing at gale force through the room.

all clapped and sang "Happy Birthday," in a happy and

7

The Restless Journey

In spite of the chaos growing around me, I still managed to hold my head high, and continued with plans for the book tour. I was in constant touch with my publishers in New York, and the day finally arrived for the presentation in Ghirardelli Square.

Much to my surprise, the party went pretty much as planned. About two hundred people arrived: booksellers, book buyers, members of the press, friends, and relatives. Mary Lou stayed close by my side, knowing how paranoid I was feeling. I knew I was being talked about, and all I wanted to do was hide; instead, I had to bear the full light of public exposure. Even though the headlines about the lawsuit would not hit the newspapers until the next day, the prospect weighed heavily on my mind. While the crowd danced to the country and western music, or nibbled Vasilis Glimadakis' *dolmades* and *soufflaki,* washed down with *ouzo,* I withdrew, talking only to people I knew well, and not circulating as I would have done in normal circumstances. Time passed, and some of the guests moved on to dine elegantly on seafood crepes and champagne at the Magic Pan, while I kept close to my friends.

Then there was a tap on my shoulder, and a familiar voice said, "I'd like you to meet Pat Michaels." I turned with a mechanical smile of greeting before I recognized the name, then froze: It was a fellow performer at KGO, who had thoughtlessly foisted this introduction on me. I turned abruptly on my heel and left the two men standing where they were. I joined the first group I knew, but I was shaken, and the incident cast a further pall over the rest of the evening.

The obscene phone calls had become unbearable. I had a listed number for the instrument on the twenty-five-foot extension the bodyguards had used and that had no cutoff bell: It was an old-fashioned machine I had been fond of and had managed to persuade the telephone company to let me keep. I also had an unlisted number and I was even receiving "dirty" calls on that line. Finally, in desperation, I took the old phone off the hook and put a pillow over the receiver so that the constant beep-beep-beep tone wouldn't drive me crazy.

I had called the telephone company—and the police—innumerable times, but discovered there was little they were prepared to do other than change the number; and I didn't think I could afford to do that, as I had many lecture brochures out just then with my number on them and would stand to lose a great many engagements if it were changed.

It was at this point that I received a letter from my editor, saying that unfortunately several of the big television shows they had been sure they could book me on had strangely not come to fruition. But the tour was to continue as scheduled anyway.

I began to feel ill. One symptom was a loss of my sense of balance. When I got up in the morning, I was so dizzy

I would literally run into the walls. Sometimes I thought perhaps my imagination was running away with me, for I would definitely feel more dizzy in some parts of the house than in others.

Mary Lou was also becoming affected, and strangely, she was experiencing some of the same sensations I was —even nausea and vertigo.

Of course we were now under a great deal of extra stress as I was due to leave momentarily for New York for the first part of the book tour. What had been an eagerly anticipated event had become an effort of will, and the house seemed sullenly resentful of my leaving.

As we planned the itinerary and my wardrobe, Mary Lou said suddenly, "I can't let you go by yourself, Patsy Lou. You aren't in any condition to go on this tour at all. I know you can't afford my fare, so I'll pay my own and go with you. I have friends there I'd like to see anyway." How like her: She exemplified friendship in everything she did. She also suggested that Dog should board at her house with Jimmy and her adult daughters Robin and Jeannie. I felt buoyed by her generous, warm-hearted gesture, with a realization of how much I should value her companionship, and with this reassurance, we prepared to leave for New York.

As we locked the door behind us, we looked at each other with astonishment, as we were quite sure we heard footsteps. I had an odd fancy: Was I really leaving everything behind, or would something follow me, to exercise its influence on me all the time I was away? Morbid imagining, I told myself, and set my mind strictly on the practicalities of the tour ahead.

Michael Gricus and Mary Ann Gigulito, faithful as ever, saw us off at the airport with a big bouquet of yellow roses. As members of my fan club, they were getting their share of persecution too, and I could only feel sympathy for them. Indeed, some people had asked them if they were members of a fan club for a prostitute! I gave them both an extra hug as we said good-bye.

In spite of my fatigue and anxiety, I could not but feel a thrill of excitement when we arrived in New York. The publisher had arranged a suite for us at the famous Algonquin Hotel; and although I would have preferred to exchange a little atmosphere for some hot water (the antiquated water pipes were being repaired), Mary Lou was tremendously excited over the idea of staying under the same roof that had housed the Algonquin Round Table. Those brilliant gatherings at which Alexander Woollcott and Dorothy Parker had scintillated, fired Mary Lou's imagination, and she gradually assumed some of that lady's characteristics. She was constantly quoting her: " 'Men,' " she recited with glee, as she removed her sunglasses from her nose, " 'seldom make passes at girls who wear glasses,' " and I would retort with, "Mary Lou, you're running the whole gamut of emotions from A to B."

We were thrilled to find the rooms decorated with crepe paper streamers and confetti. A bottle of champagne rested in an ice bucket, and a copy of my book was propped up on the bedside stand. A large sign read WELCOME TO OUR PARTY GIRL and was signed MCGRAW-HILL. I picked up some of the streamers and threw confetti in the air, whooping with joy as I opened the champagne, and Mary Lou and I each had a glass. We still had our coats on as we celebrated, filled with wonder and a sense of release. This was the first time I had felt such exuberance in many a long day. And there was even a welcoming note from Mayor John Lindsay, who had been a schoolmate of Mary Lou's late husband, Jack Ward.

Mary Lou said, with an air of summing up, "Pat, you're really on your way. This is going to be a marvelous tour . . . I can tell . . . and I *know* you feel better already." And of course, under those conditions, I couldn't disagree with her.

The next morning, Sam Stewart, from the publishing house, called to say we had a luncheon date at Sardi's and Mary Lou and I should grab a cab and come over immediately to the office of McGraw-Hill. We could meet everybody there, and then we would go off for our luncheon engagement. At noontime, six of us left the offices, to walk to Sardi's. We were in a happy buoyant mood. I was a little taken aback when, as we approached Sardi's, a fat man singled me out of the group and held out an autograph book. Certainly I was flattered, but after the treatment I had received at McGraw-Hill, it seemed only right that I should be asked for my autograph. As Mary Lou handed me a pen, but before I could write, the man peered at me more closely and said, "Are you somebody?"

"Well," I said, "yes."

He said, "Who?"

I said, "Pat Montandon." He looked at me a second and abruptly grabbed his autograph book away.

"Oh," he said, "I thought you were *really* somebody."

We all looked at each other and burst out laughing. It was a great joke on me and an instant lesson in humility.

Although my schedule wasn't as heavy as we had anticipated, I was still scheduled to appear on several national network shows. One was the Merv Griffin show, which at that time originated in New York. I was so excited about it, I even went to Saks Fifth Avenue and bought a special evening gown in emerald green chiffon. Even though it cost three hundred dollars, I was able to justify the expenditure to myself as I figured I could use it on a number of shows and wear it to parties when I got home. Suddenly I felt my old carefree self.

In New York, light-years removed from San Francisco and the crooked street, I felt the house could not touch me.

"I just needed to get away, Mary Lou, because I sure feel great now!"

She responded, "There's nothing in that house that can't be cured by the proper perspective." And we laughingly concluded that all our trauma and troubles had been caused by the anxieties of overwork and our too vivid imaginations.

It was Tuesday, October 1, 1968. I was due at the Merv Griffin theater about five o'clock for makeup. Mary Lou accompanied me as we rushed over with all my finery over our arms. We discovered the makeup rooms were in the subbasement and after going down an iron winding stairway, we finally found the right department.

A large friendly woman appeared to be in charge of makeup. As we came in the door, she looked at me and said unexpectedly, "Are you Twiggy?" I was speechless, but eventually I got myself organized and went back to a cubicle where I donned the green chiffon.

The producer came in to talk and fill me in on the timing. He asked a few questions about my book and told me some of the things Merv would be asking. He explained I would be appearing at the show's end. When I was ready, he said, I could go upstairs and sit in the green room where all the guests waited until their turn to appear. I was terribly excited at the idea of appearing on national television and was quite nervous. Mary Lou had a family friend in the advertising business, whom she had called, and he had joined us at the theater. Also, coincidentally, two friends of mine from San Francisco, Frances Moffat and Arthur Meyer, were in New York and were sitting in the audience waiting to applaud wildly when I made my appearance. I was encouraged to know, regardless of how nervous I might be, I would have my own private rooting section.

The green room proved to be a small room dominated by a large television set. We were mesmerized by the TV screen as Arthur Treacher appeared and announced, "Our guests this evening will be Zizi Jeanmaire. . . ." Of course her name was familiar, but the other names I can't remember. They are only a vague sound in my head. I do recall he introduced Twiggy and finally "Pat Montandon." I looked at Mary Lou and grinned.

As we watched Merv talk to Zizi Jeanmaire, there was a rustle in the back of the green room as Twiggy and her boyfriend, Justin, entered to await their turn. They chose seats directly in front of us. Mary Lou and I shared knowing looks. I whispered, "My look-alike," and drew my breath in sharply to make myself look skinny. I knew my time was coming. Twiggy was on with Justin and there wasn't a lot of air time left. The producer came in and tapped me on the shoulder; Mary Lou threw me a kiss, and said, "Good luck." I arranged my dress and held my book in a sweaty palm as I stood poised in the wings. I could hear the inaudible murmur of conversation. The orchestra played and I waited for my cue.

I was told to stand by. I continued to wait, growing more nervous with each passing second, and having a perverse desire for a large glass of ice water. Suddenly the house lights went up and I noticed that the curtains which had separated backstage from the interviewing area were opening. With a feeling of confusion, I realized the show was over. There was a babble of voices. Mary Lou had her arm around me and Frances Moffat and Arthur Meyer were coming up from the audience saying, "What happened?" I saw Merv Griffin come backstage. I tried to talk to him. He gave me a wave and disappeared. The producer of the show, in a tone of professional apology, said, "Well, that's the way it goes in show business. We're very sorry. We didn't expect Justin to arrive with Twiggy. We didn't have room for anyone else," and he hurried away. I felt dismayed. It was beyond my understanding.

"Come on, Pat," someone said. "I'm going to buy you a drink at Sardi's." The last thing on earth I wanted was a drink, but I felt it only fair to go with my friends and tried not to let them see how disturbed I was. I felt myself retreating into the nightmare that had surrounded me for so long. As soon as I could, I excused myself from my friends and walked tiredly out of Sardi's, got in a cab, and went back to the Algonquin alone. I scrubbed the makeup off my face, took a long, hot bath, and went to bed. The next morning I felt wretched. It was as if my feet were mired in quicksand, and the more I struggled, the more I felt I was going under.

Mary Lou acted as if she were taking care of an invalid and couldn't do enough to try to make me feel better.

After thinking it over during breakfast I decided perhaps I was making too much of it all, that although I was terribly disappointed, and it was a letdown, it certainly wasn't the end of the world and I had to pull myself together.

"Mary Lou, let's go for a walk," I said, jumping up. "Let's walk up and down Fifth Avenue to all the bookstores we can find, go in, ask for my book, and when we find it, let's put it in the window."

Well, we did. It was fun. The salespeople were a little chagrined to see what was happening but most of them went along with us. That made me feel a little better; and then I saw the spires of St. Patrick's Cathedral.

"Let's go to church, Mary Lou," I said. "I feel the need to pray."

Wednesday, October 2, 1968, was a cold, crisp day in New York City. We could see the warmth of our breath in front of us as we walked up the steps away from the clamor of Fifth Avenue, through the heavy bronze doors into the quiet of the cathedral. Someone was playing the organ as we walked slowly up the main aisle. In an alcove to the left I could see a priest in his long white robes; and I could hear the cry of a baby being christened. I had a deep sense of inexplicable sadness as we walked forward under the vaulted ceiling toward the main altar.

The church was almost empty, except for perhaps ten or twelve people. Some were sitting quietly, some kneeling, lost in their devotions, and others were looking about, in quiet reverence. The air was heavy with the tallowy smell of candle wax, and I could see the flickering lights of the votive candles in the side altars of the nave. The late-autumn sun filtered through the huge stained-glass windows, casting long jeweled reflections on the floor.

I looked at Mary Lou and whispered, "I want to light a candle, but I don't know what to do."

She whispered back, "I'll show you."

She handed me a quarter and then took me to the slot where one inserts the money and, like teaching a child, led me to the candles. I selected one, and with it in my hands as if mesmerized, I walked slowly past the side altars, seeking the right one for my candle.

There were signs indicating who the saints were: I walked past St. Teresa, who had an alcove all to herself, and came to two side by side in an elaborately carved Gothic marble niche, rising to a crocketed finial: to St. Louis, King of France, Crusader, Protector of the Weak and the Oppressed. But the one that interested me most stood beyond, *St. Michael—Great Archangel, Captain of the Army of God, Type of Fortitude, Champion of Every Faithful Soul in Strife with the Powers of Evil.*

I was reminded how my father, when he needed an answer to a problem, would open the Bible at random, and always seemed to find a passage appropriate to his needs. I felt, in much the same way, I had now been led to St. Michael, because I needed his help. Slowly and deliberately, I placed the candle in the topmost position of the iron rack, and with a long taper lit it. I liked the ritual. I felt I was doing something that needed to be done. As I watched the glow from the flame, I started to pray. I didn't kneel. I just stood and looked at the candle and prayed. I didn't know exactly what I was praying about, but I knew something evil had entered my life. It frightened me. Only God could help me and my prayer encompassed these thoughts.

I must have stared at the candle a long time. Mary Lou tapped me on the shoulder. We looked at each other and I could see tears glistening in her eyes, as they were in mine. She whispered, "We should kneel." I knelt in front of the statue of Saint Michael and bowed my head, but no prayer would come. I had said everything I knew to say.

We got up and walked down the long aisle and back down the steps out onto noisy Fifth Avenue. We were quiet as we walked along bundled up against the cold and with our hands in our pockets. At last breaking the silence, I said, "Mary Lou, I have a terrible feeling that something tragic is going to happen."

"Pat, it's just because of all the problems you've had lately. Everybody goes through things like this."

"I thought that too, for awhile, but I'm beginning to think there's more to it . . . there's something wrong in that house . . . There really is an evil force in my life."

There was a long, protracted silence between us. And then, with a sigh of acknowledgment, Mary Lou said, "I know, Pat, I know . . . I can feel it too . . . it's been weird."

"I've sometimes wondered whether it has anything to do with the Tarot reader. Do you think it's possible?"

"No . . . I think it was already there. Maybe his influence just called it out!"

"I guess I should look for another apartment when I get back."

"Well, Patsy Lou, that might not be a bad idea."

The whole conversation seemed unreal, and I vowed when I returned to San Francisco I would make plans to move.

We went back to the Algonquin. I packed my bags to continue the rest of my tour. It was time to leave New York and go on to such places as Chicago, Minneapolis, St. Paul, Cincinnati, Cleveland, and Detroit. Mary Lou was going back to San Francisco. We said good-bye and we went our separate ways.

8

The Inescapable Chain

It was during the air controllers' slowdown in 1968. I sat in an airplane at Kennedy Airport for three hours before we could take off. Finally, we lifted into the air and landed in Chicago. My reception there was pleasant enough but I couldn't recapture that wonderful happy feeling I'd had before the Merv Griffin incident. Everything I did was a great effort; the dizziness was worse and I was terribly tired. As I continued the tour I found at times I didn't even know what city I was in. I would be doing a television interview and would hardly know what I was saying. It was a struggle. I kept thinking, *If I can only get through this, I'll be all right again.* I had lost a great deal of weight and I laughed wryly to myself, thinking, *I may look like Twiggy yet.*

City after city, airport after airport flashed by, leaving little impress on my consciousness.

My last stop was Detroit. I was looking forward to Detroit. It was almost as if I had kept the only good thing until last—as though I were keeping a secret from myself. I was half afraid to think about it until I could see what was going to happen.

I had some difficulty getting a cab from my hotel in Cleveland to the airport, and as a result, I was one of the last passengers for Detroit to board.

I looked frantically for a seat in the crowded plane. The aircraft had a too-full air about it, and it crossed my mind that perhaps it had been oversold and I might have to get off. As always, those people who had seats wore the smug look of possessive interest in their terrain (the territorial imperative).

I wandered down the aisle until I saw a dark-haired older woman gesture to me from the back. There was a vacant seat next to her, the very last. I gave her a tired smile and settled gratefully into the seat, pushing my hand luggage underneath.

I turned to appraise my companion, hoping she would be pleasant and not too talkative. I was bone-weary, and did not feel up to inconsequential chatter. To my relief, she was agreeable and easy, and did not force herself on me. We half slid into casual conversation and she revealed she was going to visit a daughter who was expecting a baby. She took a motherly but nonprying interest in me, which touched a lonely chord.

I was surprised when she reached over and patted my hand. "You seem nervous, are you afraid to fly?"

"No," I said with a deep sigh, "I'm just tired, I guess."

And much to my embarrassment, I realized the tears were sliding down my cheeks. The next moment I was pouring out my heart to her. Her gentle kindliness had unlocked the floodgate of my feelings.

"I'm really not crazy," I attempted to assure her. "It's just that I've been living in a nightmare. I've had the most unbelievable experiences. . . . Do you believe in the supernatural?"

And not waiting for an answer, I went on, "I've

reached the point where I can't *not* believe it. . . . I've had so many strange things happen."

As I talked, she nodded sympathetically, interjecting an understanding word here and there, and when I had finished, I felt strangely better. I found I'd been able to talk to her far more easily, perhaps because she *was* a stranger, an anonymous personality, than I had to any of my friends. It was like going into a confessional. And at the end, when she said she understood, we were able to settle back in our seats, with our own thoughts again. At peace within, I allowed myself to think of Detroit, and why I was looking forward to arriving there.

I had met the mayor of that city, Jerome P. Cavanagh, or Jerry as I called him, shortly before the fanfare about my book had burst on the scene in San Francisco. We had been introduced to one another by David Sacks, and that same evening, Jerry and a friend of his, also from Detroit, had taken Mary Lou and me to dinner at Doros, an Italian restaurant on Montgomery Street. Before the meal was over, somehow word had gotten out that Jerry was the mayor of Detroit, and wine appeared at the table. (It was funny to remember that before Jerry arrived to pick us up at my house, I had said to Mary Lou, "Do you suppose I should offer to loan him my old Oldsmobile? He probably won't have a car." While we were debating what to do, the doorbell rang. I'd been looking out the windows, and could see the outline of a long, black limousine: I knew immediately my offer of transportation was superfluous.)

The four of us hit it off beautifully together. Jerry Cavanagh, a tall, broad-shouldered man with a good sense of humor, appealed to me at once. Mary Lou, in her bright way, was obviously completely at ease with the Mayor's friend, and conversation weaved in and out between the four of us. Mary Lou, as usual, lost no time in telling Jerry that I had a book coming out soon, and that Detroit was one of the major stops on the tour. I could see he was digesting this information, as I was to find out later. There was something likable about him, and I soon summed him up as someone I would like to know better. He must have felt the same way about me, since he called the next day and asked if I would go with him to Tiburon for lunch.

Once again, the black limousine made its appearance, and as I sank into the cushions, I thought, "This is really the way to travel."

Jerry was entranced with Tiburon. We walked up and down its picturesque Main Street, poking into the shops, busy with tourists. I thought that, for lunch, it would be nice to sit on the deck of a place called The Dock. It has a nautical air about it, with great ship's timbers, and marine memorabilia, and there are always children gazing wide-eyed at a ship's model or a stuffed swordfish. It overlooks a little harbor, with a constant traffic of yachts that come dipping and bobbing across the Bay, and beyond, across the water, rises the sparkling skyline of San Francisco.

As we sat enjoying our lunch, we watched seagulls alighting hungrily near the tables and swooping down at intervals for scraps when no one was looking; although it wasn't a warm day, it seemed cozy to me, as we sat and talked for hours over lunch and silver fizzes. Time passed all too quickly, and we left reluctantly and headed back to the city. He left me at Lombard Street, but not before he asked whether he could take me out to dinner that night.

I don't remember now where we went. What did it matter? We were enjoying each other's company, and Jerry couldn't have been nicer. He said I was to let him know as soon as I knew what date I would be in Detroit. He knew all the media personalities, of course, and assured me I would receive royal treatment. I was thrilled at his thoughtfulness, for the prospect of the tour at that time was still alarming, and I needed reassurance for the program ahead against the insecurities that had been building up in me. Mary Lou beamed when I told her what he had said, identifying as she always did, with my career, and anything she regarded as good for my welfare or morale.

After our second dinner together, I knew this was for me more than a casual acquaintance with a stranger; it was a friendship that could easily grow, and be more rewarding at each meeting.

Mary Lou wrote a letter as soon as he left, outlining my itinerary and emphasizing the date of my arrival in Detroit. We received a letter back saying that Jerry was looking forward to seeing me and was pleased to have all the information about my schedule and where I was staying.

Now I was approaching Detroit at last, and it was understandable that in spite of everything else that had happened that city held something special for me. Here at least I would be assured of welcome.

We touched down at last.

As I fumbled for my belongings, I was taken by surprise to hear my seat companion's tone of voice as she turned and put her hand on my arm, saying with urgency, "It's going to be all right for you. Don't worry."

Had I misunderstood? "I'm sorry, I didn't hear you," I said.

"It's going to be all right," she repeated. "I've been working on it." Then she dug into her voluminous brown bag and handed me something, and then we were in the midst of debarking, and I hastily put it, whatever it was, into my coat pocket. A moment later she had hurried away down the plane's steps and was immediately lost in the surging crowd of travelers.

I finally found a cab and as I was driven away from the airport, I was amazed at the spirit of joy, of celebration that was going on. The pilot had announced that the Detroit Tigers had just won the World Series, and the whole city was exploding in a paean of triumph. As we inched our way along the thronged streets my driver, too, joined in the celebration, and in spite of myself, I found I was caught up in it. Leaning out the window, I yelled, "We did it!" with the rest. I pretended, at first, that it was all to welcome me. My ego needed a little salve, and the harmless make-believe raised my spirits. But there was a sturdy reality to this rejoicing. The city that morning belonged to the Tigers, and to the Tigers alone.

It was with a sense of relief that I reached my rooms, and could rest and prepare myself for the next day. When I awakened, I called to see whether there were any messages. I found there were a few from the publishers, as well as a letter from Mary Lou. She was writing to let me know that things were pretty much the same at home . . . there wasn't any need to hurry back . . . she had been by the house, and it was so freezing she had called again about the boiler . . . Nothing to worry about . . . say hello to Jerry. . . .

I refused to allow myself to think about the house and turned away to get ready for an early morning newspaper interview, the first on my schedule. The reporter from the *Free Press* was waiting for me in the lobby, with a staff photographer. They introduced themselves as Jennifer Jarratt and Jim Tafoya, and after an exchange of greetings we settled down in a quiet corner where we could talk undisturbed. Jimmy began snapping away, taking candid shots, as Jennifer started asking questions:

"Is this your first visit to Detroit?"

"What do you think of our baseball team?"

"What kind of parties do you like best?"

"How did you get the idea for writing your book?"

"How long did it take?"

"Do you have a TV show in San Francisco?"

All innocuous questions. I was answering in a relaxed way, by now quite accustomed to this sort of interview, when the bombshell exploded.

"What's this about you and our mayor, Jerry Cavanagh?"

There was an awkward pause as I hesitated, not knowing how to field the question, and then stammered, "What d'you mean?"

She silently handed me a newspaper clipping, a copy of a Herb Caen item which had appeared in the San Francisco *Chronicle*. It had been picked up by the Detroit press, and said that Pat Montandon and Jerry Cavanagh were a romantic duo. While I was digesting this, she handed me another clipping, in which Jerry stated that he had met me only once—and briefly—and that any talk of a romance between us was part of my publicity campaign for *How to Be a Party Girl*. He didn't know me. . . .

I hoped I didn't show how upset I was. Jennifer kept pressing me for some kind of comment. I threshed about mentally. What could I say? I was entirely unprepared. At practically the very moment of my arrival to be subjected to this. Hurt and disappointed, I blurted out the first thing that came into my head, which happened to be the truth.

"Jerry and I are friends," I said, "certainly not a romance. We did go to dinner in San Francisco, and I found him charming and considerate, a man of great character and sensitivity."

I went on to say that I thought the office of mayor weighed heavily on his shoulders. . . . ("Good heavens," I thought to myself, "I'm overdoing it.") Jennifer, however, appeared satisfied with this rigmarole, and we exchanged friendly goodbyes.

Left alone with my own thoughts, I was crushed. I couldn't understand what had happened until I faced the realization that everything I had touched had fallen apart. Unwillingly, my mind went back to a phrase in Mary Lou's letter, ". . . The house was so freezing." Perhaps what was happening to me now, in Detroit, was an extension of that old ominous sequence of events, a link in an inescapable chain that seemed to have no end. I tried to shake myself free of these thoughts. It must all be nonsense. How could malign forces reach me across the thousand miles of distance? And why?

I looked at my schedule with a sigh. As unhappy as I felt, still I had better pull myself together and get on with it. Because of the national affiliation of all the ABC stations, I had been booked on a number of the local shows. There was a camaraderie between the stations, and I was asked by one of the staff to go to a banquet, which Joey Bishop was emceeing, the night before I left Detroit. I certainly did not have any other plans, but I was still having recurring bouts of dizziness and was far from being in a party mood. And yet I needed some distraction from my own thoughts—I forced myself to tell him I'd be pleased to accept.

As I dressed for the party, the last of my book tour, I took special care. I was determined not to admit to the world that I had caved in under pressure. I put on the soft green evening gown from the Merv Griffin debacle and pinned a long blond fall on top of my own long blond hair, swept the front of it up, and took extra time with my makeup.

My escort was well aware of the situation with Jerry. It had, after all, been in all the papers, but he had only asked a few discreet questions. However, he tugged at my arm, as we were seated at our table, which was placed directly in front of the speakers' platform. He leaned over and whispered, "Look who's here, Pat . . . Jerry."

I followed his glance, and there, on the dais, was Mayor Cavanagh. We could hardly miss each other as I was seated almost directly in his line of vision. And throughout the evening, he kept looking at me and even gave me a surreptitious wave. I tried to ignore him, and as soon as the party was over, I suggested to my new-found friend that I would like to go back to my hotel. I had to pack, as I was catching an early-morning plane home.

When I reached my room, the red message light on the phone was blinking. I picked up the receiver and called the operator.

She said, "Yes, you have a message. 'Jerry called.'"

I said, "Did he leave a number?"

"No."

"Anything else?"

"No. That's all—Jerry called."

As I put the phone back in its cradle, I smiled cynically to myself as I started packing.

I didn't care how I stuffed my clothes back into my worn suitcase. Wrinkles no longer mattered. I merely shoved everything in, sat on top of the last bag, fastened it, and the next morning left Detroit for San Francisco.

As I settled into my seat on the plane, homeward bound, I felt in my coat pocket and encountered a small, round object. At first I thought it was a coin, except that it had a little hook or loop on it. Then I remembered: the woman on the plane—she had given it to me, and I had never looked at it. I examined it curiously. It was a flat disk of metal, a medallion. It bore a winged figure with a spear, standing above a dragon; and the spear was thrust into the dragon's mouth. Around the rim was an inscription in French: *Saint Michel.* It was *St. Michael, Champion of Every Faithful Soul in Strife with the Powers of Evil. . . .*

figure against the darkening skyline. I went c.. up broad

9

As the House Is Pleased to Direct Me

It was late in October when I arrived back in San Francisco. The sun was just setting. I don't remember how I got home from the airport, whether I took a cab or whether someone met me. I recall looking vaguely at the city as familiar landmarks came into view, partially shrouded in a chilling fog rolling in billows down over the higher ground from the ocean, and lying in a slowly stirring blanket over the Bay. In the past when the beautiful silhouette of the city appeared along a curve of the freeway, I would identify myself with it, but now I felt a stranger, wholly alienated from it. Before I had always belonged, in my own mind, to that strangely romantic and irregular skyline, and all that lay within it; but now I merely felt defeated.

As the panorama of towers unfolded, I caught sight of the Equitable Building, truncated by a swath of fog, with the temperature, 62 degrees, startlingly bright in lights against the darkening skyline. I went on up Broad-

117

way, passing Enrico's sidewalk tables on the right, and recognizing a familiar face or two, sipping a cocktail, yet feeling disinclined to wave. As I approached, I could see the Bay Bridge, half wreathed in fog, and knew the Golden Gate was equally cloaked in mist, for the bridge foghorn was hooting its mournful warnings; and when I reached the house I could see that the hedges of hydrangeas along the crooked street had been cut back, and now wore their bare and bleak winter livery.

I wrestled my suitcases up the steps to my apartment, half carrying, half dragging their heavy load, and pausing at each twist in the stairs to catch my breath.

I was fatigued to the point that each action required its own conscious effort: I put down the bags at the front door, fumbled for my keys, found the right one, and turned the lock. I dragged my luggage into the foyer, found my keys again, and opened the door to my own apartment. Standing in the doorway, I took in the familiar scene. How cold it was. I gave an involuntary shiver. At first all was dark; the Roman shades of ecru linen were down and only the light from the foyer filtered past my own shadow. Even after I had switched on the lamps, the shades, cutting out the view, gave a gloomy aspect to the living room. I took in every detail: the long white sofa under the windows; the antique console table to the right against the wall, beneath the fragile antique mirror, with its two small crystal sconces on either side, each holding two long thin white candles; the marble topped coffee table, piled high with books waiting to be read; and at my feet the expanse of impractical white carpeting. That handpainted chest recalled an afternoon's explorations through the antique shops of Sausalito; and the west wall, covered with gaily-colored bird prints, testified to the kindness of an old friend, Wally Wood, who had helped me to arrange them.

Down two steps, past the built-in planters on either side stood the French provincial dining table, and lined up around it, six chairs upholstered in white linen. Beyond were two eighteenth-century English corner cupboards. Jogging out unexpectedly into the ceiling on the left was part of the upper flight of the main staircase, giving the room an odd, lopsided shape.

The apartment had a gloomy air, exuding a closed-up, dead odor. A thin film of dust covered everything. When I walked into the bedroom, I sensed, even before turning on the light, that it would be as bleak as the rest, although, in that moment, I also detected an unexpected fragrance. When I turned on the light, I saw a magnificent bouquet of out-of-season flowers, placed in the middle of the dressing table, opposite my bed. The blooms were reflected in a large, heavy mirror, which still had a piece of the frame missing from the time when it had crashed to the floor, just before my book tour. (Oddly enough, it had been securely fastened by two extra-large hooks firmly attached to a 2 x 4 board nailed into the studs in the wall. The glass had not shattered when it fell. At the time I thought it might have been caused by a minor earth tremor, common enough in San Francisco, but nothing else in the house had been disturbed.) The bouquet, a combination of spring flowers, freesias, iris, tulips, and baby's breath, cascaded over the top of a wicker basket. A note in red ink read, *Welcome back. See you tomorrow—Mary Lou.* It was the one cheerful touch in my homecoming.

I didn't even unpack; all I craved was sleep. I left the suitcases at the door, rinsed the dust out of the tub, and ran it to the top. I poured in some bath oil and took a long, soothing bath. As I dried myself, I slowly realized I wasn't cold anymore; and as I stepped into the bedroom I was conscious that the entire apartment was warmer, or at any rate felt warmer, than it had for months. To my surprise I noticed that the flowers on the dressing table were already drooping as though the heat of my bedroom was too much for them. Then I got in between my crisp white sheets and fell asleep instantly.

I was awakened abruptly by the insistent shrilling of the bedside telephone. The room was in darkness, freezing cold, and I fumbled for the receiver, realizing, as I did so, that I had forgotten to shut the bell off. I mumbled a hello into the mouthpiece, and my eyes flew open as a male voice whispered, "I'm watching you. . . . You're going to die. . . ."

I reached over and pressed down the receiver bar to cut off the conversation, and fumbling still, shut off the bell. I lay back staring into the blackness until sleep again mercifully overtook me.

The next morning Mary Lou came over at daybreak and bustled around, making coffee, offering to unpack my suitcases, and catching me up on the latest news. She showed me a letter from Carolyn, still in Honolulu, and a postcard from Vera Scott in Las Vegas. Dog was much better than he had been for some time, and we decided to leave him at her home on Webster Street a while longer.

I stayed in bed, listless, with no interest in what was going on around me. It was hard for me even to feign a show of attention. The momentary warmth of the night before had gone. It was as though a tacit truce between the house and me were over.

I knew I had to pull myself together and get ready to do my show again. KGO had been more than generous in giving me time off for my book tour, and I still had to make some incidental trips to Los Angeles, but those I could spread over several afternoons. What I most needed was a new impulse of energy, and yet even the need for it did not matter to me. I didn't care anymore. I had cared all my life, and that I didn't now held no strangeness for me. That was the way it was.

I lay in bed the entire weekend, only rousing from my lethargy to have a bowl of canned soup or fry an egg;

and on Monday, still in the same apathetic mood, I went
to work. I did my show and came home, only to fall into
bed once more, complaining of a wicked headache. It
had started that morning and had grown steadily worse. It
was centered over my right eye and extended to the back
of my neck in soul-destroying pain. No amount of aspirin
controlled it and the accompanying dizziness was growing worse.

I realized I had to see a doctor. I made an appointment
to see Dr. Robert Blau, who along with Warren Arnold
had been my physician for some time, although up until
now I had rarely needed his services. After examining me
he suggested I might have a disease called "tic doulou-
reux" which paralyzes the face and creates excruciating
agony. He gave me some medication, carbamazepine, to
relieve my suffering. It was in the form of little white pills,
and I took them regularly as prescribed, but the pain
was reduced only to a dull ache. I would thrash about
on my bed, until, helpless before the pain, I would double
the dosage, then fall into a stupor. When it had brought
me to a state of total exhaustion, I was sent to see five
other specialists, all of whom in turn gave me a clean
bill of health or suggested I see somebody else.

After days of fruitless and expensive visits, it was at
length decided that I had, of all things, a bad tooth,
which needed a root canal. A Dr. Marsh performed the
work, and I was relieved to have my headache immediately disappear, although I was concerned that the
dizziness remained. My tonogue felt thick, my speech
clumsy, and I felt an inward vacancy.

The days went by like shadows against a cloud, without making any particular impression. I just wanted to
live through them and have them behind me. Oddly
enough, the house no longer bothered me. It had become
strangely innocuous. Nothing about it jarred my nerves or
made me fearful—colorless and uninviting, yes, but
accepting. I no longer found drafts coming from windows

that should have been firmly closed. The fire escape stayed where it belonged. The locks on the doors remained locked. I felt as though I should never leave the house; indeed, it was an effort to go anywhere or do anything. I became more and more a recluse—or as much a recluse as my occupation would allow.

Mary Lou would talk to me for hours on end about recovering my spunk and doing something. I had always been a doer. I couldn't just lie down and die. To all her attempts to rouse me, I would merely shake my head and say, *In time, Mary Lou.* It was two months before I dared tell her I had resigned my job. My contract with KGO would expire on April 4, 1969; it was now December, 1968. I didn't know what I was going to do. I had no plans; and very little money saved. All I knew was that I didn't care anymore.

Meantime, I took refuge in sleep, in a state of suspended animation. It was as though the house and I had accepted each other, although I still dimly felt I had to leave it and with Mary Lou's encouragement had on two occasions requested over the air that anyone knowing of a small, quiet place to rent please let me know. I had been sharply reprimanded by the program director for making this personal appeal during my show, but not before I'd heard from several real estate agents and private persons claiming to have idyllic refuges of one sort or another. I even toyed with the idea of a Chinese junk listed in the want ads, and then I remembered I still had a year and a half to go on the lease, and would have the additional expense of moving. It was too much for me; I couldn't cope with it.

It was almost Christmas. I have always loved the holiday season, and no one could celebrate it with more enthusiasm than I had in the past: Now, I found I didn't have the energy even to send out cards, although Mary Lou had bought some and signed my name to a few.

At last she could stand it no longer. She said, in a tone of finality, "Pat, you've got to decorate for Christmas." She brought box after box up from the basement and into the living room. She unpacked them with great abandon, strewing the brightly colored ornaments over tables and chairs, hoping she could at least capture my interest. Just to please her, I took some of the lights out and draped them over a rubber-tree plant ensconced on a ledge in back of my sofa; and with the addition of a few colored balls, I thought it served nicely as a Christmas tree. I laughed helplessly when, from the sheer weight of the ornaments, the whole thing toppled onto the middle of my white sofa, breaking bulbs and scattering dirt from the pot and leaves from the plant all over the floor. After perfunctorily vacuuming up the debris, I decided it wasn't worth the effort. Perhaps next year I would have a Christmas.

During the month of December I began to receive calls from a man named Alfred Wilsey, who always insisted on speaking to me personally and invited me out to dinner. I found he had got my telephone number from a business partner of his called Gerson Bakar, whom I had met some years before. The last place I wanted to go was to dinner with a stranger, so I begged off, telling him I was much too busy with the Christmas season, and perhaps he could call another time.

I was seeing only a few of my old friends, and really not very often. Alfred sounded pleasant over the telephone, but I had no inclination to go out. He called me again a few days after Christmas, to tell me he was going to Borrego, a remote little place in the desert beyond Palm Springs and would call me when he got back. I said, "Fine, please do. Bye."

I didn't expect he would call again, but he did. It was during the first part of January, 1969: "I have invited some friends over for dinner. Now they can't come, and I have a rack of lamb and only my son, Lad, here to help me eat it." He went on to explain that the boy had broken his leg in an automobile accident and he was nursing him back to health—and wouldn't I please come over and join them. "I don't live very far from you, Pat . . . only about six blocks." I felt resigned to the whole thing and said, "All right, yes . . . why not?"

I was still wearing what I called my tablecloth outfit. It resembled an old-fashioned lace tablecloth, like one my grandmother used, and it consisted of palazzo pants with an over-blouse in ecru lace. I had worn it on my show that day and hadn't even bothered to change. In fact, I still had traces of television makeup on my face, something I seldom allowed to happen. But in my state of lassitude, I didn't care as much as I should have.

As I waited for the ring of the doorbell, I wondered why I was seeing this stranger at all. I supposed I simply couldn't make the effort of refusing anymore. I would go once, and that would be the end of it. The more I thought about it, the more I thought the evening would be tiresome, as I still occasionally had a throbbing head-ache and my dizzy spells continued. *He'll wish he'd never asked me out,* I thought. At least I had made it perfectly clear over the telephone that it would have to be an early evening, and he had been agreeable to that: I had an out if I needed it.

The doorbell rang exactly fifteen minutes after I had hung up. As I opened my apartment door and peered into the foyer, I could see the man who was waiting. I got an impression of dark hair, heavy eyebrows, and nicely assembled features—and a general air of kindliness, hard to pin down. I thought he was good-looking in a strong way, without that "too-good-looking" quality I instinctively mistrust.

When I opened the door to greet him, I noticed he had a gentle way of speaking too. "Pat," he said, "I didn't think I was ever going to meet you."

I grabbed my coat and off we went, down the steps and

out to his car. He was driving a battered old station wagon. I have always had a thing about cars. I suppose it stems from my childhood of always having cars that didn't quite work or were falling apart; and it was a sharp disappointment to see that he was driving such a dilapidated old wreck.

We got in and quickly drove six blocks to the apartment building where he lived. I was surprised when he pushed the elevator button for the penthouse on the thirty-third floor, and I looked at him questioningly.

"Do you live in the penthouse?" I asked.

"Yes, I've lived here for a year."

'Well, you must have quite a view."

High double doors marked the entrance. We walked in. I could see the view was truly magnificent. The windows in the living room looked about twenty feet high and framed the entire Bay, taking in the Bay Bridge and Oakland, and then sweeping all the way around past Alcatraz, Angel Island, to the Golden Gate Bridge, far to the west. I stood and gazed, absorbing the shimmer of lights on the distant shore and the beauty of San Francisco stretched out below, like a scale model in color.

We were immediately comfortable with each other, Alfred and I, with no awkward silences between us. His son, Lad, was lively and friendly, and we all chatted inconsequentially until dinner was served. Afterward we went into the living room and talked a while longer, until Alfred looked at me consideringly, then said, "Pat, you look terribly tired. I am going to take you home."

Well, that was certainly a switch. In the past I always made that kind of decision. I couldn't recall anyone ever asking to take me home so early before and gratefully obeyed. It was only half past nine as he took me firmly back down the hills and over to the crooked street. He escorted me up the stairs to my front door and said, looking directly at me, "I don't remember when I've been able to talk to anyone so easily. May I give you a call to-morrow?"

"Yes . . . that would be nice."

The feeling of pleasure lingering with me from the evening evaporated when I entered my apartment. Its influence again seemed to surge up and envelop me.

The next day Alfred called, as he had promised. He asked me to go to dinner with him again. He refused to take no for an answer. In spite of my negative frame of mind, I wanted very much to see him. We chose a tiny restaurant in North Beach, The Golden Spike, where they serve family-style meals, and over a bowl of mine-strone, served from a large tureen, he started to ask me some probing questions. I realized that in spite of all the press coverage I had received, he knew nothing about me. He had never seen my television show, and in fact didn't know I had one. He already instilled in me a senes of so much confidence that I had no qualms about telling him anything he asked. And I made no secret of having been married before.

"How old are you?"

I hesitated, not knowing whether to tell the truth. I had always been truthful about my age until the last few years, and now felt a lie might be in order.

"Thirty-two," I said. He looked at me with a twinkle in his eyes and said, "Oh? Well, then, you are much too young for me, I'm forty-five."

I quickly amended the number to thirty-five.

Alfred threw his head back and roared with laughter. I laughed with him, warmed by the rapport we had estab-lished, the kind of rapport I so badly needed.

When I discussed Alfred with Mary Lou, she looked at me with caution in her eyes and said, "Honey, don't get carried away . . . you hardly know him. I hope he's all you say—you know how easily fooled you are."

I quickly reassured her our relationship had only just begun. I didn't feel it had reached the stage of being a romance, but it was certainly heartening to have someone to talk to, someone I felt I could trust, and I was now looking forward to each meeting.

I still found the dreariness of the apartment inexplicable and wondered whether it was because it needed redecorating, though it had been only six months since the last refurbishing. I discussed this with Mary Lou, who was enthusiastic at the idea of redoing the place, and even said she would help with the financing; although she would have liked it even better if I had been able to move.

We began looking for workmen: luckily, the landlord was able to find me a painter who was prepared to repaint the whole apartment for a reasonable fee.

For new material, we went to Home Yardage, to recover the sofa in white linen, and had linen pillows in pinks and reds as color accents. The dining room chairs were reupholstered in fresh white cotton; a French chair in the living room was covered in a beautiful, soft beige leather, and I even went the whole hog and bought new white wall to wall carpeting.

The effect was bright and attractive at first, and yet, as fast as the smell of linseed oil and turpentine evaporated, the brightness of my refurbishing seemed to fade with it and the pervasive grayness returned.

In spite of this, I decided to give a belated birthday party for Mary Lou. I also wanted to see Alfred again, hoping to draw some strength from his serenity and confidence, and I could use as an excuse that he hadn't seen the apartment's new face lift. Mary Lou had had her birthday while I was on my book tour, and her little son, Jimmy, also had just had his in January. I decided to give a combined party for the two of them.

Little did I realize this would be the last birthday party I would ever be able to give for Mary Lou.

I planned it to be small and intimate. I asked Alfred and his son, Lad, if they would come, and Susan Weber, the producer of my show at KGO. Olympia Martyn came too.

Olympia was an old, old friend of mine, who had gotten to know Mary Lou through me. Paul Robinson was there, a longtime friend of Mary Lou, and of course, "The Boy Friend," who by this time was in his dotage. I didn't want many people: I just wanted a few close friends around to show Mary Lou how much we treasured her and to try to do something that would be a little bit of fun after the long dreary months we'd lived through together. Mary Lou was delighted, as much delighted, I think, that I was at last doing something as that it was her own birthday party.

I remember selecting a present for her. I knew exactly what it should be: opera tickets. She loved the opera, and I thought back with amusement to that evening when she had so openhandedly given away my opera pass. Opera tickets would have been perfect, yet when I stood at the box office to purchase them, I had a feeling, a premonition perhaps, that the opera season was too far away. I had to get her something more immediate.

Instead, I bought her tickets for the remaining concerts of the San Francisco Symphony's season. I knew she thoroughly enjoyed Seiji Ozawa, so I searched out an album of records on which he conducted Bach's *Christmas Oratorio*. I wrapped it, with the tickets, in some gold fabric I had, that Mary Lou had always admired. I gave the rich-looking little parcel to her at our little celebration. She was so pleased. And giving me a hug and a kiss, she waltzed around the room, telling me how much she would enjoy the concerts; she thought she might even take "The Boy Friend" with her.

The party was a success, in spite of the overmastering fatigue which would periodically envelop me.

I had hired a caterer, who had brought his own silver chafing dish and cart, and demonstrated his sleight of hand with the banana fritters like a master magician. We all clapped and sang "Happy Birthday," in a happy and sentimental mood. Jimmy loved it all and gorged himself unrestrainedly.

Olympia Martyn had asked if she could bring a friend, who she said, was a pleasant, inconspicuous woman, and an amateur astrologer. I wasn't too keen, after the horoscope Mrs. Armstrong had sent me, to be drawn into this subject again, nor did I want anyone at the party to be upset by unfortunate predictions. But I reasoned that she would know it was a birthday and would only tell fortunes in fun.

As it turned out she read almost everybody's fortune, but concentrated on Alfred and me. She made us acutely embarrassed by some such phrase as "his Mars was in the ascendant, and was descending into my house of Venus." Alfred's sign was Libra, while both Jimmy Ward and I were Capricorns and Mary Lou was a Scorpio.

I tried to steer the soothsayer in Mary Lou's direction, as she had studiously avoided her, but she seemed not to notice, and ignored her throughout the evening. (I didn't attach any particular significance to this until later.)

It was a quiet, loving evening, and over by ten o'clock. As we said goodnight, Mary Lou and Jimmy walked down the stairs and out to her car to drive on home. The other guests departed about the same time, but Alfred lingered on. He sat on the sofa and talked for a while, surprising me when he said, as he reached over and held my hand, "Pat, I'm worried about you. You don't look as if you feel well."

I said, "I don't. I haven't felt well for months."

He said, "Don't you think you should get away? Perhaps a vacation would be good for you."

I knew I couldn't afford a vacation, particularly after that long book tour. And I couldn't tell him that I wanted to lie down and sleep forever, not caring whether I woke up or not. Alfred must have sensed some of this: and what I did tell him was that I had resigned my job at KGO. Naturally I couldn't tell everyone why I wanted to leave my once delightful, beautiful apartment. It would have sounded so neurotic. I didn't want people to think I was unbalanced, some kind of a nut, so I kept my feelings about the place to myself. But Alfred wasn't just anybody, so I told him the whole story and ended by saying that as limp and exhausted as I felt, I knew, as soon as my lease was up, I would have to leave.

As I told Alfred all this, I watched closely for his reaction: Would he look at me in dismay? Would he think I was losing my mind? But as I talked, he merely nodded his head. When I got through, he put his arms around me and said, "Pat, I think what you are doing is absolutely right. I don't like this place. I never have. It bothers me. I'll be relieved when you get out of it." He went on to say, "D'you mind if I put my own telephone in, so that you can call me if you need me?"

This surprised me enormously. I had two telephones already, but with one shut off and the other off the receiver at night, it was impossible to get through to me. He wanted me to have this extra phone kept exclusively for ourselves. I was touched that he would care.

Two days later a red telephone was installed at the side of my bed and Alfred Wilsey was the only one who had its number.

I knew I was beginning to fall in love with this kind, gentle man, and the more I heard about him, the more my feelings for him increased. I had found out through a number of friends that he had been married some years before to a woman who, as he was well aware, was dying of cancer. In fact, he had been the one elected to tell her the heartbreaking news, and they had been married shortly afterward. He had looked after her for nine years.

Now he had been widowed for over a year, and apparently all his friends had tried to fix him up, as a highly eligible man, with someone to take out, but he had so far refused to date at all. Why had he made me the exception?

It emerged that he had been visiting a mutual friend,

Lois Woods, who had just bought my book. Looking at my photograph on the jacket, Alfred had had a strange feeling that he had, somehow, to reach me—to see and talk to me. It was almost as though he had been sent to me. He made no advances, did nothing more than hold my hand. It was immensely comforting. He was the kind of person who wanted to take care of people, and indeed, he seemed to regard caring for others as his mission in life and he lived his religion. He went to church every Sunday, and had once called to ask me to join him. We went to St. Francis' Catholic Church, in North Beach, not far from where both of us lived. I liked looking at the candles, and I enjoyed the service, although it was still largely unfamiliar to me. Having been brought up as a Protestant, I found the Catholic ritual presented me with a huge mystery.

Increasingly, as I came to know him better, I appreciated more the feeling of reality he gave me, and especially the sense of security. I felt safe only in his presence —Alfred was my St. Michael.

10

A Lower Deep Still

Alfred told me he had to go away for a few days to play in a golf tournament. I hated to see him go; it was as if I were losing my only lifeline, but I didn't want him to know I felt panic at his leaving.

I hadn't mentioned to him the severe dizziness I was experiencing. I had talked to my doctor about it again, but he didn't seem to know what was wrong with me, and I began to think it was psychosomatic. My headaches had returned, and when I said good-bye to Alfred I had the beginnings of a cold. Still, his red phone next to my bedside was reassuring; he was only to be gone a week.

It was San Francisco's rainy season. I was forcing myself to carry on with a number of lecture engagements, and I thought the rain would never stop. Not having the proper wet weather gear, I was repeatedly drenched as I made my way from one lecture hall to another, out of heated rooms into the cold outside; and when I reached home, squishing up the twisted steps, my shoes almost fell apart, my stockings were soaking wet. The cold of the house was even more insistent than ever. I have always been susceptible to respiratory infections, and now the inevitable consequence of my repeated exposure followed. I started coughing and my temperature began to rise, hovering around 101 degrees and climbing alarmingly at night.

I administered all the home remedies I knew, but at last admitted defeat and telephoned my doctor. He prescribed antibiotics, a strong cough medication, and sleeping pills to get me through the night. Work, of course, was out of the question. I had to have complete bed rest.

I started coughing so severely I couldn't sleep. I would doze, and when I wakened, I would be drenched in perspiration. Once again, I fancied I could hear the eerie laughter echoing through the house, and the phones ringing, sometimes separately, sometimes in a discordant jangle of sound. It was an effort to get out of bed. I could hardly manage to move around the house, even to get a cup of tea; and as my strength ebbed, I began to lose track of time and of what medicine I was taking and how much.

Mary Lou, of course, was always faithful, running errands for me, plumping the pillows, and doing all she could to make me comfortable, and I kept reassuring her I was all right. I didn't want her to know I felt I was going to die.

About the fifth day of my illness, the red telephone rang. It was Alfred. He was home.

"I'm so glad you're back."

"You don't sound right. What's the matter?"

"Oh, Alfred, I'm so sick."

"Have you called a doctor?"

"Yes."

His voice was concerned. "What did he say?"

"He said I'll be okay and gave me some medicine."

"Isn't there anything I can do for you?"

"No, nothing," I said.

"Are you sure? There must be something, and you must let me know if you need anything."

He wanted to come over right away but I said no. I felt such a nothingness. I didn't have strength for anything outside myself. My universe had shrunk to the confines of my bedroom.

As I hung up, I was seized by a sudden spasm of coughing and reached for the cough mixture. I had already taken at least four teaspoonfuls of a powerful, vile-tasting green cough medication, which seemed to have had no effect on my cough at all. I crawled out of bed and paced slowly up and down, coughing ceaselessly. Nothing afforded relief. I got back into bed, exhausted by the effort, and propped myself up with pillows so I could breathe more easily. I couldn't remember whether I had taken the antibiotics on time, and took some more, only to be racked by fresh waves of coughing; I reached again for the cough medication. My only wish was for some respite for oblivion. I took two sleeping pills, hoping for healing sleep.

I was in a graveyard—everything was misty-gray. I tried to run and could not, and just as a gray veil was about to envelop me, I broke free and ran and ran until my breath was coming in short burning gasps, filling my lungs with fire. I fell on the ground and felt it crumble beneath me, and then I saw I had fallen into an open grave and a gray cadaver was beneath me. I screamed and screamed but no one came to help.

I awakened screaming and crying until I realized I had been dreaming. I got a drink of water from the bedside table, sloshing some on my face and the front of my nightgown.

I dozed again for perhaps twenty minutes, only to awaken with paroxysms of coughing and uncontrollable convulsive shuddering, so that the entire bed shook. I got up, drenched in perspiration, although the room was freezing cold, and I continued shivering. I went into the bathroom. The reflection in the mirror was that of a total stranger. My eyes were sunken and hollow; my skin looked sallow; and my hair hung in limp, dank strands. My nightgown clung moistly to my body, and as I held onto the sink, bent double in a fresh seizure, I fancied I saw an amorphous form reflected in the mirror. Turning, I was overcome by the feeling of another presence.

I was crying weakly as I got into bed and took yet another sleeping pill. I knew I must have sleep. In my dazed condition, I had left the lights on throughout the house, and had failed to lock my bedroom door. I got up and stumbled into the living room to turn off the lights, and as I did so, I was racked with another fit of coughing. I doubled up and fell to the floor. Instinctively I knew I had to make a phone call; I must get somebody to help me, but I couldn't get up, I couldn't move.

I lay there in a half stupor and finally by an effort of will managed to crawl back to the bedroom. Somehow it seemed terribly important that I bolt the bedroom door. After repeated tries I reached up and turned the dead bolt into its socket. I managed to crawl back to bed and groped for the telephone on the bedside table. A number came to my hazy mind. It was my eldest brother's— Carlos. I hadn't talked to him for over a year, but I wanted my family. I needed help.

The phone rang and a voice said, "Hello."

"Carlos?"

"Who is this?"

"Carlos, it's Patsy. I'm so sick . . . please come."

"Where are you?" He was clearly alarmed.

"I'm at home. . . . Please come . . . I need you."

I dropped the phone onto its cradle and with numb fingers and a foggy brain managed to dial one more time, Alfred. I didn't give him a chance to say hello.

"I think I'm dying."

"What!"

"I'm so sick . . . I need help."

I don't remember the rest of the conversation. I was growing numb, slipping away. Alfred said he kept trying to talk to me and got a mumbling sound and finally, nothing. I had dropped the receiver. He immediately called the police and an ambulance, dressed, and raced over. He told me later that he arrived outside the gates just as my brother and his wife did. They compared notes hurriedly and rushed up the steps. The police and ambulance arrived almost simultaneously. They rang the doorbell but there was no answer. Alfred took the initiative and decided to break in through the sliding glass doors off the library. They were now in the house, but they still had the problem of getting into my bedroom. The door was bolted and locked. Alfred put his shoulder to it and broke it open.

When they found me, lying on the bed in a complete stupor, the receiver from the red phone was still in my hand, I was breathing stertorously, and there was an overpowering sour odor throughout the house.

I have a vague memory of someone bending over me, as I slipped in and out of consciousness. My next recollection, equally vague, was of being in an ambulance. Then, someone was pressing on my stomach and there was a bright light overhead . . . I'm afraid . . . I'm afraid. . . . And next I was vomiting repeatedly. Blackness again, and snatches and bits of memory of riding in a car and of Alfred carrying me in a dead man's hold up all those stairs.

I woke up late the next day in my own bed, with my sister-in-law in the bed next to me, and I remember how funny I thought it was that I should crash into the walls on the way to the bathroom.

All through the afternoon the telephone rang—newspaper people calling to find out what had happened. Had

I tried to kill myself? I was horrified that anyone would even conceive that I had attempted suicide.

It would be all too easy to say it had been the cumulative effect of mental and physical strain, a severe attack of influenza, and my susceptibility, in a weakened state, to the antibiotics, strong cough medication, and sleeping pills. But I felt the overriding cause was the house. Combined with the rest, it was a lethal combination, to be sure. But I hadn't taken the medication all at once, or with any design to do away with myself. I was certainly so ill I had felt I was going to die, or rather that it was inevitable I should die in that bedroom.

Alfred was my earliest visitor the next day, kind and solicitous. He busied himself around the house, answering the telephone and attending to my wants. I clung to him for support and reassurance.

My recovery was slow. Mary Lou was at my side now most of the time. She would even spend the night in the house until I was able to be on my own again.

One of the worst things I had to face was the newspaper publicity. Staring headlines across the front page read BEAUTY'S FLU PILL BOUT; with a four-column photograph and story. I was cruelly embarrassed, and more than ever I wanted to get away—away from people—and hide.

Red roses arrived unexpectedly from my younger brother, Jim, whom I hadn't seen or heard from in five years; and telegrams and phone calls poured in from the rest of my family. Warren Arnold called, with a gentle concern in his voice; and Merla Zellerbach sent me a thoughtful note. Michael and Mary Ann, my devoted fans, talked to Mary Lou to find out what they could do for me. But from the hundreds of people who had attended all those glittering galas under my roof—not one word.

Thinking it would cheer me, Mary Lou brought Do back. He came into my bedroom wagging his tail ec statically, an indubitable smile on his face, and began jumping on and off the bed and chasing himself in circles in the middle of the room. Then, with complete abandon, he would tear back and forth through the house, to settle down at last by my side, licking my face periodically, and falling fast asleep. Yet, by the next day, there was an unmistakable change. He began to droop and his tail hung between his legs. He slunk about, cowering under the furniture, and began to gnaw his fur again. Within three days he had started to urinate all over the apartment, to the ruination of the new white carpets.

Alfred, who loved animals and had two dogs of his own, suggested that he would find a home for Dog. He obviously should not stay in the house. He called a friend, Doris Cherin, and with her consent, took Dog over to her house for a visit to see how they would get on. She immediately fell in love with him. I hated to give him up, although I knew it was for the best.

I sadly packed up Dog's papers, his dish, an extra leash, and the remainder of his food. He now had a new home, where he was to live happily ever after, a healthy and contented dog. (Whenever I visit him now, he is always pleased to see me; and has never had a return of the terrors which once afflicted him.)

As I gathered his few belongings together, many memories crowded back from happier days. Dog was my constant companion on my television show, and it was even suggested by one viewer that the program should be called, *Pat and Dog,* or even *Dog and Pat.*

I thought of the time when I was chattering away on the air one morning and Dog, who always sprang into instant life as soon as the red "on" lights of the camera lit up, was cheerfully carrying on a little snuffling, throat-clearing monologue of his own on the sofa at my side. Suddenly, a voice came over the intercom. "Your sound has gone out." I continued to talk, oblivious of the interruption, until I heard, "Pat, your sound has gone out

. . . we're going to a commercial."

The studio director, engineers, and floor manager all huddled around my microphone, trying to find out the source of the fault—and then they discovered the happy sounds Dog was making came from the fact that he had chewed completely through my thin plastic microphone cord. The next day, Herb Caen's column bore the item "A dog biscuit to that nice animal."

I remembered, too, another morning in happier days when I was racing to get to the studio, Dog bounding along down the steps of the crooked street in front of me. I was fully made up for the cameras and wearing an evening gown of yellow chiffon. My hair was pulled back in soft curls, and I was carrying my shoes in my hand, rushing, always bordering on being late.

As usual, I put Dog on the back seat of the Oldsmobile, and he immediately stuck his head through the partially rolled-down window. I started the motor and had just begun to move off, when I was startled by Dog's sharp, excited barks. I realized, sickeningly, that he had jumped out and was gleefully chasing the mangy white dog of uncertain origin that I had often seen next door. I stopped the car in the middle of the street, with the engine still running, and set off in hot pursuit, my shoes flying, ringlets falling, and crying out, "Dog, come back here! Dog, come back!" to no avail. I chased him down the driveway of the apartments opposite, and like a scene in a Mack Sennett comedy, we made three laps around the garden before Dog eventually dashed through the open doorway of one of the lower apartments, with me close on his trail.

As I finally caught up with him, I came upon the mongrel's master, in pajama top and a startled expression, standing in the middle of the living room.

For one long, eternal second, we looked at one another, then I swept Dog up under one arm and said haughtily, "You really should keep your animal on leash. " Dog, a little intimidated away from his own territory, managed a few defiant barks. I made an exit with as much dignity as I could muster. Scolding him all the way to the studio, I made it just as I was getting my air cue, and before I could put on my shoes or tuck my hair back into place. "Good morning," I said trying to appear relaxed, but breathing heavily and still clutching Dog under my arm. "Guess what happened to us this morning!"

It's a mistake to linger over memories. The doorbell was ringing. It was Alfred, and Dog was soon on his way to a new, more secure home.

On one of the days after I was up and around, although still feeling weak, Alfred took me for a drive along the coast to Pacifica. It was a bleak, dreary day, foggy and overcast, and made all the more so by my state of mind. I could scarcely talk, nor did I have any wish to. The gray ocean crashed onto the rocks along the beach, with only a few bedraggled seabirds wheeling and crying, and the heavy fog hung over everything—everything, I thought, including my soul. I was still shaky and nervous, and the mirror told me I looked pale and washed out. My hair was lifeless, all my sparkle gone. I had lost so much weight that clothes hung limply on me. It was even hard to find anything to wear. I, who had been full of ambition, wanting to make something of myself, now had no wish for anything beyond surrendering to whatever Fate had in store.

We were silent all the way down the coast. Alfred would occasionally reach over and pat my hand. He seemed to sense my sadness and appreciate that this was no time for words.

We pulled off the road and found a parking place overlooking the pounding waves of the Pacific. I could see drops of spray settle on the windshield and grow larger, until, like my hidden tears, they would slide down the glass. We must have sat silently watching those drops of salt water for as much as ten minutes. When Alfred at length put his arms around me, I nestled my head into his shoulder, and felt I never wanted to leave that warm, protecting haven. He took my face in his hands and kissed me.

"Pat," he said. "I don't want anything to happen to you. . . . You've got to get out of that house."

For the first time in days I felt an emotion other than sadness and despair: a dawning blend of love, and hope, and courage returned.

"I know I do . . . and I will," I said.

My contract at KGO had now expired. I decided I would take what savings I had, throwing caution to the winds, and sit on a warm beach in Mexico. There I would recover my strength, and be healed of my terrors. I chose Mazatlán, as an inexpensive place to go to.

My spirits rose as I quickly made the arrangements to leave, already seeing in my mind's eye those long, sweeping beaches, the loveliest in Mexico, bordered in foam, and the tropical foliage receding into a blue distance. Mazatlán is at the mouth of the Gulf of California, level with the Cabo San Lucas, at the tip of the California Peninsula, and only a few miles south of the Tropic of Cancer; to go there from San Francisco is to enter a new world.

Both Mary Lou and Alfred applauded my decision, knowing I needed time and distance to heal my bruised body and spirit. They came to the airport to see me off, as I left the rain of San Francisco behind. I flew first to Los Angeles on PSA, changed to Mexicana Airlines, and in two and a half hours landed in the caressing warmth of Mexico.

My hotel, the Playa del Sol, lay at the beach, sun-bleached and aged, and the wide archway of the cobble-stoned entrance framed a view of the ocean and the beach, dotted here and there with a *casita de palapa,* a round, thatched umbrella-shaped shelter from the sun.

An open checking-in counter stretched along the right wall of the hotel foyer, and seeing an impatient line of people already there, I preferred, rather than wait my turn, to walk out onto the beach. I kicked off my shoes and waded out in the sand, away from the people and the chaffering around the local vendors and let the warm, silvery grains cling to my unaccustomed feet, and well up between my toes. The air enveloped me softly, and I began to feel soothed and peaceful.

I chose a palm tree, which was stirred by a gentle breeze, slid down gently into the sand, and stretched myself out at full length, oblivious of my clothes, and fell sound asleep. I was awakened two hours later by a gentle tap on my shoulder, and a voice saying in broken English, "*Señora,* you burned. *El sol muy* hot."

I rose hastily to my feet, brushing the sand from my dress, and realized the hot sun had already done a great deal of damage. I had been lying face down; the backs of my legs were beet-red, but I didn't care. It felt good.

I made my way slowly back to the hotel, to find the lobby deserted. My luggage stood forlornly by the counter. The sun was almost setting. No one seemed at all surprised or concerned at my delayed arrival.

After unpacking my few belongings, two long muumuus, a caftan, and a couple of bathing suits, I took a warm bath and went to bed, dinnerless, and did not wake until I heard the sound of voices next morning. I had slept for fifteen hours.

I went out through the window doors of my room opening onto the balcony and looked down at a group of bartering fishermen. They had brought their nets up to the first rise of the beach above the tide level, and had spread out their glittering haul of silver fish. As I watched, a procession of village women filed down to the assembled men and began filling great, flat baskets with the early-morning catch, which they carried away up the beach again, perched on their heads, moving with easy grace.

I dressed slowly, putting on a white caftan, rubbed sun lotion on my burned legs, and for the first time in weeks realized I was ravenously hungry. The leisurely elevator, breaking and creaking as it passed each floor, bore me downstairs; and after asking my way several times, I was eventually guided to the dining room. I ordered a larger breakfast than I had eaten for months. I had the appetite of a person recovering, at last, from a long illness.

By the time I had finished breakfast, I felt as though I had had no sleep at all. I returned to my eyrie at the top of the hotel and slept for six more hours. It was by then the full heat of the afternoon, the time of siesta. I slipped on a white bathing suit and a long pink cotton beach cover, purchased a huge straw sunhat from one of the vendors, and without any plans at all began slowly walking up the beach.

The lush vegetation grew down in many places right to the shore; hibiscus and azalea and many other flowers, nameless to me, interrupted the shrubs, palms, and banana trees. A solitary heron contemplated a shrimp-filled pool; sandpipers drifted and nodded; and high over the trees the buzzards wheeled and seabirds sped out over the ocean, to dive recklessly for their prey.

I turned toward the town, and walked along a broad sweeping avenue, the promenade of the local inhabitants. The evening strollers had not yet emerged from their afternoon rest, and I had the way to myself. I came to a vast church up a narrow cobblestoned side street. There was no one about, and I wandered through the cool stillness, looking for a statue of St. Michael, but found none. I knelt and said a prayer, and again felt the stifling oppression that had become so much a part of me. I prayed for deliverance from the evil permeating my life.

As my strength came back, if not my peace of mind, I found energy to explore the shops, brimming with folk artifacts. And the simple dignity and good manners of the people were unchanged from a previous visit.

When Sunday came, I made my way back to the church, remembering to dress modestly: The Mexicans notice, even if they do not criticize, the brash foreigner. I wound a silk scarf about my head and climbed the weather-beaten steps. All the doors were wide open. Even the window to the right of the pew where I sat was open; and as the jangled bell summoned the congregation, its deep diapason sounding as if it could shake the church to its foundations, a cloud of doves fluttered from the eaves of the house outside, only to return and settle again during the intervals of silence.

As I prayed, my mind turned back again to my unresolved problems. I still needed help, and I prayed for guidance. The service began, the candles were lighted, and the priest stood at the altar. I found it difficult to follow the ritual, but the earnest simplicity of the people, young and old, was affecting. Old, old women, as ravaged by time as Goya's withered crones, sat and alternately chided or smiled benevolently at their grandchildren. Babes in arms slept soundly through the sermon, while I thought of the strange catastrophes which had befallen me. And I thought of Alfred, my St. Michael. I had been writing to him and missing him as often. But mostly I tried to shake free of the shadow of the house, which seemed as though it would never leave me.

I looked around the church for an answer. Painted statues of saints, with votive flowers of paper or tin at their feet; altars draped in scarlet and green cloth; martyrs and archangels, apostles and cherubim, filled the pandrels of the vault. Alien as these symbols of the cult were to one of my simple faith, this was still my Father's House, and I found a measure of peace from my devotions in it.

The days passed. I spent them sleeping, sunbathing, and walking, interspersed with meals. And I often went back to the church. I was reminded, as I sat there one

day, of a Mrs. Braken, who had always been regarded as
the best pray-er in my Father's congregation; she, like
my mother, had a direct line to God, and I made up my
mind there and then, to call her. To get in touch by phone
in Mexico, requires an act of faith in itself, but eventually
I succeeded, and heard a surprised old friend acknowl-
edge me in comforting and sincere tones. I told her about
my troubles and how much I needed her prayers. She said
she would start a prayer chain on my behalf, and I left
the phone booth, knowing she would already be on her
knees, and many more would follow.

As the week drew to a close, I found myself renewed
and strengthened.

I was looking tanned and fit. On the day I was leaving,
as I waited for my plane at the airport, I heard a mes-
senger boy paging, and as he came nearer, I realized he
was trying to pronounce the name Montandon. It was
a telegram from the CBS television station in Los Angeles, asking if I would do their *Boutique* show for them
for a week. Mary Lou, knowing my schedule, had been
enterprising enough to have me paged at the airport. The
Boutique show director was surprised when I called him
less than two hours later from the Los Angeles Airport.
And as I talked to him and reread that welcome telegram
I recalled the words of an old hymn remembered from
my childhood: *"I know the Lord will make a way for
me."*

11

Lifeline

I returned to find the apartment engulfed in flowers. Blue and yellow birds-of-paradise, the enameled vermilion blooms of anthurium, and a profusion of sprays of Vanda Cymbidium orchids, like so many butterflies about to take flight, and showy cattleyas, filled every room. Alfred had had them flown in from Honolulu, as though to exorcise, with their exotic colors, the underlying melancholy of the house. He had met me at the airport and we were extravagantly happy to see one another again. He was delighted to find me looking so well, and we discovered a new bond: We had missed one another with equal intensity.

Bright as the flowers were, and the basket of fruit that had come with them, the apartment still challenged me. I felt it closing in on me once more, and I was restless and uneasy.

I wanted to see Alfred every minute of every day. I felt he was my only safe harbor; yet I had to plan how I was to organize my life. I had in prospect the week's work in Los Angeles and a scattered series of lecture engagements, but I knew the all-important task before me was to summon up the energy to get out of the house.

Mary Lou was equally happy to see me restored to something like my former self and delighted I felt well enough to undertake *Boutique*. As I still had a week free, we now had a little spare time, and on one of those days I suggested we go to lunch together at Los Gallos, a Mexican restaurant on Union Street. I suppose my Mazatlán interlude prompted my choice. The owner, Rubin Medina, cheerfully acknowledged our presence, and we settled down to a little celebration over a pitcher of sangria.

Almost at once Mary Lou sprung a surprise. She had clearly been bubbling over to tell me something. And yet she still approached it in a roundabout way. She led the conversation to her children: She was so happy that her twenty-year-old daughter, Jeannie, had fallen in love with Frank "Chip" Rose, a young lawyer and amateur photographer. They were ideally suited, both gentle and loving. And then there was Robin. Mary Lou was a little disturbed about Robin, who, like her name, was seldom still, and was now, at seventeen, living in a commune. Mary Lou felt she had done all she could for her, but Robin's ways distressed her all the same.

And Jimmy? Jimmy had grown into an independent thirteen-year-old, and she didn't know how to handle him. How fortunate she had gone to see Bishop Myers and managed to get him enrolled at the Cathedral School. At that age he needed a father. . . .

She broke off and said brightly, "That's my family settled. And now you're back and well again. . . . I really don't think anyone needs me."

I protested, but she went on. "But I've got a marvelous idea." Her large blue eyes took on a fresh sparkle. "I'm going to go to Europe . . . Italy . . . the Tower of Pisa . . . Florence . . . Dante . . . the Pitti Palace

. . . the Uffizi . . . Montegufoni . . . Fiesole. . . ."
And, mischievously, "and lots and lots of Chianti and
romantic Italians waiting to pinch me at every corner—
you know, honey, how much I've always wanted to go,
and I've discovered I can get a reduced fare through the
symphony on a charter plane, and I shall only be away
a month." Although her news took me by surprise, I was
delighted for her, as she now looked more strained than
I did. We had been through all the troubles of the house
and my illness together, without a break, and she needed
a rest and a change of scene. I knew she had always
harbored a longing to go to Italy. It was time she thought
of herself.

We now prepared to go our separate ways temporarily,
in a physical sense, at least. I told her a little more of
Alfred, and she rejoiced that we were happy together.
"Honey, I do hope everything works out the way you
want it. It's time things went right for you." And she began
to help me pack for Los Angeles, running around in her
work skirt and blouse, with a long pink feather boa
improbably draped around her neck and trailing on either
side, and a pencil behind her ear. Evening dresses were
strewn around the apartment everywhere; hairpieces
jostled cosmetics and jewelry.

Taking in her extraordinary appearance, I said, "If
you were only pregnant, Mary Lou, you'd be straight
out of *Auntie Mame*."

"And that *would* be some miracle," she retorted. We
both collapsed in helpless laughter on the sofa.

The days telescoped in excitement and I was soon
in Los Angeles, swept up in the bustle and hypertension
of that ugly-fascinating metropolis. I installed myself in
a small hotel near CBS Television City, where the show
was to be taped. It was fun to be working again.

Alfred called me every evening, sometimes as often as
three times; and I always called him back before I went
to sleep. I ached for his company. I had learned I could

not do without him, and I was as dissatisfied as he was by the inadequacy of telephone exchanges. My week's work was ending and we would be able to meet again, but I still had unresolved problems. I'd been offered a continuance of the show in Los Angeles, and I had to go home to decide what to do there; and some lecture engagements were still pending in northern California. The television offer had introduced a confusing element, as I did not want to be separated from Alfred and I certainly did not want to go back to that house.

On my last evening in Los Angeles, he telephoned earlier than usual. I do not remember all we talked about. It is forgotten in the joy in which we exchanged our love. He wanted to marry me, he said, and I opened my heart to him unreservedly in return. I'd done enough thinking about him to realize he was the only man I had ever loved so deeply. He was different from anyone else I had ever known, with a steadiness about him that came from an unshakable inner core of goodness. The next day I flew back to San Francisco, floating on a full tide of happiness.

We selected a date late in June for our marriage—June 24, after Mary Lou's return. It was now May 7, 1969.

We spent every possible moment together, making plans for the future, in a delirium of happiness; but when he wasn't with me, depression would still come down on me like a cloud, and the house insidiously take hold once more. A strange development was the sound of the ticking of a clock. I could hear it when I awoke, at around half past two in the morning, and I could not understand where the measured metronomic sound was coming from. I told Alfred about it, and we ransacked the rooms, but could find nothing.

We did silly, childish things together. We boarded the Hyde Street cable car and, careening down to the little terminus by the beach, jostled our way into the crowded

Buena Vista café, and ordered Irish coffee, happy just to be in each other's company. But always, as we turned homeward, my spirits would droop.

When Alfred saw these changes, he said with finality, "We are not waiting until June to get married. We're getting married now. I'm going to get you out of that house as fast as I can." He heard no protest from me.

We selected May 14—only three days away; and although I had a lecture at Lake Tahoe for the General Motors dealers on that day, I had a far more important date to keep. I got in touch with my friend Merla Zellerbach and asked if she would fill my speaking engagement, and in her customary nonprying way, she said she would. I had only one more lecture left on my calendar for the entire year, and that was for June 20, at Mills College. We would be back from our honeymoon by then, so it presented no problem.

We were married quietly in the Malcolm McNaughtons' house on Jackson Street. Their offer of the house for the wedding had been gratefully accepted, as we were fond of them both.

We sent, of course, a telegram to Mary Lou, who was staying in Fiesole, in the Tuscan hills above Florence: ALFRED AND I ARE BEING MARRIED TODAY. WE WISH YOU WERE HERE TO GIVE THE BRIDE AWAY. WE BOTH SEND OUR LOVE.

It was an early morning ceremony, at nine o'clock, so that we could leave immediately afterward by plane for Hawaii. We were bound for Mauna Kea, on the island of Hawaii.

Happy as I was to be with Alfred, away from all familiar associations and transported to a new, exotic environment, I naturally had not changed overnight. I had not left all the shadows behind in San Francisco. I had thought that after our marriage I would relax, but I had not completely escaped from the malign influence of the house on the crooked street, and I clung instinctively to Alfred as my sheet anchor. Fortunately, he was wholly understanding of my dependence upon him. If he merely left the room, I became anxious; and when in the natural course of events he went to the barbershop one day, leaving me to my own devices, my hands started to perspire and tremble and I grew short of breath. I had always been independent, but now I had a rising feeling of panic if I was separated from him for a moment. It was almost three years before my mental wounds were to be healed.

We stayed a little short of two weeks on Mauna Kea. We swam in the circular pool, took long walks through the lush, flower-strewn landscape, and dived through the crested waves. We also spent long hours talking about how we happened to meet; what made him feel he had been sent to me. And I unburdened myself more freely than I had ever before to anyone about the unnatural pattern of incidents I had lived through in the previous year and a half, besieged in my own house.

"Do you really think there's something strange there?" I would ask. "I've not imagined it all?" And it was reassuring coming from someone so practical and down-to-earth, to hear him say, "Yes, Pat, I do think there is something beyond our understanding in that house. I'm convinced of it."

Toward the end of the two weeks we decided to fly to Honolulu, to spend a few days there and see my cousin, Carolyn. We were housed in exceptional grandeur at the Kahala Hilton in the Presidential suite on the tenth floor.

We called Carolyn and asked her to have dinner with us in the Mailé Room, which with its graceful kimono-clad women, soft Hawaiian music, and the little stream that runs through it to one side, made a gentle and sympathetic rendezvous. Carolyn, tanned and bare-legged, wearing a short blue cotton shift, looked fresh and pretty. But I detected an underlying restlessness—a tension beneath her animated talk of her job and her new island friends. We spoke of her stay with me in San Francisco, and the eerie incident of the music, and she confessed she had often heard it subsequently, as she was drifting off to sleep. . . . "I really wasn't very comfortable in that place, Pat," she said. As we continued to draw her out, she revealed that the married boyfriend was in Honolulu and she was still seeing him. She implied he was in the process of getting a divorce and seemed quite sure they would soon be married.

I felt saddened in comparing her situation with our shining happiness, and feeling helpless to advise her, instinctively took off the magnificent double ruffled pink carnation lei Alfred had given me and placed it around her neck, telling her that I loved her.

My own happiness was dimmed as I said good-bye. I wondered afterward if there was anything I could have done to help and I realized Alfred had perceived the same telltale signs when he said, as we turned away, "Under all her brightness, Carolyn is a sad girl."

12

Encirclement

My skimpy-looking wardrobe was now neatly arranged in Alfred's enormous double hanging walk-in closet; it not only had hanging space, but special slots for handbags and shoes, a dressing table with a three-way mirror surrounded by lights, and at the far end there was a tall window with a spectacular view of Alcatraz. My clothes hung there like forlorn and lonely waifs. In my old closet, on the north wall of my old bedroom, they had been jammed in, helter-skelter, giving the impression of overflowing abundance. When he saw them, Alfred suggested I go shopping; not a difficult suggestion for me to act on at any time.

The housekeeper, Helen, had brought over my clothes from the old apartment. I had given her a vague list, based on which she had gotten, along with my wardrobe, essential things like my telephone list, personal knickknacks, and a small bench, covered in red silk, that I thought would be useful in my dressing room area. I had been using it in the old bedroom as a support for my television set, which, having no stand of its own, then had to be placed on the dressing table and plugged into a wall outlet directly beneath—a fact which later proved significant.

I had no inclination to go near the house or even to make an inventory of its contents, and I made no decision about the remaining year of the lease. I pushed that to the back of my mind, to be resolved later. Marriage always entails many adjustments; and my new surroundings were different enough to demand my full concentration. For a long while, I'd had only myself to think about; and I would sometimes go off on my own for a few hours now that I was feeling more secure, not telling anyone when I would return. "Single-girl habits," Alfred characterized them, pulling me to him and kissing me. "You've got to get over that, Patsy. I worry when I don't know where you are—and you mustn't go back to that house unless I'm with you—promise?" I readily agreed, as I had no desire to go there alone, or indeed at all.

The house was clearly visible from my vast new penthouse, and I was often drawn to the windows to stare down at it, hoping, I suppose, to penetrate its secrets. I could see the red canvas awnings over the three bedroom windows and patio, their fringes fluttering lightly in the wind. And I could make out the two-foot-wide ledge extending beyond the floor off the balcony, where I would often sunbathe because it was such a protected spot; and as a result, had been able to keep a year-round light suntan, leading people to think I had been on exotic winter vacations. I could also see the spreading top of the magnolia tree.

I could not make out the entire length of the crooked street, as taller buildings blocked portions of the upper half, but I could see the endless stream of traffic, and could imagine the delighted shrieks of excitement as the occupants of the cars careened down its irregular course.

My gaze swung back to the house. I could not see the

front steps—only the wall that marked their ascent. I knew those steps by heart—the slippery ones, that had often led to my downfall as I rushed to work in the early morning, and the ones that always collected water on rainy days. I would have to leap over them, trying to land gracefully on a dry spot beyond them. I once missed and sat down in a puddle with a resounding splash. The house now had an abandoned look although there were new occupants in the top floor ballroom apartment. They had moved in shortly before I was married, and while seemingly nice enough, Mary Lou and I quickly realized we were annoying to them. In an effort at neighborliness, we had brought their mail up to them from their box, only to be told firmly not to do so again. Dog was equally anathema to them, and they constantly complained of his barking. Thereafter, we only exchanged cool greetings as we passed on the stairway or in the foyer.

I did not know whether Evelyn Walker was at home or not, but the curtains appeared to be drawn. I assumed she was away, as usual, on a business trip.

I was pulled from the window and my thoughts by happy news. Mary Lou was home, and I expected a ring of the doorbell at any moment. I was in my bedroom on the upper floor when I heard it sound, and she rushed through the unlocked front door just as I ran down the winding stairs. We met halfway, smothering each other in hugs and kisses and greeting one another with staccato exclamations.

"You're married!"

"Yes!"

"You look wonderful! So relaxed!"

"Did you have a good time?"

"So happy for you!"

"Love your dress!"

"I'll get one for you!"

"So much to tell. . . . Did you meet anyone special?"

"Yes!"

"Not *really?*"

"A wild Italian!"

"Really?"

"Yes!"

We sat on the stairs, not even taking the time to go to a more comfortable spot. She told me she had stayed in a small *pensione* at Fiesole. It seems the son of the owner, a man of about forty-two, had taken a great interest in Mary Lou and she in him. She regaled me with stories of picnics in the Tuscan hills, expeditions to Siena and Arezzo and many-towered San Gimignano, rooting in antique shops, visiting endless churches, palaces— and Chianti and more Chianti wine.

"You're in love, Mary Lou."

She hesitated, and said quietly, "I think I might be." And as she brought out photographs of Angelo, she said, tenderly, "He's paralyzed from the waist down."

I saw he was a handsome, darkly Italian man, always posed being supported by crutches, with Mary Lou standing beside him.

"But tell me about *you* . . . let me see your new clothes."

As I showed her around the apartment, not omitting a single detail, like the marble bathroom and the bathtub overlooking the Bay, she said, "I can't believe it . . . and I thought we were going to spend our old age in those rocking chairs together!"

This was a reference to a standing joke between us. During those all too frequent times of loneliness and depression, I would say, imitating the cracked voice of an elderly woman and bending over at the waist with my hand on my back, "Mary Lou, did you take your Geritol this morning?" And, cupping her hand behind her ear, she would reply, "Eh, what's that? . . . Your rocking chair's making too much noise, Patsy Lou." We could laugh now at those days.

We visited all afternoon. Mary Lou had to catch up with my news; and of course I was eager to hear more about her travels. She reported happily that Jeannie and Chip were being married the very next week.

"You and Alfred will come, won't you?" she asked.

"Of course." But on later inspection of my calendar, I realized a party was being given in our honor on the very same day, and we had regretfully to miss the wedding.

When at length we said good-bye, I felt we had come back from a long distance in a short space of time; and from then on I spoke with her on the telephone every morning. We were like close sisters, and shared our innermost thoughts. She was still concerned about Robin, but felt Jimmy was doing much better, and she was, of course, delighted about Chip and Jeannie. We discussed at length what she should wear at the wedding. We decided on a peach-colored sheer wool dress, the perfect choice for our usual cool San Francisco summer weather.

Then Mary Lou asked, "What are you going to do about your apartment?" She knew very well it was still sitting there, fully furnished, with the rent paid up and a year to go on the lease.

"I don't know, Mary Lou. . . . I've been ignoring it, but I'm going to have to make a decision soon."

"I'll make a deal with you," she said. "Jeannie and Chip can't afford much of a honeymoon. Why don't I stay in your apartment and get everything taken care of while they stay at my house?"

"Are you sure you want to, Mary Lou? I wouldn't go back on a bet."

With a small laugh, she said, "Of course I want to— there's still a lot of odds and ends of work to clear up and I can do it very nicely there."

"You're sure you're not afraid?"

"I wouldn't want to stay there alone, but with the new

tenants living upstairs . . . and Jimmy with me, too, I won't be afraid."

"All right, if that's what you want to do, it's fine with me. I'll bring the keys over to you. I want to stop and see Jeannie before the wedding anyway."

Alfred and I went to Mary Lou's narrow Victorian house at 2249 Webster Street, en route to our own party, the day of Jeannie's wedding. Mary Lou looked excited and beautiful in her peach-colored dress, with a string of pearls around her neck. Her hair had been freshly done in her usual soft style of short brushed curls all over her head. I had brought with me the heavy, shammy-colored key case and handed it over to her with mock ceremony. The case contained my safe deposit key, extra keys to the car, three keys to the house, and a key to the television studio, which I had forgotten to return—all my old keys, in fact.

The wedding was to take place in about an hour, and Mary Lou's little house was humming. I went up the dark, cramped stairway to the upper floor to see Jeannie. She was sitting at her dressing table, languorously brushing her long brown hair. When I said good-bye, I kissed her and told her how much I would miss being at her wedding, and then sentimentally misty-eyed, went back downstairs.

I can't now remember exactly when Mary Lou moved into the house on the crooked street, but the very next day, whenever it was, she called me excitedly over the telephone to say, "We're here!" It must have been about Wednesday, June 18, 1969.

I seized the moment to tell her I wanted her and Jimmy and Gerson Bakar to be our first dinner guests, and set the date for the next evening.

Mary Lou reprimanded me teasingly for not coming to pick up my mail, which included a refund from the Internal Revenue Service. She said she would deposit it for me, and went on laughingly to tell me about Jimmy's adventures with my monstrous, heavy old Webcor tape recorder, which I hadn't used for at least a year. It had been replaced by a much more up to date model. She asked whether I hadn't psychic gifts of which I was unaware—the seventh daughter of a seventh daughter, perhaps, as the first tape Jimmy had put on revealed my voice, describing me living in a resplendent penthouse apartment. I was quite taken aback until I remembered: The tape was for a television pilot in which I was supposed to be a hostess entertaining famous people at a party. I said I thought it must be Jimmy who had the second sight to pick out that particular tape.

I was still curious to know how they had settled in to my old apartment and I went on to ask her, "Does the house bother you, Mary Lou?"

She replied quite firmly, "Not at all. We have a full house. Evelyn is home for a change, the new tenants are upstairs, and Jimmy and me. Of course there are always noises one has to get used to. . . ."

From that moment onward, events moved in an inexorable pattern, the significance of which I had no inkling or premonition.

The following day, Thursday, June 19, was the day set for taking my deposition in the "Call Girl" lawsuit. As I had to make my appearance before the court reporter and attorneys in the afternoon, I asked Mary Lou to come over in the morning to help me refresh my memory about that period and to try to recall any details that might be important for me to remember. She reminded me in turn that I still had an outstanding engagement to speak at Mills College the next night, June 20. There was to be a dinner first, to which Mary Lou had also been invited. She said she would call the secretary to tell her that Alfred would be taking her place. That would be the very last of my lectures, the end of my former life: *the* final act.

Mary Lou arrived the next morning at about nine o'clock to go over all the details of my deposition. I suppose it was as a result of our having to go back and relive all the ugly incidents of the *TV Guide* libel that made us both pensive and sad. We sat on the large bed that Alfred and I share, with papers strewn all around, alternately lounging and sitting, with long reflective pauses as we gazed unseeingly at the vast view stretched below us.

We fell to reminiscing, as if we were indeed old women in our rocking chairs.

Our thoughts darted from one thing to another. "Mary Lou, I shall never forget the time we went to Anton La Vey's and you drank that pink and purple liqueur. It didn't seem to bother you at all, and I was scared to death."

Mary Lou smiled and said, "I thought of trying the love potion on 'The Boy Friend,' but I don't think it would have worked anyway."

Then the subject of the strange happenings in the apartment came up, but before we could explore it we were startled out of our reverie as Al's married daughter, Susan, popped into the room. She had come by unexpectedly to say hello, and apologized profusely when she realized I had company. I introduced her to Mary Lou, as she had not met her before. Realizing I was busy, Susan said she would see me the next day and abruptly left the room. She told me later that, strangely, as she walked down the hall from our bedroom, she had such a sense of inexplicable sadness that she started crying, as if she were in deep grief.

We left our reminiscing behind, as I had to get ready for the deposition; and Mary Lou went back to my old apartment.

Alfred took me down to the Mills Building, where the deposition was to be taken, reassuring me on the way of his love and support. I knew I was going to have an unpleasant interview, but I did not dream how unpleasant it was to become. Never having been involved in a lawsuit before, I was completely unprepared.

My attorney, Charles Morgan, met me in the lobby, and escorted me to an upper floor and into a small cell-like room. I was introduced to two male attorneys and a court reporter. The attorneys started out gently, but soon began to make me feel as if I had committed a crime and were on trial for my life. The deposition took four and a half hours, and I was left wrung out and limp. I had shed my dress jacket after the second hour, and the perspiration rolled down my forehead as the inexorable questioning continued.

At the end of the time, Alfred was waiting for me and I got into the car. He reached out to hold my hand. "Pat, you've got to be tough." That was perhaps the last quality that could have been attributed to me at that moment.

We arrived home with barely enough time for a shower before our guests arrived. I'm afraid I was a rather draggy hostess for our first dinner party. I don't remember what I served, and much of the conversation floated by me. Mary Lou, of course, was extremely interested in everything I had been asked about during the afternoon session, and Jimmy had great fun running around our balconies and picking out landmarks with binoculars. I was more than ready for an early evening and didn't hesitate to say so, consequently the party broke up about nine thirty, but not before Mary Lou and I arranged to see each other the next morning for breakfast.

I was at last to go back to the house on the crooked street.

We selected ten o'clock as being a good time; and we planned to go over some papers the lawyers had requested.

Mary Lou and Jimmy lingered for a few moments after Gerson Bakar had left, and as Al and I walked them to the elevator, she turned to me in an agitated manner and said, "When are they going to take my deposition? I'm your star witness, you know."

I said, "They'll get around to you. These things take time, as you've so often told me."

"I know," she said—and I remember her words as if they were said ten minutes ago—"but they'd better hurry."

When I asked her why, she just shrugged her shoulders, got into the elevator, which had now arrived, turned and repeated, "I don't know, but they'd better hurry."

13

The Victim

*I was walking through a beautiful garden of spring flowers;
it had many mossy walks and winding ways, sometimes
opening out into a greensward surrounded by flowering
shrubs, sometimes leading into a garden enclosed, a secret
place, which sheltered more tender plants. I was wearing
a floating white gown, and I turned with delight first to
one side and then to another, inhaling the fragrance that
welled up from the flowers on every side. I went on and
on, deeper into the garden, where the flowers were bigger,
and had more vivid colors, but as I came nearer to them
I realized they were not flowers, but grotesque gargoyles,
leering at me and spewing filth from their mouths, soiling
my pretty dress and threatening to drown me; and just
as they were about to overwhelm me, they changed again
into wild beasts, savage and terrible, with flames coming
from their fingertips, which were reaching toward me.
I tried to scream, but could not. . . . I awoke, to realize,*
thankfully, that I had been dreaming.

I got out of bed and splashed cold water on my face, trying vainly to clear the nightmare from my mind. It had seemed so real that I was even fearful to go downstairs and get a glass of milk. Alfred, who had been awakened by my thrashing about, asked me what was wrong. "A bad dream," I said.

"Probably that business of the deposition," he replied, getting out of bed. "I'll get you some hot milk."

"We'll both go," I said, not wanting to be left alone; and we sat at the kitchen table together, Alfred holding one hand as I drank the cup of milk held in the other, talking all the time about ordinary, everyday things; and soon I was able to go back to bed, where I slept quite soundly through the rest of the night.

It seemed odd to be ringing the doorbell on Lombard Street again. I gave our old coded ring, four longs and one short. There came the dull burring sound of the release buzzer, and then I was inside the marble-floored foyer. I noticed there was a pane missing from the stained-glass window but the entrance hall was even darker than I remembered. My own recessed doorway was in shadow, and Mary Lou was standing in the entrance. It wasn't until I entered the living room that I noticed her appearance. She was still wearing her bathrobe; her hair looked disheveled, and she had dark circles under her eyes.

"What on earth's the matter, Mary Lou?"

"I've been up all night," was her reply.

"Why, are you sick?"

"No, I couldn't sleep and I felt it absolutely necessary to get your papers in order."

"Are you crazy, Mary Lou? You know those things can wait."

"Perhaps . . . but I put a big stack of your books and things in the trunk of my car."

"During the night?"

"Yes."

"Good heavens, Mary Lou, that's dumb. It's dangerous to go out at night alone."

"Well, it's done," she said wearily, "now let's have some breakfast."

We cooked together in the outmoded old kitchen. When I had lived there, I dared not complain about it, even though it lacked a dishwasher, a garbage disposal unit, or even an up-to-date stove. The landlord had lowered my rent years before with the understanding that I accept the apartment "as is," and it still was "as is." I couldn't help glancing down to the glass pane in the back door, half expecting to see the fire escape ladder rolled down, and I was relieved there was no sign of it.

Mary Lou cooked the bacon, and I did the eggs. She had made a pot of coffee, and its fragrant aroma titillated my nostrils pleasantly, and mingled with the other good breakfast smells. I have always been a breakfast person, and delaying it until so late had made me ravenously hungry.

Mary Lou's spirits rose as we sat in the small dining room eating. The sunlight was shining through the windows and occasional glints were reflected from the small crystal chandelier overhead, and cast prismatic colors on the wall.

Otherwise, the apartment seemed as dreary and depressing as when I had left it. I looked around the living room, two steps up from where we were breakfasting, and saw that the white carpet still bore the evidence of Dog's misbehavior. The soft pink and bright red throw pillows on the sofa looked faded and did nothing to brighten the room.

Mary Lou brought up the subject of her vacation, and mentioned she had had a letter from Angelo a few days before and hadn't yet gotten it translated; but she could make out a few words and phrases here and there. He missed her, and hoped she would hurry back to Italy. She smiled as she told me about it.

Jimmy was off somewhere with his friends, but he would be back in time for dinner. I asked what she was going to do all day, and she didn't know. She was so tired, she thought she might sleep.

We talked aimlessly, until Mary Lou asked, "Are you happy, Patsy Lou?"

"Yes, I am . . . except for the lawsuit thing. I'll be glad when it's over."

"I'm glad you're pursuing it."

"I have to . . . you know what a fighter I am."

"Don't forget your speaking engagement at Mills College tonight."

"Why don't you come along, too, M.L.? I'm sure they wouldn't mind."

"No, it's Alfred's place to go, not mine."

We finished breakfast and went to the bedroom. I wanted to get a stack of lingerie Helen had overlooked during the move, and I noticed the television set looked much larger, perched on the dressing table, where it obscured a portion of the mirror, than when it had rested on the red-covered stool.

The bedroom, with its soft gray-painted walls and gray sheer curtains, looked tidier than when I had lived in it, when huge piles of books, magazines and television scripts lay everywhere. The tables were orderly now; and the bed, with its pink velvet canopy and quilted linen cover, was neatly made. I noticed that the bolts and locks on the doors and windows were still in place, and an involuntary shiver ran down my spine.

Jimmy slept, as Carolyn had, in the office-library; and that room, unlike the bedroom, was a shambles of business papers strewn over everything—the outcome of Mary Lou's night of work.

"Please get some rest, Mary Lou," I said. "You did too much last night—I still don't understand why."

"Just a whim, combined with insomnia, Patsy Lou— you know how that is."

It was almost time for a hair appointment I had at Don Lindahl's. I picked up my stack of lingerie, gave Mary Lou a quick hug, and dashed out the door, yelling over my shoulder, "I'll call you this afternoon, M.L."

"Bye, honey," she said.

It was half past four when I got home from the hairdresser. We were due for dinner at Mills College at seven, and it would take, leaving time for parking, an hour to get there. I took a soothing, warm bubble bath in my marble tub, being extra careful to keep my hair dry. I put on a bathrobe and decided to rest a little while, before starting my makeup. I stretched out on top of the bed with a big down pillow under my feet; and after I had myself comfortably arranged, reached for the telephone to check with Mary Lou. I dialed my old number, Grayston 4-0200, and after about three rings, Mary Lou answered.

"Did you rest?" I asked.

"A little," was her reply.

"I'm getting ready for Mills College. Do you suppose they are getting ready for me?"

"No one could get ready for you, Patsy Lou," she said with a laugh.

"What are you going to do tonight?"

"I think I'll go to a movie with Jimmy, but I'm awfully tired . . . maybe I'll just go to bed early."

"I'll talk to you in the morning and give you a complete report."

"Yes, I'll be anxious to hear."

She was making a special point of this as she knew it was a rather important and prestigious speaking engagement for me. I was to address the California Writers' Guild, and I felt ill-equipped to tell other writers about writing. However, now that I had Alfred beside me, I had regained some confidence in facing an audience. The engagement was not only prestigious, I was being paid an honorarium as well.

"Say a prayer for me," I concluded to Mary Lou.

"And for me, too," she said with a half laugh.

"Bye bye."

"Bye, Patsy Lou."

Those were the last words I ever heard her say.

I felt ill at ease as we headed for East Oakland and the college. Something wasn't right; perhaps it was because Alfred would be hearing me lecture, and I was feeling a little self-conscious. Whatever it was, I didn't like it. Like an animal before an impending storm, I felt I wanted to cower under the nearest available shelter.

A large crowd was already assembled in the dining room when we arrived and we were graciously shown to our seats.

"Couldn't Mrs. Ward come?" a lady asked. "We have a place for her."

"I'm sorry," I replied. "Didn't she let you know?"

"I thought there would be three," she said.

"No, just the two of us."

I felt a pang of regret that I hadn't insisted Mary Lou come too. This lecture rather tied a red ribbon on our association together, in the sense that it was the very last one. After tonight my calendar would be blank.

I was distressed that Alfred was seated away from me at the far end of the table. I sat near the center, alternately chatting with the woman on my right and the one on my left. The place for Mary Lou was glaringly empty in the crowded hall, to my left, near the end opposite from Alfred.

I was unusually nervous. Normally, speech-making is fun for me, and if I feel a momentary qualm, it is quickly dispelled by the warmth of an audience. I was glad when the chairperson announced we could now go to the lecture hall, which was across the campus, a short distance from where we were dining.

Alfred quickly came to pull my chair back and escort me over to the hall. As we walked along arm in arm, he said, "You're shivering, darling. Are you cold?"

It was a balmy June evening, and the East Bay, quite unlike San Francisco in summer, was softly warm. I felt chilled, however, and Alfred took off his rough tweed jacket and put it around my shoulders.

We sat waiting in the back row as the chairperson opened the proceedings. One of their member writers said a few words; then came my introduction. Alfred gave my hand a squeeze and I smiled, reassured, as I walked down the aisle to give my talk. The auditorium was strangely different from most lecture halls I had seen. The room was fan-shaped with the speaker on the same level as the front row, but lower than the remaining rows of seats. At first I felt uncomfortable because of this odd shape; it seemed weird to be lower than most of my listeners. The ham in me took over, however, and I was soon in full swing, perhaps a little overanimated, and a trifle loud, due to my attack of nerves; but I felt effective, nevertheless.

Shortly after I started speaking, I noticed an older, gray-haired woman enter the hall with three younger-looking people. They made a slight disturbance as they found seats in the center of the room. I continued talking as if I had their rapt attention, but I was keenly aware that this little group was whispering loudly among themselves.

I spoke for approximately forty-five minutes, and as I neared the end, the gray-haired woman and her entourage made a noisy and disturbing exit.

"Oh, well," I thought, "it takes all kinds—I suppose I was boring them."

At the conclusion of my address I was asked the usual questions:

"How long did it take to write your book?"

"Where did you learn to write?"

"Who was your publisher?"

The audience gave me a resounding round of applause when I finished, making me feel much better about the old woman who had left in so rude a fashion; and Alfred leaned over and whispered, as I joined him in the back row, "You were great! Now let's get out of here."

The Writers' Guild had more business to conduct and we were to meet the members shortly afterward at yet another building nearby, where I was to autograph copies of my book. We could leave and wander over at leisure. We tiptoed out the double doors, and had just got beyond the forecourt, when I heard a voice from the shadows at the corner of the building. Several figures emerged from the darkness and surrounded us. It was the gray-haired old woman and her little gang of followers.

"You bitch," she screamed. "How dare you show your face here? You're nothing but a slut!" I stared at her; her features were twisted with vitriolic hatred. I was completely stunned. All the past injuries and hurts which were, even now, barely under the surface, came flooding back to me. Somehow, I was taken full circle, back to the Tarot card reader—and the venom in this voice was the same.

Before I could say anything, Alfred took my arm, as the woman continued with a raised fist, screaming epithets at me. Her little group merely looked smilingly on, as Alfred led me firmly away, on down by a curving wall, under some eucalyptus trees, whose pungent smell assailed our nostrils as we passed by.

"What caused that, I wonder?"

I couldn't talk; I was so near tears. I couldn't possibly sign autographs now. What if "she" turned up and started berating me again? I felt humiliated, too, that Alfred should have heard such abuse heaped on me, knowing he didn't deserve such an affront to his wife.

We went to our car, and just sat there for a while, trying to decide what to do. We soon saw people coming slowly across the grass from the auditorium, and I knew they would be expecting me. We strained to make out faces, to see whether the gray-haired woman was among those making their way toward the library. I would hardly have been surprised if she had come looking for me with a gun, so intense was her evident malice toward me.

We decided at last to go in for a few minutes, and then leave; and after I autographed four or five books, I excused myself with the plea of a headache, and we left.

We talked all the way home about "that woman," and we concluded her objection to me was inspired by the old libel. I was hurt to the quick and could hardly wait to discuss it with Mary Lou.

We arrived home at about ten thirty; and although I was achingly weary from tension, I did not feel sleepy.

"I think I'll call Mary Lou and tell her what happened, Alfred," I said.

"You told me she was awfully tired, sweetheart . . . she might be asleep."

"I'll check," I said, and opening the draperies from our bedroom windows, I peered through the blackness down toward the house on Lombard Street.

"There aren't any lights on that I can see," I commented.

"You kept that place so buttoned up, Patsy, you couldn't see a light if there was one."

"Well, I guess I had better wait until morning," I concluded.

We both took a long hot bath together in the large marble tub trying to relax and unbend. Alfred looked strained, too, and I knew the old woman's abuse had affected him as well. Our bed felt cozy and comfortable when we climbed into it. I glanced at the bedside digital clock; its luminous numbers read 11:45 and in smaller letters and figures, June 20. 1 snuggled close to Alfred, feeling the tension slip from my body, as with my head on his chest, we both fell soundly asleep.

The phone was ringing loudly, insistently. Was I dreaming? Had I forgotten to shut the bell off? It took me a moment to remember where I was.

"I'll get it," came Alfred's sleep-heavy voice.

"No, I will," I said.

The white Princess phone was on the table at my side of the bed. As I reached for the receiver, I noticed the clock glowing silently in the dark room. It read 4:01— June 21.

Who could be calling at this time of the morning? I wondered groggily, as the phone continued its piercingly shrill ringing.

"Is this Pat Montandon?" came an authoritative male voice.

"Yes," I said, suddenly wide awake, and aware that Alfred was sitting up in bed next to me.

"Are you the lady who lived on Lombard Street?"

"Yes"—my voice rising—"what is it?"

"There was a fire there early this morning and we have a female body. Can you tell me who it is?"

His words stabbed into my consciousness with the force of a sharp blade.

"Mary Lou," I gasped. "Oh, my God. . . . No. . . . No."

Alfred took the phone from me and continued, taking charge in his usual calm manner I couldn't bear to listen. I put my hands over my ears, as if by blotting out their voices I could make what was being said untrue.

I was rocking back and forth when the conversation ended, and Alfred took me in his arms and gently made me listen. There had been a fire. No one at that time knew the details, except that it happened at about 2:30 A.M.—and Mary Lou had died in it.

"No," I said. "I don't believe it. It's a cruel joke."

I turned away from Alfred, picked up the phone, and dialed my old number. Alfred watched me patiently as I waited vainly for an answer to the soft ringing. There was none.

14

But for Those Obstinate Questionings

"No, it isn't true. No—no—no, I don't believe it. Mary Lou isn't dead." Racking sobs tore at my throat. I cried out, "Oh, no—oh no—no—no," I repeated the words over and over again, as if by forming the words, I could stay the fact.

Alfred washed my face with a cold washcloth. He held me close and I lay sobbing on his chest until I could stand it no longer and would break away again to moan, "It's not true. It can't be true. I don't believe it."

"Patsy, I'm afraid it is true," Alfred said.

"No, no, no."

"Yes," he said, and moved over to the green silk draperies, which he pulled aside. Pointing down toward Lombard Street, he told me to look. It was still dark but I could see the ominous, swirling red lights of fire engines, like futuristic monsters, blinking against the garden wall. They continued in a constantly searching pattern, an unceasing accompaniment to tragedy.

I could no longer deny the truth. Mary Lou was dead.

Alfred dropped the draperies back into place and put his arms around me.

"Patsy, the man from the Fire Department said she was already dead when they found her. She probably didn't suffer."

"But what started the fire?" I asked between sobs. "Did he say?"

"Just that it started in your bedroom."

"But how, Alfred? How? I don't understand."

"He thought maybe a cigarette."

"A cigarette!" I screamed. "Mary Lou didn't smoke. You know that. She didn't smoke," I repeated. "She didn't smoke."

I crouched on the floor in an embryonic position, curled in on myself, alternately sobbing softly and crying hysterically.

"We have to go to the children," Alfred said.

"Oh, my God, what about Jimmy? My God—my God —what happened over there?"

Alfred got a dress for me and pulled it on over my head. He patiently put my shoes on, found a coat for me, and dressed me as if I were a child. It was still dark when we left our apartment for Mary Lou's house on Webster Street. The streets were quiet and deserted of traffic. I wondered illogically why all the lights in the city weren't on and why everybody wasn't weeping with me. How could they be so callous? How could they not know? How could they not feel what I felt?

Occasionally I would regain some rationality and know I had to pull myself together for the sake of Mary Lou's children, but there were so many questions and the only possible answers seemed to lead inevitably to other inexplicable questions. We drew up in front of Mary Lou's little Victorian house and just as we approached the door, Chip opened it. No words were needed. We could only mirror each other's misery. Jeannie was sitting in the dining room alone, just sitting there. She was obviously in a state of shock. I put my arms around her, but couldn't say anything.

"Where is Jimmy?" Alfred asked. They had been calling, trying to find him and had, at last, discovered he was at a friend's house. Apparently it had been decided late that evening that he would spend the night away from the Lombard Street house.

The Coroner's Office called. Jeannie had to go to the morgue to identify her mother's personal effects. Not much—just two rings—a gold wedding band, and a simple birthstone ring.

Dawn was streaking the morning sky with brilliant red and gold. It was going to be a beautiful day.

We sat with heavy hearts in the little dining room, calling the people who should know, accepting phone calls, and drinking coffee. A newspaper reporter called to talk to me.

"I don't feel like talking," I said. "Please don't ask me to."

"Did she smoke? Did the fire start from a careless cigarette?"

"She didn't smoke," I answered dully. I hung up and the questions again started circling in my brain. *What could possibly have started the fire in my bedroom?*

Jimmy was brought home. Robin, too, came, and after the family of Mary Lou had gathered and closed ranks in their sorrow, we left.

As we entered our bedroom, I realized someone had opened the draperies. I quickly closed them, averting my eyes from the scene of the fire below.

That day is a blur to me, remembered only vaguely. At some point, Alfred took me to his church. As we walked into the St. Francis Catholic Church and I lit a candle for Mary Lou, I remembered the time only nine months before when I lit one in St. Patrick's Cathedral in New York City with Mary Lou teaching me how. I touched the Saint Michael's medal hanging from a chain around my neck, and knelt and prayed for my friend.

The days were a haze of sorrow, of not knowing what to do and of getting bits and pieces of information. There was going to be an inquest. But first there would be a memorial service for Mary Lou. I wanted to show my love for her, yet I felt there was no way to express it. There would be no funeral, no place even to send flowers. I thought of the time she brought forms for both of us to sign, willing our eyes to help some sightless person —even this final gesture of caring was denied her. Alfred and I went to the service and I sat sobbing throughout. I remember only one prayer, and one line from it stayed with me: "She is relieved of her burdens."

I couldn't talk to anyone. I leaned heavily against Alfred and in the back of my mind, becoming more clear as the numbness wore off, was a chilling feeling that there was more to this tragedy than anyone knew or suspected.

A few days after the memorial service, and before the inquest which was to take place exactly two months after the fire, Alfred insisted I go back to the house on Lombard Street. He felt if I didn't see it, I would wonder all my life what it had looked like. He is very practical—a realist —and I rely on him completely. If he thought I should go back, I would.

It was the usual cold foggy San Francisco summer day. The foghorns were hooting mournfully in the distance and as we walked toward the house, I felt myself trembling from head to toe. I looked up at the building. The awnings were in charred shreds. There was a stench even from the garden—the acrid smell of smoke and burned wood. There were a few pieces of furniture which had been thrown out from the balcony and were now in unidentifiable masses in the garden.

"Are you sure this is a good idea, Alfred?" I said.

"Yes, Pat, you have to be strong and you've got to learn this is the best way; to face up to whatever there is to face up to in that house. And I will be with you."

He had his arm around me and I was leaning on him as we walked slowly up the stairs. The glass was broken in the windows. I could see temporary plywood had taken the place of the panes in the doors off the bedroom as well as the library. We walked into the foyer and turned left, into a place I had never seen before. There was nothing familiar about it. The living room area was blackened with smoke. The shades were hanging in tatters, and underfoot the wetness of the now charcoal-smeared gray carpet penetrated the thin soles of my shoes. The unremitting odor of burned wool and wood, smoke and water, made me dig in my purse for a handkerchief, which I held over my nose and mouth. The once white sofa looked like some huge, overstuffed monstrosity, waterlogged and ash-streaked. Most of the furniture had been badly damaged. Some worth saving had already been removed. I stood in the living room and steeling myself, looked reluctantly toward the bedroom. There was nothing there: just outside walls, charred and blackened.

The wall between the library and my bedroom where the head of the bed had originally been was burned through completely so that the two rooms appeared to be one large room. There wasn't a single recognizable stick of furniture—only charred wood and ashes. The closet was just no longer there, its back wall had burned through to the connecting bathroom.

Alfred led me by the hand into the dining room and on to the kitchen, which was a blackened, soot-ridden chaos. Dishes were broken on the cupboard counters. Everything was in disarray. I looked on out to the back door which I could see was securely locked, and noted that the metal fire escape from upstairs was down on the back porch.

"Alfred, I just can't bear it anymore," I said, crying now.

"Okay," he said, "I'll take you home, darling."

I had seen quite clearly that while the fire had damaged the entire apartment, the flames themselves had been confined to the bedroom. I stumbled blindly down the stairs. By the time we walked out through the gates, I could no longer think, feel, or hear. I had pulled a curtain in my mind and it was several days before I started to react again.

We had a parade of people coming in and out of our apartment—a man from the Arson Squad, a man from Homicide. Questions . . . questions . . . questions. They were trying to find answers. They had none. But the inquest was coming up and we felt certain everything would be resolved there and our questions answered.

I learned that the fire had been reported at about 2:55 A.M. by the upstairs tenant. Apparently, he was roused by a neighbor returning home early in the morning who noticed flames coming from my old apartment. He called the police and they, in turn, called the Fire Department. According to Arson Inspector Lucas, the fire apparently originated in the master bedroom—my bedroom. Mary Lou was found in bed. They said examination at that time revealed she was found in a prone position, face down. She was covered with third-degree burns and there was extreme charring of the lower extremities, below the knee.

I hated hearing the reports—I hated it, but I had to know. There was something so strange about this whole thing. I wondered if she had been murdered and then a fire started. No, I was told, she couldn't have been murdered.

"How do you know?" I asked.

"Because we did an autopsy and it would show if she had been murdered."

"Are you sure?" I said.

They went over all the details, trying to make me feel better, trying to reassure me.

"How do you know she couldn't have been murdered?" I would ask again.

"If she had, it would have shown up in the autopsy—besides, the house was so securely locked from inside the Fire Department had to break the doors down."

In spite of all their patiently given explanations, I felt something was amiss.

It was August 21, 1969, the date of the inquest. In the Coroner's Court of the State of California in and for the City and County of San Francisco, Dr. Henry W. Turkel, Coroner, presiding. We arrived about nine thirty in the morning and those of us who were to appear at the inquest gathered in a silent little knot outside the coroner's hearing room, waiting to be called: Jean Eileen Rose (Jeannie), Mary Lou's daughter, was there. Evelyn Walker, my neighbor downstairs, was also present; Pauline Kendall, an old, old friend of Mary Lou's; Inspector George Lucas from the Fire Department; Inspector David Toschi from the Homicide Division; Alfred and I.

I had never been to an inquest. I didn't know what to expect. Several reporters were hanging around, and one, as a matter of routine, asked if he could take my photograph. I just turned my head and said, "No." We went inside.

I can't remember much of the room, except that there were seven people who made up the jury, and they were seated in courtroom fashion along one side. We sat silently, our little group, and waited for Dr. Turkel to come in to conduct the inquest. I had no *real* reason up to that point to think there was anything strange about the manner of Mary Lou's death; except for my own gnawing intuition. It did seem uncanny that I could have lived in that apartment so long and have so many catastrophes and strange happenings occur during the last year and a half—and now this, the culminating horror.

I wondered about the compulsion I'd had to get out. I had only been out of that fateful apartment for one month—Mary Lou had been there one week—none of it made sense to me. These jumbled thoughts were going through my mind when the coroner entered the courtroom. After seating himself behind a large desk, he addressed the jury: "We will now go to the matter of the death of Mary Louise Ward"—(*At last*, I thought, *we will get some answers*)—"and first we will call Pat Montandon. Would you come forward, please?"

I went forward and took the chair that was indicated, facing the jury.

What now follows is taken verbatim from the official transcript of the inquest. I have italicized the portions which seem to me to be especially significant.

The coroner asked me of my acquaintance with Mary Louise Ward, and I told him she was my friend and secretary. The next question: "I see. I understand that she had occasion to be occupying your apartment or an apartment you had."

Answer: "Yes."

Question: "This was with your permission and understanding?"

Answer: "That's right."

Question: "You know now that she died as a consequence of a fire on the premises on the 21st of June?"

Answer: "Yes."

Question: "When did you last see her before this fire occurred?"

Answer: "The day before."

Question: "When did you last talk with her? Was that the same day?"

Answer: "The afternoon of the day before, which was the 20th."

Question: "That was the last time you spoke with her?"

Answer: "Yes."

Question: "What was her mood then? Was she her usual self?"

Answer: "Yes. She was happy."

Question: "Did she indicate what her plans were for that day or evening?"

Answer: "She said she was going to a movie with her son or she thought she would, but she was so tired, she really didn't want to go."

Question: "That was which night—Friday night?"

Answer: "Yes. Friday afternoon, about 4:30."

Question: "You have learned since, I presume, she did not go to the movie?"

Answer: "Yes, sir."

Question: "Her son visited with some people and decided to ask permission to stay there, which was granted?"

Answer: "Yes."

Question: "Do you know these people?"

Answer: "No, I do not."

Question: "Had you lived in this apartment some time yourself?"

Answer: "Eight and a half years."

Question: "In that time, had you had any difficulty of any kind with fire or concern over fire?"

Answer: "No concern whatever over fire."

Question: "You never had a fire?"

Answer: "No." [The awning fire of the maharishi party did not enter my head at the time.]

Question: "Some question arises as to whether Mary Louise Ward did or did not smoke. Would you now answer?"

Answer: "She did not smoke."

Question: "Did you know her well enough to say with certainty she did not smoke?"

Answer: "Yes, sir, she did not smoke."

Question: "Would you have any knowledge as to whether anyone visited in the apartment that night?"

Answer: "I don't think so."

Question: "To your best knowledge, no one did?"

Answer: "To my best knowledge, no one visited."

Question: "Did she sometimes have callers—people

who might come and visit with her—men or women?"

Answer: "Yes."

Question: "Have you known any to stay through an evening on occasion?"

Answer: "No."

Question: "I don't mean through the night. Through the evening? Perhaps spend some hours there."

Answer: "Well, in her own home, I'm sure she had visitors who did."

Question: "How long had she lived in this apartment?"

Answer: "In my apartment?"

Question: "Yes."

Answer: "She had been there one week."

Question: "Then you really wouldn't know what her practices were?"

Answer: "No."

Question: "I see. All right."

And then the next statement which was made to the jury confirmed all the feelings I had had, but hadn't been able to put into words.

Dr. Turkel said, *"I should explain to you and particularly to the jurors, that we have examined Mary Louise Ward as carefully as we know how and at great length, and we cannot establish any reason for her death. She did suffer severe burns and we believe she was apparently dead when these burns did occur, but we don't know why she died."*

(*No reason for her death!* I repeated to myself, what is he talking about? Didn't she die from the fire? *No reason, no reason,* kept resounding in my head. And yet I cannot say I was surprised—I was not.)

I was thanked and dismissed from the stand.

The next witness called was Mary Lou's daughter, Jeannie—Jean Eileen Rose. The questions continued in the ordinary routine kind of way until Dr. Turkel said to Jeannie, *"You have heard me say we have not found any reason for your mother's death—that she apparently died or collapsed and then suffered burns that some fire developed. Can you help us understand the sequence of events? You probably can't, but we wonder, maybe you have some ideas?"*

Jeannie answered, "Well, it was my understanding that she never woke up and that she probably suffocated before she suffered any pain."

Dr. Turkel: *"That is not quite what we find, Jeannie."*

Jeannie: "Oh, I didn't know."

Dr. Turkel: *"Initially we thought that would likely be the case, but our tests, etc. do not demonstrate this. Do you have any reason to be suspicious that there's anything wrong with your mother's death or do you feel that it's just an unfortunate accident?"*

Jeannie: *"Well, it's just terribly freaky, but that is all I can think."*

Dr. Turkel: "Sure. All right. Thank you. You may step down."

The next witness who was sworn in was a longtime friend of Mary Lou's, Pauline Kendall. Dr. Turkel asked her, among other things, "I understand that the evening before this fire, you spoke with her on the phone for some time."

Answer: "That's correct."

Question: "For how long, roughly?"

Answer: "Perhaps an hour."

Question: "Now, any two women who get together and talk for an hour at a stretch generally talk about things very close to one another."

Answer: "Yes."

Question: "Did she confide to you she was having any problem [sic] of any kind?"

Answer: "No."

Question: "Would you know was she a chronic user of sleeping pills?"

Answer: "I don't know what you mean by chronic."

Question: "Well, if you take as many as two a day,

you are addicted to two sleeping pills a day."

Answer: "I wouldn't say she was."

Question: "Did she take one a day, regularly?"

Answer: "She took sleeping pills but she tried not to take them unless they were necessary."

Question: "Right. The criterion is if a person can skip a few days, she is not addicted."

Answer: "She tried to do that."

Question: "Did she, though?"

Answer: "I heard her mention at times she did get along without them."

Question: "This is what we need now. Do you know of any illnesses she suffered which might have caused her to collapse?"

Answer: "She had encephalitis once. She also had low blood pressure."

Question: "Was she treated for this?"

Answer: "She took pills for it. I know it got very low and she would get weak when it got low."

Question: "Did you ever go to Dr. Gamble's office with her?"

Answer: "I never went with her. I did go to Dr. Gamble because of Mary Louise."

Question: "Then apparently you did know her rather well?"

Answer: "Yes."

Question: "Would you know, did she smoke?"

Answer: "No."

Question: "Let me ask, did she have callers sometimes in the evening at the home?"

Answer: "I am certain that she did not because she was very tired that evening."

Question: "That particular night? Did she sometimes have callers? I don't mean to be prying."

Answer: "No."

Question: "But we are trying to establish—"

Answer: "She didn't have any privacy, really."

Question: "I see. This particular night, she had expected her son to be home. Is that not right, until it was decided that he was going to stay elsewhere?"

Answer: "Well, there were kind of plans in the air, like Pat said, she was planning to go to a movie with Jimmy. Then, I had tentative plans with her and nothing firmed up, so . . ."

Question: "Then, you have no reason to think that someone did spend the evening there, who did in fact smoke, and who might have left a cigarette on the premises."

Answer: "No."

Question: "Then you have no knowledge of this and no reason to think that that did happen?"

Answer: "Well, from what I know of Mary Louise, I don't think she would have allowed anyone to come over any time of the night, at the last minute."

Question: "Very good. When did you finish your conversation with her?"

Answer: "About 9:30."

Question: "Well, it would seem impossible that anyone would be coming, but they might have. We just don't know. You don't think they did?"

Answer: "I doubt it very much."

Question: "Very good. Do you have any information which would help us explain this event in any way?"

Answer: [Witness shrugs shoulders]

Question: "*You don't know. We don't either, so we all have to shrug, as it were, and we are hunting for what we can find. This is a very unusual case. In my sixteen years I have run into something like this only very rarely.* All right. Thank you very much. You may step down."

The next witness who was sworn in was Evelyn Walker, the downstairs neighbor.

Question: "Miss Walker, you lived downstairs from where Mary Louise Ward died?"

Answer: "That's right."

Question: "I understand your apartment is such that if people walk about above you, you can hear it?"

Answer: "Well, occasionally."

Question: "Did you know Mrs. Ward?"

Answer: "Not well, just an acquaintance."

Question: "You knew she was living there?"

Answer: "Yes."

Question: "Did you know her son was living with her?"

Answer: "Yes, she had told me."

Question: "I am given to understand that you at times could tell whether there was one person or two persons above, depending on the movements. Is this correct?"

Answer: "Well, I couldn't answer that exactly except that evening I just remember that I heard footsteps earlier in the evening. I had gone to bed early and watched television but I just remembered I had heard these footsteps earlier in the evening, which didn't bother me at all. I just recalled—I thought, 'Mary Lou is home.' That was all, but there was nothing out of the ordinary."

Question: "There were no unusual sounds?"

Answer: "No."

Question: "No sounds of a struggle?"

Answer: "Oh, no."

Question: "Nothing of an undue stomping about?"

Answer: "Not a bit."

Question: "Anything to suggest more than one person?"

Answer: "Not at all."

Question: "Do you think there was just one person home from what you heard?"

Answer: "Yes, as far as I would know."

Question: "Of course it would be entirely possible for one person to walk and then the other."

Answer: "That's right."

Question: "But you didn't hear two walking at one time?"

Answer: "No—no—no."

Question: "You have no reason to think that anyone else was on the premises during the evening?"

Answer: "No, not a bit."

The next witness was Inspector Lucas from the Fire Department.

The coroner: "Inspector Lucas, you have investigated this matter for the Arson Squad of the Fire Department?"

Answer: "Yes, Doctor."

Question: "And you were at the scene of the fire?"

Answer: "Yes, Doctor. In fact, I was with two of the firemen when we discovered the body."

Question: "Is it your practice in the Arson Squad to go out always when there is a death?"

Answer: "Well, this happened to be a second alarm and we responded automatically."

Question: "I see. That was the reason you were there?"

Answer: "So we were there a lot sooner than at a normal fire. If there is a death, there might be a delay of twenty minutes or half an hour before they would call us."

Question: "I was coming to that and the reason you were there was because of the intensity of the fire?"

Answer: "The heavy smoke. The fire itself was not too intense. *It was that the apartment was so, as we say, buttoned up, that there was no place for the smoke to go until the two windows on the [. . .] side broke and that allowed more air—oxygen—to get in and then everything burst into flame.*"

Question: "This suggests that it was a smoldering fire?"

Answer: "It was a long, smoldering fire, Doctor."

Question: "Have you been able to establish the source of the fire?"

Answer: "Yes. The fire started in a closet which would be on the north side of the bed and burned out through the closet and up into the attic—the attic space across the room—and then into the bedroom where Mrs. Ward was found—throughout that room completely."

Question: "I understood you to say the closet was next to the bed?"

Answer: "It was about four or five feet from the bed in the same room."

Question: "It went up through the attic?"

Answer: "It went up through the attic and also went out through the bedroom at the same time."

Question: "From the closet?"

Answer: "From the closet. Now, Ms. Montandon, when I talked to her, she told me that when she had lived there, she was in the habit of sleeping late some mornings and she had heavy drapes on the windows, which would explain the fact that the fire wasn't discovered for so long—that the fire had to burn through those drapes and nobody on the outside could see in, and that when the window burst, that was the first sign of anybody having any knowledge of the fire."

Question: "You say it started in the closet. What started the fire? Can you say?"

Answer: "It was most likely the wiring, Doctor, because there was a television set in the bedroom and the outlet was in the closet itself. I went through the debris, looking for the outlet. *I could not find the outlet.* I even looked downstairs in Miss Walker's place in the debris and I couldn't find the outlet and we have to presume in a case like this; and I presume that Mrs. Ward had gone to bed. She had taken a sleeping pill and gone to bed, leaving the television on. [The television set was not plugged into the outlet in the closet. I had seen it sitting on the dressing table the day before the fire. It was plugged into the baseboard approximately eight feet from the closet.] The wiring in the place—a lot of it was illegal—that wouldn't necessarily mean that it was defective, but there were places in the ceiling where the wiring had been illegally spliced before, and I presume that the wire became overheated and it traveled back from the television right into the closet where all the wires were; and those wires started burning and they burned and a fuse was found to be blown in the closet out in the hall where there was a small fuse box. One of the fuse stats was blown and that would show there had been a fire, because that is all that would blow a fuse like that is a fire." [As a result of the fire inspector's report the landlord had to have the entire building rewired.]

Question: "Do you think if there was enough heat being generated to start a fire, it would have blown a fuse? That's what they are for, I understand."

Answer: "Yes, they are, but if it's a slow rise heat. For a fuse to blow, it has to be a rapid, sudden thing, but a slow rise in the heat, the fuse would hold it for quite a while until something in the closet ignited. The closet had a shelf on it and according to Ms. Montandon, there had been a fluorescent light in there that did not work and there is a similar closet in the other room—the other bedroom—and I have a picture of that if you would like to see it, Doctor."

Question: "All right."

Answer: "*I checked everything. I mean, as you know, I have been in this business for quite a while and I was so concerned that I called you up and told you about that, if you remember.*"

Question: "Right. I do."

Answer: "Because the position of the body, for one thing, Doctor."

Question: "Let me interrupt. What you are showing is—?"

Answer: "This is the other closet, Doctor."

Question: "The other closet with the wire coiled up to demonstrate?"

Answer: "No."

Question: "What does this demonstrate for us?"

Answer: "It just shows the shelf. There was a shelf in the main bedroom similar to that in the closet, but it wasn't quite as big a closet."

Question: "But this doesn't demonstrate anything in relation to why a fire would start?"

Answer: "No, I'm just showing you the other closet in the other room."

Question: "May we keep this? We will see that it comes back to you. I will leave this for the jurors."

Answer: "Yes."

Question: "All right. Anything else you would add before I ask a few questions?"

Answer: "No, go ahead."

Question: *"In this case the carbon monoxide level in the blood was 1.5 percent saturation of carbon monoxide in the blood which is nothing. We get two or three times that much from a cigarette."*

Answer: *"I was very amazed when I called up and found that out from Mr. Scannell."*

Question: *"That is why we are still amazed.* [To the jurors] *Whenever there is a fire of the type described here and the person is alive while the fire is in progress, they will wind up with high levels of carbon monoxide, since that is always produced in fire, and the level in a case might be 30, 40, 60 percent saturation. This is less carbon monoxide than you get from standing on a street corner from traffic fumes, so this suggests to us that at the time of the fire the person was dead.*

"Secondly, examining the body, even though extensively burned about the lower extremities, the internal organs were all in good order, and *we find no way to account for why this person would be dead when the fire started.*

"The sleeping pills that are said to have been taken, that sometimes prevents a person from responding to the smoke, really doesn't enter here because *the level is so small in the body that she may not even have taken a sleeping pill that night.* That could be a little bit left from the day before.

"There was only a trace of Secobarbital.

"Inspector, you suggest the most unbelievable coinci-

dence, that this would be an electrical fire occurring by chance after somebody is dead for no apparent reason."

Answer: "Well. . . ."

Question: "You see what I am saying?"

Answer: "I see what you mean."

Question: "This raises questions in my mind."

Answer: *"I don't know whether— Well, that is one of the reasons why I called you, Doctor. I have seen so many bodies, I mean after twenty-one years in here I have seen so many bodies burned at fires, and this one just didn't strike me right for the simple reason the position of the body. She was face down on the bed. Well, that doesn't mean anything, but it looked like her legs were over the end of the bed, as if maybe she had gotten up and then just fallen back on the bed. That is the thing that I—"*

Question: "This is true. She may have, but why she collapsed, we can't say.

"The whole thing is unusual, and I didn't expect we'd come up with an answer, but I wanted to air it and let everyone have their say and see where the difficulty lies."

Answer: "In regard to anybody else being in the place, definitely, in my opinion, no. The front door had a sliding bolt on it, which was a very big bolt, and it took the Fire Department quite a while to break in that door to get in."

Question: "No other entrance?"

Answer: "No other entrance. I mean there was a back door that was locked, that was opened by the Fire Department."

Question: "Deadbolt?"

Answer: "No. One of these round knobs and you screw it. You turn it and it goes into the other part of the door. It's a bolt."

Question: "It's a bolt?"

Answer: "Yes."

Question: "Nothing you can slam shut and leave?"

Answer: "No."

Question: "So the apartment was indeed secure?"

Answer: [Nodding affirmatively] "Nobody could have gone in there and gone out."

Question: "My first concern was that someone might have left a cigarette or she in fact might have been smoking but we learn she was not a smoker."

Answer: "Definitely not a cigarette, Doctor."

Question: "She would have had no callers who would have left a cigarette?"

Answer: "Definitely not."

Question: "*Well, I must confess for the jurors and whoever is listening that we cannot give a suitable explanation. We can only tell you that we have made a very determined effort to solve the case, as to what caused the death and so on, and we simply cannot with our best effort.*

"You apparently are unable to tell us how it is she came to be in this position?"

Answer: "That is the only thing that bothers me."

Question: "You are indeed satisfied it was an electrical fire?"

Answer: "Definitely, Doctor. I had the electrical inspector up there with me several days after."

Question: "Was he of the same opinion?"

Answer: "He was of the same opinion, yes."

The coroner: "All right. That is all I ask. Thank you." [Witness excused.]

The coroner: "Inspector Toschi."

Inspector David Toschi, having been duly sworn, testified as follows:

Question: "*Inspector Toschi, you investigated this matter for the Homicide Detail in response to our request?*"

Answer: "Yes, Doctor."

Question: "*And the jurors should understand this is because of the irregularities in the case and not because we have any immediate suspicion, but we felt it would be wise to let the Homicide Detail know of this case and let them study it.*

"Inspector, you did carry out an intensive investigation along with Inspector Lucas?"

Answer: "I did, Doctor."

Question: "Or at least paralleling his in part?"

Answer: "Yes, sir."

Question: *"In essence, do you find the same things he has related, apart from his official opinion?"*

Answer: *"Everything that has been said today from all the witnesses, including Inspector Lucas, who was at the scene, is consistent with information that I have.* I have contacted all these people, spoken to them, gone into background on the deceased, spoken several times with Inspector Lucas. I can find no one who can say that Mary Louise smoked. I have spoken to quite a few people that have known her for several years. She did not smoke. She was a moderate drinker.

"According to Mrs. Kendall, as she stated, Mrs. Ward was home for the night, that Friday night, June the 20th. Her son had gone out to spend the night with friends in the area. She did take sleeping pills. There is evidence of it in your autopsy. However, I did talk to Dr. John Gamble, who has known her for about twelve years, and he said that he has prescribed only Nembutal for her these last few years, and he couldn't understand why there was Seconal, but it's very possible she has gone to another doctor to obtain this."

Question: "Let me explain to the jury that we are talking about two types of sleeping pills and this doctor didn't prescribe the particular type that we found, but you can get them from friends or another doctor. There is no problem here. Go ahead."

Answer: "Her last prescription for the Nembutal was on April 17th of this year and apparently she had asked for some more Nembutal in May, but it was turned down by one of his associates, a Dr. Smith, because they didn't want her to have too many over such a close period of time.

"According to Dr. Gamble, she was in good health. He hadn't seen her for several months. She was a very hypertensive person."

Question: "Hypertensive?"

Answer: "She was something . . ."

Question: "High blood pressure?"

Answer: "Yes."

Question: "She had high blood pressure?"

Answer: "No. No."

Question: "Hypertonic? She was keyed up?"

Answer: "Yes. She was a very nervous type person. But as far as he knew, her health was good and he couldn't give any specific reason as to what might have been wrong with her recently.

"We know she had encephalitis approximately twelve years ago and occasionally did get headaches from this and as a result of this took sleeping pills when she felt she would probably have a bad night.

"Lately I learned from the family and friends that she was in the habit of taking a small glass of wine before retiring to calm her down.

"Now, as Inspector Lucas says, the apartment was quite secure that evening. The front door and back door. She apparently was alone. ["Mrs. Walker"] said that she thought she heard only the one set of footsteps, which was about 9:30 or so.

"At this time I don't find any evidence of any criminality coming out of that apartment, Doctor."

Question: "All right. Then you are entirely satisfied there is no crime in relation to this death?"

Answer: "I am, sir, at this time. Yes, sir."

The coroner: "Very well. That is all we would ask you to establish. You may step down."

Answer: "Thank you, Doctor." [Witness excused]

The coroner: "Are there any questions from the jurors? Any comments?" [No response]

The coroner: *"If not, I would point out that the cause*

of death in this case must remain undetermined. We have made an exhaustive study to find something which would account for the death. We cannot relate it to the encephalitis, either. This doesn't appear to be the cause of death.

"We did find extensive burns of the body. The carbon monoxide in the blood is not consistent with one being alive in the presence of a fire. The amount of sleeping medicine in the body was infinitesimal and there was none in the stomach to suggest she had recently taken a dose.

"The blood alcohol level was .04 percent, which in the average person is consistent with having one drink. It can only remain for you to conclude, as we cannot account as to the cause of death properly or the circumstances of the death, you could not say she died as a consequence of the faulty wiring because we don't know why she died, and it would appear she was dead already when the fire occurred.

"While we leave the case in doubt, I felt obliged to hold the hearing. We wanted to make a permanent record under oath and see what others might offer, and sometimes we learn things in the course of the inquest we don't learn otherwise.

"Is there anyone who would like to make comment in this case?

"If not, we thank you for coming and this is as far as we can go in this matter.

"Thank you again."

[Testimony closed]

15

Clues to the Labyrinth

It was difficult to grasp what the coroner had said. The verdict, and the evidence leading up to it, had created more questions than had been answered. Not all the inconsistencies occurred to me at the time, as, in the shock and tensions of the inquest, I was in no state to analyze details. And within months there was more terrible news to face. It was as though the mindless evil, the blind malevolence of the house had reached out to strike at all those who had stayed or worked with me there in the last few years.

First came word that Carolyn had killed herself in Honolulu. I remembered so well with what high hopes she had set out to make a fresh start when Mary Lou and I saw her off at the airport; and then later, when Alfred and I visited with her in the Islands and we had both felt there was a weight in her heart, and a foreboding of unhappiness to come. It was dreadfully sad: she was only twenty-four.

Then came a phone call from Vera Scott's mother. She told me Vera had taken her own life, the victim of an unhappy romance. Believing, I suppose, that there was no hope, she had shot herself. Poor child, she was so young—like Carolyn, in her twenties. My heart was heavy thinking of the three women who had been a part of my life and were now dead. If it hadn't been for Alfred and my new strength in him I might have been overwhelmed. And but for him, too, I undoubtedly would have been the first of the victims.

I started to have a recurring dream. It always began the same way, and followed the same unchanging pattern: *Mary Lou appears at the side of my bed. She is dressed in some kind of gray robe; and after shaking me to wakefulness, motions me to follow her. I get out of bed and walk down the hall, and just as we reach the top of the stairway, I abruptly find myself back on Lombard Street, and the steps become the ones ascending to the foyer. In the same instant, blood-curdling screams come from the stairway leading up to the apartment on the third floor above. I call out to Mary Lou, but she has disappeared. I rush into the apartment to find her. I look everywhere, calling her name. I hear more screams, broken by moans, coming from behind the closed door to the bedroom. I run to it, and throwing it open, see Mary Lou gasping for breath, as some formless entity envelops her, choking her. I run forward, screaming, "Get away! Get away!" but I, too, become enveloped, and can feel myself starting to strangle. And then for the first time, Mary Lou speaks to me, in a rasping voice, "Get out, Patsy Lou, get out!"*

That was the end, always. I would awake suddenly, shaken and depressed, and would move closer to Alfred, for the comfort of his warmth against me, and eventually I would fall asleep again. The dream always left me vaguely unhappy for a few days, only to sink back into my subconscious until the next time.

At first I had the dream perhaps once every six weeks;

after a year it began to increase to once or twice a month.

Then another strange thing happened. It was November, 1972. Alfred and I went to Honolulu for the first vacation there since our marriage, and stayed for a few days at the Kahala Hilton. I went one morning (and it is fixed in my mind because it was the day before Thanksgiving) to the beauty salon to get my hair done, while Alfred was sunning on the beach. There were only about five people, including two hairdressers, in the shop at the time, and I became keenly aware of a lanky, attractive woman who was being attended to near me. She had something tomboyish, friendly and outgoing about her, and as her hair was being dressed, she was telling the stylist a string of stories about psychic phenomena in a singularly down-to-earth way.

As she got under the hair dryer, she turned to the woman seated next to her.

"Young woman," she said in a brisk voice, "you should put those cigarettes away. You've had a serious throat cancer operation and you shouldn't be smoking at all." We all looked in the same direction, wondering how the object of her advice would respond.

A startled face emerged from under the dryer. "How could you possibly know?"

"Oh, I knew all right, I was getting some bad vibes. Let me see your hand . . . Yes, there it is . . . that cross on your hepatic line . . . You have had a difficult time with your mother . . . quarreled with her . . . fought a bit . . . You've been married about ten years . . . You come from somewhere where there are a lot of horses . . . and you lost your only child at birth. You're English, of course, but that I can tell by your accent."

I listened, fascinated, as the youngish woman (she was in her mid-thirties) confirmed the truth of everything our candid friend said. I heard her ask the seer for her name and address and invite her to the Flamingo Hotel in Las Vegas the following October when her husband, an entertainer, was to perform. She had obviously been bowled over by the unhesitating truths she had just heard, spoken without any suggestion of mumbo-jumbo or mystery.

After this extraordinary incident the conversation became general, and we learned that the psychic was in the Islands for a medical convention. She explained that she often worked with doctors in the area of paranormal research, and also cooperated with the police in solving crimes.

When my hair was done, I joined Alfred for cocktails; later, over dinner, I regaled him with the story of the beauty salon psychic—and really thought little more about it until the next day.

We had strolled to a lovely stretch of beach below the hotel and settled ourselves with huge towels on the warm sand. I was lulled by the sounds of the surf breaking on the coral reef in the distance, and soaking up the sun.

I had been lying on my stomach for some time, when I decided to change my position. I sat up and looked around, and caught sight of the tall woman of the day before. I waved to her and was pleased to see she was coming over to us.

"I'm Gerri Patton," she said. "Weren't you in the beauty shop yesterday?"

"Yes," I said. "You were telling fortunes."

"Not fortunes," she corrected me. "I was explaining about psychic vibrations."

I introduced her to Alfred and she sat down on the sand next to us and started an animated conversation. I was curious to know exactly what she did. She said she was an investigator involved in psychic research, and would be going to Maui the next day to lecture. We listened, fascinated, as she told us about some of the cases she'd worked on.

Acting on a sudden impulse, I asked her, "Read my husband's palm, will you, Gerri?"

"Sure," she said, "but remember it doesn't always work. Sometimes I just can't do it."

Saying this, she took both Alfred's hands: and after some mild protestation on his part, proceeded to give us a reading. I can't remember exactly what she said in detail, but she pinpointed facts of his earlier life and zeroed in on current aspects of his career as well. We were both surprised she was so accurate.

Our curiosity whetted, we started to question her. She mentioned the word "psychometrizing."

"What does that mean?" I asked.

"Well, it's kind of hard to explain," she said. "I would say it's the ancient art of object reading. There are two forms: A psychic can read the object itself, or you can read through actual physical contact. You get vibrations. One is called precognition—that means discerning the future; the other is retrocognition—getting vibrations from an object and telling about the past from it. Of course, if it's a really old object, I can have all kinds of trouble, because I get many different vibrations from different people. And then, of course, it's very hard to prove, because the present owner generally can't tell me if what I find is right or not, as what I am responding to may have happened long before the object came into his or her possession—I'll show you how it works."

She was looking at a ring I wore, a large pearl mounted in a plain gold setting, which I had owned for about seven years.

"Let me have that and I'll see if I can psychometrize it for you," she said, and I slipped the ring off my finger and handed it to her.

"Fine, that's fine, that's just fine. Okay, okay," she said, repeating herself as she held the jewel in her hands. "Now, let's see," and she closed both hands over the ring and shut her eyes, rocking ever so slightly back and forth in the sand.

"You live in an apartment house up lots of steps."

I looked at Alfred and winked. *She was sure off the track*, I thought.

"You enter a hallway with a marble floor," she stated. "That's right—marble." And then she started gesturing, holding the ring in one hand and directing with the other.

"You turn this way—left—and then you are in the living room, and then off to the left [still gesturing] is a bedroom. . . ." Then, feeling the ring with her fingertips over and over again, she said, "To the right, a small room for eating and beyond, a rather old kitchen . . . now I'm back in the living room . . . there's a fireplace in the corner. It's different. It has—it has two sides to it. Yes, yes, two sides and there are three big windows to the right and you can see water, lots of water and some little boats."

I couldn't believe it. I looked at Alfred. He seemed thunderstruck. She was describing the house. She had been talking incredibly fast, almost as if she were on a tape recorder turned to the wrong speed. Now there was silence, and after perhaps ten seconds she opened her eyes and looked at me.

"Someone was killed there," she said. "A woman."

"How could you know?" I asked. "Is there . . . anything more you can tell me?"

"It's just the vibrations I get," she said, and then, "No," with a sigh, "I can't tell you any more."

She looked tired now and said she thought she had better get a drink of water. She would see us back at the hotel later.

Alfred and I sat and stared at each other. How could she have known? How could she have described the apartment so fully? I had given her not one single clue: On the contrary, I'd been careful not to tell her anything about myself.

That night I had the dream again.

I looked for Gerri Patton the next day but didn't see her anywhere; then I remembered she had said she would be on Maui. I do not recall exactly when I finally did see her again, but it was shortly before we were to return to San Francisco. I wrote down her address and telephone number, because something was working at the back of my mind, and I thought I might want to get in touch with her later. I was haunted by all that had happened, and felt a kind of personal obligation to investigate it as scrupulously as I could. At first, my ideas of how to go about it were barely formulated, but the passing months strengthened my conviction and I began, with Alfred's encouragement, to make plans.

It was almost a year later that I used the number to call Gerri Patton. She answered brightly, remembering me at once. I said, "Gerri, I'm still shaken by what you told me on the beach in Honolulu."

She remembered the incident clearly and said she had made a tape of everything she had told me. She explained she always did this for verification, because, working as she did in a field full of crackpots and phonies, she felt it important that anything she did be above suspicion.

I told her I would like it very much if she could put me in touch with a person of psychic ability—someone above reproach—who could perhaps go to the old apartment with me. Although I knew it was a longshot and might not prove anything, I wanted to take that step.

Gerri said, "Sure, I can give you a name—and I'll try to come along too, if you like."

She gave me the name of a man called Frank "Nick" Nocerino and she added, "You know, he's licensed by the State Board of Education. He teaches classes in parapsychology and psychic research, and is called in on all the important cases of disappearances . . . He's a remarkable sensitive."

"Okay, Gerri. Thanks. I'll get in touch with Mr. Nocerino and then I'll get back to you. First I'll have to talk to the people who live there now and find out if I can get their cooperation."

"Fine. Whenever you arrange it I'll try to make myself free. . . . We'll work something out."

I immediately called my old landlord, and went straight to the point.

"I would like to know who lives in my old apartment," I said.

"Why, the Reillys," he said. "He's a surgeon, you know. . . . James and Phyllis."

"Do you have their phone number?"

"No, but I can get it for you."

"Oh, I can look it up. . . ."

"Well, I don't know if it's listed—but I'm sure you can get it from his office." And he gave me the number. "I don't own that building anymore, you know."

"No, I didn't know that. When did you sell it?"

"Oh, just a little while ago . . . that place sure was a voodoo for me. It had a hex on it, Pat. I had more trouble there than I've ever had in my life. It was hard to unload. Of course, I wouldn't want to say anything that would cause anyone any problems, but that place sure had a hex on it."

I thanked him for the information and looked in the telephone book for James Reilly's number, and placed a call: It hadn't been necessary to check with his office. I couldn't help but remember the last time I'd tried to reach that apartment—in such anguish—and gotten no answer.

The phone rang several times, and I was ready to hang up when a soft female voice answered.

The woman identified herself as Phyllis Reilly. I told her I would like to come over sometime if it was all right with her, just to see what the old apartment looked like. I had lived there for so long, I had some curiosity about it.

"Sure," she said. "How about Saturday around ten o'clock?"

"Fine. I'll see you then. Thanks so much."

I didn't want the psychics to go over until I had laid the groundwork. It was a delicate situation and one I hardly knew how to handle.

I got in touch with Allan Carr, an understanding Englishman and a friend of mine, who had agreed to help me in any way he could during this investigation.

It was almost ten o'clock on a Saturday morning. As I parked my car at the curb, I felt a little uneasy. I was afraid the experience of seeing the house again after almost five years might be an emotional one for me. There were too many memories.

As we walked into the garden, it seemed normal and was in good shape. The statue was still on the first landing of the steps. The magnolia tree had plump buds ready to burst into bloom, although it was the wrong time of year. It was the first of September, 1973.

As we walked up the steps, I noted they had a different type of finish. They obviously had been redone. Walking past Evelyn Walker's door, I wondered who lived there now, because I knew she had moved out after the fire. We were now on the top landing and I automatically gave the old coded ring, feeling slightly abashed when I realized what I had done.

An attractive, petite, blond woman who looked like Eleanor McGovern answered the door.

"You're Pat," she said brightly.

"And this is Allan Carr," I said. "You must be Phyllis."

"Right," she said. "Won't you come in?"

"You're very nice to let us come over this way. I do appreciate it."

She was warm and hospitable and asked me to look around and to make myself at home. The pleasantries over with, I could concentrate on my surroundings. I'd expected to be disturbed on returning to the scene of so many problems, then the ultimate tragedy of Mary Lou's death, but strangely I was not. The apartment seemed pretty much the way it had been before the fire. I peered into the old library and could see it was nicely furnished and was not doubling, as it had for me, as an office.

I hesitated to go into the bedroom, yet I felt I had to. Allan walked with me as we looked around. The room seemed much smaller and the furniture was arranged differently. The bed was now against the east wall, whereas when I had lived there, it had been on the west. It seemed changed, but not unsettling.

I walked back into the living room and Phyllis asked if we would like some coffee.

She went to the kitchen; I was standing by the side window in the living room. Allan was seated in an over-stuffed chair. We were talking idly about the way I had furnished the apartment, as opposed to the way it was now, when suddenly I smelled smoke—old smoke. That's the only way I can describe it. It was quite strong. I looked quickly about the room to see if there was a fire in the fireplace, knowing full well there was not. No one was smoking a cigarette. There couldn't be smoke coming from any known source.

I said to Allan, "Do you smell smoke?"

He looked sharply at me and said, "Yes, I do."

Before we could comment further, Phyllis Reilly walked back into the room with the coffee.

"Phyllis, do you smell smoke?" I asked.

"No," she said. "I don't smell anything."

"Are you sure?" I still smelled it very strongly.

"No, I don't smell anything at all, except the coffee."

"Allan, do you still smell it?"

"Not as strongly now," he said. And I became aware that I could no longer detect it. I was wondering how I could get around to asking Mrs. Reilly about bringing psychics into her house. It semed so improbable. I decided to say nothing about it but rather to discuss it with Alfred and have her come over to our house and explain what I was doing.

Allan and I walked into the foyer together. I was telling

the story of the dope people who'd lived upstairs and as I paused by the stair landing. I was again suddenly enveloped in the acrid odor of old smoke. It was much stronger this time—overpowering. I abruptly ended my story, saying nothing about the sensation, thanked Mrs. Reilly, and left.

I was disturbed. As we walked down the steps, Allan and I were both silent and remained so until, as Allan opened the car door, he said, "Pat, I didn't want to say anything, but when you were standing in the foyer, talking to Mrs. Reilly, I smelled that overpowering smell of smoke again. It was extremely strong—stronger than the first time."

I got in the car and just sat there a few minutes, all the while looking up at the gray building.

"Allan," I said, "I smelled it, too, but it seemed too much to say anything. I don't want anyone to think I'm some kind of kook, but it was very real. I wasn't imagining it. I'm glad you smelled it, too. Apparently Phyllis did not."

We talked about it all the way back to my house. We didn't know what to make of it, if anything, and we wondered whether it could possibly be a residue from the fire. But after almost five years? And the fire, after all, had been confined to the bedroom. Did I have an overactive imagination? But why should Allan smell it? And why didn't Phyllis? Why were we the only ones?

"Well, I've got to find out more about this whole thing. That's for sure," I said.

I called Phyllis Reilly the next day and asked if she and her husband would come over to our house for cocktails the following evening. She said her husband was busy but that she could come.

The next evening, we sat in the living room, sipping cocktails and making light conversation. Alfred was there, Allan, Phyllis, and I.

"Phyllis," I said, "you know, of course, about my best

friend dying in that apartment in a fire."

"Yes, I know, Pat."

"I've always felt there was something more to be explored about it all—and if it's all right with you, I would like very much to bring over two psychics and let them see what they can discover. I feel silly even talking about it, and yet, I feel that I must do this."

I told her about the strong aroma of smoke the second time. She said, not unexpectedly, that she hadn't smelled it.

"I don't want to frighten you. I don't want to create a difficult situation for you or your husband," I said. "Nor would I want you to think I am off my rocker, as it were. . . ."

"I don't think that," she said. "I'm a skeptic, but I do want to tell you something, Pat. We've decided to move out of that place."

"You have?" I said.

"Yes, we decided about a month ago."

"Why?" I asked.

"I don't really know why. James is a very pragmatic man, so practical. He would never admit to anything supernatural; but, strangely, lately he has started smelling smoke and has commented on it several times. There's a feeling about the place he doesn't like, so we're going to move."

"I'm glad you are," I said. "When can we arrange to come over with the psychics, if you're quite sure it's all right?"

"Any time before we move. Just let me know," she said.

We concluded our conversation on that note. I called Gerri Patton and she got in touch with Nick Nocerino, and we made arrangements to meet on Saturday morning, September 15, 1973. Allan Carr said he would come with me, as Alfred was busy that day. I felt a bit foolish, yet I knew what I was doing was right.

And that night, I had a dream again. Not the bad

dream; I never had it again. Rather, this time I was writing with a red pen and suddenly someone or something else took over control of my hand and the writing became different from my own. It was in red ink and there were two lines. The first line I cannot remember but the second said—and it all ran together like automatic writing—

We-are-very-proud-of-you.
Mary Lou

I awoke feeling good about the dream. I began looking forward to Saturday morning. I went over early. It was misting rain. I sat in my car, watching the traffic, as unceasing as ever, come down the crooked street. People with umbrellas, shielding their cameras, were taking pictures—a normal scene for the famous street.

Allan arrived, having come on the Hyde Street cable car. We waited awhile and the psychics apparently hadn't arrived, so we decided we had better go on up and tell James and Phyllis Reilly they were late. We bounded up the steps and as we got to the top we realized the front door was wide open and sitting inside, on the steps of the stairway going upstairs from the foyer, was Gerri Patton. A man was taking photographs in the hall. We'd gotten our wires crossed. They had arrived shortly before I did and had gone on up and been at work for some twenty minutes.

It was an informal, breezy sort of situation—not at all mysterious or suggesting anything occult or out of the ordinary. Phyllis was busily serving coffee. We were introduced, of course, to Nick Nocerino. Gerri Patton was there, Nick, James Reilly, Phyllis Reilly, Allan Carr, and I. Gerri and Nick then resumed working, quite independently of each other. It was very businesslike until I suddenly heard Gerri yell for Nick. She was standing stock-still on the top landing of the steps from the foyer.

"Come here, Nick. I've got something. I've really got something," she said.

Nick went dashing out the door with his camera. They both carried tape recorders as well. I walked out into the hall to watch. Gerri was leaning against the wall.

"I was almost pushed down the steps," she said. "There are two forces here."

All the while, she was talking into the tape recorder. Then she and Nick went along the walls touching them with their hands and Nick said, "It's very hot here. Do you feel it? It's very hot. And here's a cold spot."

I couldn't make head or tails of what they were doing. I knew at the end of their work they would tell me what they thought about the house. I sat talking to Allan and Phyllis, trying not to get in the way. In the back of my mind, I kept thinking something would happen, something obvious—that *I* would smell smoke again or the windows would fly open. But there was absolutely nothing—not even the faintest tinge of a smoke smell, except perhaps for Gerri's husband's pipe. (I failed to mention her husband, Pat Patton, was also present. He occasionally accompanies her on her fieldwork.)

Nick was taking many rolls of film and he and Gerri were dashing around the house from room to room, again quite separately, out in the hall, up the stairs, and even onto the back porch. I could hear Gerri saying, "There's nothing here in the kitchen," but as she entered the enclosed back porch area she grew dizzy and had to sit down to keep her balance. As the morning progressed, Gerri went into the bedroom. Now you must remember, as I pointed out before, that the bedroom furniture was arranged very differently from the way I had done it. I could hear Gerri saying over and over again, "I'm so hot, I'm so hot, I'm burning up. I am so hot."

I walked to the bedroom door and could see she was leaning against the wall in exactly the spot where Mary Lou would have been during the fire. She was flushed and perspiration was rolling down her face and she kept repeating, "I'm so hot, I'm so hot." She did not know, and *could* not have known, of the arrangement of furniture. I walked back to the living room, disturbed and saddened.

Nick and Gerri worked for perhaps three and a half or four hours and at the end of that time we all gathered in the living room to hear the tape recordings.

It was a strange experience to hear the two voices, talking in an unbroken stream, as though they'd laid themselves wide open to every sensation and impression the house had to give them.

Nick was describing, his eyes closed, some of the emotions he experienced in going through the house. Suddenly his voice became tearful, his face altered radically, he looked entirely changed. Sobbing, he said, "I felt myself being drawn down to the floor [bedroom]. I went to the floor and, as I went down to the floor everything got kind of bad. But I didn't do it either."

Gerri said, "Are you okay?"

[Weeping]

"How are you feeling, Nick?"

"I'm very sad."

"Why are you sad?"

"I don't know. I just didn't do anything."

"What do you mean, you didn't do anything?"

"I didn't do nothing. I don't know."

"Nick."

"What?"

"What went on? Why are you crying?"

"I'm not crying, am I?"

"What went on, Nick?"

"I don't know, I just found myself on the floor, and there was warmness all around my hands and from about six inches up my arms. I just lay there."

"Did you fall, Nick?"

"No, I actually found myself being pulled to the floor."

"Did somebody push you?"

"No."

"Are you there alone?"

"I was there with somebody, but I was alone when I went to the floor. I was real depressed."

"As you went to the floor, did you have the sensation of, say, that this was it?"

"Yes. Pretty much."

"Do you have manic depressiveness?"

"I didn't care anymore."

"In other words, what's the use?"

"Yes, I was useless, very depressed. I'm sorry."

"That's all right. That's how we work. Anyway . . . you okay now?"

"Yeah, I'm fine. Wow, where were we? We were in the bedroom, bathroom."

"Want to stop for a minute?"

"No, while it's going on in my head, I'll go through it. I'll make notes later. . . . Then came into the front room, sat down. . . . Felt like I was kind of floating. . . . Very strong floating feeling like somebody could constantly be pushed through the air. . . . I could very easily have the feeling of going through any one of the windows, at any time. I went into the tearoom and we sat down. I went into the bedroom and Pat was in the bedroom with Gerri. They were in the corner we had noted earlier. I didn't like to be in there. Emotions are very strong. Someone had knocked the table over and the teapot was on the floor. There's a lot of yelling. Got very warm, very hot. Didn't want to stay in there. Left. Decided to quit. Male, definitely a male in the bedroom or the tearoom or whatever we're talking about. The tea, the bedroom was a definite male. And the male seemed to be the violent one."

What was he talking about? "The tearoom?" *What tearoom*, I thought. I was disturbed, too, that Nick had changed so much both in manner and in speech. He was not the same person I had met earlier. As I sat there trying to digest what I'd seen and heard, the old sense of deep depression settled over me, and I began to weep.

16

Unseen Witnesses

My whole being was heavy, oppressed with sadness; the words of Gerri and Nick could not penetrate my clouded, resistant mind. The misting rain on the triple windows partially obscured the view and made the apartment appear dismal and uninviting. Time had reversed itself and I was again enmeshed in the sinister web of the house. I started to panic; I had to get out of there. Nothing was making sense to me. My breath was coming in short gasps and my sobs were just under the surface.

I was shivering with cold as I got my coat and made my forced good-byes. Alfred would be home by now, I said, and I really had to go.

Nick volunteered to send me a complete report of their findings as soon as they'd had a chance to analyze what was on the tapes and had the photographs developed. I thanked them and left.

It was essential, I felt, that I not allow myself to think about the house and its unsettling effect on me. I deliberately put my experience with the psychics out of my mind until I could calmly read their report in the more secure surroundings of my own home.

A month later a package arrived for me, a brown wrapped parcel. The return address said, "The Institute of Psychic and Hypnotic Sciences, P.O. Box 1614, Vallejo, Calif. 94590." It was Nick Nocerino's report.

With eager hands I unwrapped it—it was much larger than I had expected—about 8″ x 11″ and an inch thick. It was a notebook with hard oxford brown covers. As I opened the pages I could see it was a businesslike presentation, cut and dried, and divided into six categories:

1. Personal Comments
2. Photographic Observations and Comments
3. Photographs
4. Tape Copy #1 (Gerri Patton)
5. Tape Copy #2 (Nick Nocerino)
6. Recommendations

Without hesitation I turned to the section on photographic observations and comments, and read:

September 30, 1973
Photographic Report . . .
for Ms. Pat Montandon
PAGE #1.

After we departed . . . I was able to hire Mr. John Traina to develop and process our black and white film. All film used was Eastman Kodak 400 ASA black and white. All color slides used were also Eastman Kodak 25 ASA.

It was decided that all black and white film would be boosted to 600 ASA, while the color slides would be boosted as high as Eastman Kodak would recommend. All prints made would be standard 8 by 10. Per past test they would be glossy for maximum results. Paper to be used would be water resistant, or resilient. Paper decided on was Eastman Kodak Poly Contact "N" Resin Coated R C Paper.

As it is impossible to have photos such as these done through a developing machine, as such machines are set for a maximum low and high reading and reject most of our type of pictures, we set up a team of three observers to see that all normal rules were conformed to.

Next it was decided that the film would be developed that day 9/15/73, the first prints would be made on the next day 9/16/73, and the last run would be before 6 P.M.

The second printing would be on 9/29/73 under the same rules. The third run would be on 9/30/73 same rules to apply.

We would pay all expenses for first printing and developing only, the second and third printing would be credited to research, unless there was a change in printing.

Mr. Traina would take the slides to Rapid Color Inc. for hand processing. Cost was not to exceed $10.00 for slides. Slides were if possible to be pushed to 400 ASA.

The negatives were run through the analyzer and gave an incorrect reading of 5 seconds for dark parts of negative and a 30 second reading for the light part of negative. This might have been correct if it was reversed. But in the actual exposure of each print the time ran to 1½ minutes to 4½ minutes for each exposure.

Mr. Traina was not aware of what he was to work on, or who it was for, or where the pictures were taken, yet while doing the first printing he smelled smoke and ran out of the developing laboratory thinking there was a fire. After we examined the cellar and developing room and convinced him there was no fire he finally resumed his work. See Photograph Report for more details.

[Signed:]
F. R. Nocerino

I quickly turned to the pages of black and white 8″ x 10″ photographs. There were twenty-six.

The first was of the enclosed porch area where Dog had slept and where he had endured such torment. There were vague blotches on one side of the print and the typed caption read: *"This picture came out on third printing (Sept. 30, 1973). Very dizzy here, sweet smell and some odor of smoke. Feeling here overpowering."*

As I continued looking through the photographs I was

stopped short by #2A; there was the ghostly figure of a woman getting something out of a drawer. Her features were indistinct, though one could definitely tell it was a woman. When the pictures were taken there were only three women present—Gerri, Phyllis and I. It was not one of us.

Some of the pictures had huge purple swaths of color, pierced with jagged patterns of brightness. Photograph #21 was taken from the top of the stairs, looking down into the foyer. There was such a pattern of light that it would appear the area had been floodlit. Yet the foyer had only a small chandelier, and was never a bright place at any time, and I knew Nick Nocerino hadn't used any flashbulbs. The light was so strong near the newel post that it had virtually eaten into the silhouette of the upright. The caption to this photograph read: *"Gerri Patton and I [Nick] at top of stairs feeling of plunging down very strong hard to control, almost want to jump into air and tumble down stairs, pushed feeling very strong."* I was especially curious about #22—it was of the foyer stairway and gave an extraordinary impression of violent emotion. A deep purple spread across most of the picture. All the details were quite clear—the steps and railing—the paintings on the walls. But a Rorschach-like blob of translucent white pierced the center of the purple color, giving the impression of tremendous force, like a lightning flash. The caption read: *"Getting ill both Gerri and I [Nick] too much activity. We left top of stairs. Strong swaying motion, feeling of very hot water, smell of blood, tumbling sensation. This picture was the first to change, about 1½ hours after developing."*

A chill of apprehension went through me as I looked at the strange pictures. But where were the photographs of the bedroom? They must have taken at least twenty, yet not one of them had come out.

I put the pictures aside for a moment and turned to Personal Comments:

September 15, 1973
Psychic Report
for Ms. Pat Montandon

I arrived at the address. . . . at 9:45 A.M. At about 10 A.M. met Mr. and Mrs. Patton and went into house. Were met by tenants Mr. and Mrs. James Reilly, who invited us in and served coffee.

This time was taken up by moving about house and making notes. Our host and hostess were quite willing to allow us to move about as we desired. Cold spots, energy spots, hot and cold spots were noted. Also feelings of people not present. Initials and many names also noted. I often get initials or partial names, and do not get names like Gerri Patton. My letter symbols and initials have been tested to be about 92% correct, while Gerri's name symbols have been recorded to be about 98% or better on correctness.

Colors present were strong reds and shades of gray and black. After 10:40 or so, when Ms. Pat Montandon and her friend arrived the auric colors changed. Where Pat walked the red increased. There was no doubt that the house had a strong emotional effect on her. While her friend Mr. Allan Carr brought in a strong violet to purple and orange auric color. There is not doubt that Mr. Carr is a psychic, whether he is aware of it or not!

My feelings about names are as follows: Eve, P.M., P.W., P.B., R.W., Lee, George, G.G., Pet?, Fen-?, Ferne, Fan, or what could have been Fanny? De Lucca, De Lucci?

Symbols or things I felt or saw; Lots of water like rain, or a shower, or fountains, tub with water. Lots of plants, feeling of horses and a buggy or wagon? May have been a large photo or painting? Definite fire and smell of wood and something burning. Pressure at back of head, dizziness, feeling of being picked up and hurled or pushed through the air, fight, very loud argument from staircase, severe pain in chest mostly stronger on the left side, found myself out of breath often in the hallway and at front door, strong odor of lilac, violet and some other sweet odor. False walls as if the whole place had been remodeled, walking through a garden. Death and smell of blood, extremely hot water, body powder, sadness and feeling of hopelessness. (See also the photograph report.)

[Signed:]
F. R. Nocerino

I thought about the initials Nick mentioned and I could readily identify most of them. P. M. and P. W. could of course be me. I also knew there had been fountains on the deck at one time, and a veritable garden of plants on the top floor. Many of the other things he talked about were to be verified later.

Tape #1 was recorded by Gerri Patton. She had mentioned several names:

["James Hub or Hubble"]
Angela or Angelina
Peter B.
Jac 1
Contessa or Contina
Ralph
De Lucci or De Lucca
"Fern" or "Fanny"
Felicia, Fidelity
Yvette
["Lemaire" or "Mark Lemar"]
["Joanna Drew"]

Not any of the names meant anything to me. It was clear I was to have quite a large field of research ahead.

Both Nick and Gerri repeated again and again that there was an overpowering sweet odor of violet or burning eucalyptus coming from Apartment 3.

I immediately thought of the sickeningly sweet smell that had emanated from that place when the dope addicts lived there and burned furniture on the sun deck, and smoked marijuana amid a sea of filth.

The report was confusing and somewhat disturbing, but before putting it away, I wanted to read the final section, Nick's summing up and recommendations:

September 15, 1973
Confidential Report Concerning
The . . . house
for Ms. Pat Montandon

Dear Pat, I have been in a lot of active houses, but this was one of the "better" ones. After spending several hours at the house and then studying the negatives I would suggest that if possible you do not go to this house alone for any reason as it seems to want to force its emotions on you. This is called obsession and usually will be the first step toward possession. This house is not safe for you! Further I allowed it to reach inside me and almost tear me up. And I am trained in this sort of work. It is not hard to understand the misery you must have gone through.

Further I would suggest that there were two people killed here since 1960. I would further suggest that before this a young lady whose body was being sold or used committed suicide. I would further suggest that another young woman attempted suicide. [It is not hard to see in this passage a possible allusion to my cousin Carolyn and to Vera Scott.]

It is my feeling that a great deal of what we said and what is in this report may already be known to you, and when we sat in the front room that I left a lot out. Also the others heard your normal voice but I did not. To me you were going into a state of obsession, your voice became very rapid and was unintelligible. You picked up a large woman on your right. [This triggered a memory of an experience I had with a large woman who persistently dogged my footsteps, and of whom there is a record in the police files.] I will have to hear the tapes to see if I am correct. As the force is energy it will definitely be on the tapes. I may also suggest that your friend was put away before the fire, and then put in the bed or on it to be destroyed before the fire.

Further may I suggest that you sell or give the ring [the pearl and gold ring which Gerri had psychometrized in Honolulu] away as it has very negative vibrations in it, and if you will excuse my saying it not of this world. [This ring had been given to me in about 1965, by a man who proved to be a very negative influence in my life.] You are and will be protected from anything in the house by an exorcism that my group and I have done from a distance, and from symbols left behind in the house itself.

I can only again suggest that you do not go there if at all possible, in particular never go alone.

God be with you and yours,

Frank R. "Nick" Nocerino

17

Conclusion Without End

My first reaction to the information received from Gerri Patton and Nick Nocerino had been one of bewilderment, tinged, perhaps, with skepticism. And yet, as I went back to it again and again, I felt it was imperative to find out everything I could, not knowing where the trails would lead or what they might reveal.

I found I was having a recurrence of disturbing dreams. I would wake up and see the book of photographs lying on a table near my bed, the photographs developed from the pictures taken at the seance at the house. The light of my bedroom lamp falling on it seemed to focus on it, as though it were the source of my broken sleep. From time to time I forced myself to look at it once more; and it seemed to me that some of the pictures had already changed. Nick Nocerino had told me that the strange one with the lightning flash effect in it had originally appeared to have two indistinct forms at the head of the stairs. Perhaps these photographs contained some secrets I had not yet uncovered.

I didn't know what to make of them, and decided to show them to Edgar Mitchell, the famous astronaut, who was now director of the Institute of Noetic Sciences in Palo Alto.

On examining the pictures, he said that a photograph might be the easiest way to prove the existence of psychic phenomena; but because it was so easy to distort photographs, they were not accepted as hard proof.

I hadn't seen the photographs developed. I couldn't accept them at their face value. I had to see the whole developing process for myself. I called Nick to explain what I wanted to do and arranged to have the negatives developed again one evening at a laboratory in Santa Rosa under circumstances as carefully controlled as I could manage.

There were six of us present: Daniel H. Kutz, instructor at Santa Rosa Junior College; Bob Bode, engineer; Frank H. Walston, writer for Murdoch Publications; Ricardo Joseph, instructor at Santa Rosa Junior College; Alfred Wilsey, and I.

Elaborate precautions were taken and the entire proceedings were tape recorded. I personally opened the sealed envelope containing the negatives and closely inspected each one before and after every printing.

I saw that all the chemicals were fresh, and the negatives brushed with a static free brush before printing. The time of exposure was recorded and I watched every step of the developing process. It was eerie to see things come out on the prints that were not seen in the negatives; and many of the photographs looked as though artificial illumination had been used—as though, in fact, light was coming from some unknown source. In some prints there was a curious accretion of details not present in the first printing. Others had even changed in shape and area. Bob Bode, who had adopted a nonchalant attitude throughout, and was clearly skeptical, recoiled at the photograph in which a woman's ghostly figure appears and explained, "I wouldn't like to hang that on my wall!"

I find that the book of photographs continues to disturb me today, and it is only with the greatest reluctance even now, that I can bring myself to open it and turn the pages.

After much concentrated and persistent enquiry, punctuated with many dead ends and false leads, the search into the past history of the Lombard house and its tenants became of absorbing interest, for the names Gerri Patton had mentioned so casually during her visit to the house began to assume a far more significant shape.

In the first stages the results were a little discouraging. My former landlord gave me the name and address of a woman, a Mrs. Murphy, who supposedly knew all about the house. I rang her doorbell—there was no answer. My mail to her was returned—a dead letter. I reached a doctor whom I hoped would have some illuminating information. He was at least helpful about some details. His uncle, Vernon Cranston, an attorney, and aunt, Sophie Cranston, had built the original house in 1909. The basement, he said, had been a treasure house, as his aunt had been a collector of Oriental art. His uncle and aunt had both died of natural causes in the building. I asked whether any of the names, De Lucca, etc., meant anything to him. No, he said.

My researches had revealed that the house had been split up into the three apartments in 1949, and had had a number of owners. I expected, or hoped, that they might be a fruitful source of inquiry, but meanwhile one interesting fact emerged through a friend's introducing me to a Mrs. Violet Humber, who had lived at one time on the top floor. I had asked her to describe the original floor plan: To my surprise I learned that my preconceived idea of the upstairs ballroom was incorrect. The upstairs area had been used by the Cranstons as their living quarters.

I asked the woman to describe my apartment as she had known it. She explained that it had been the dining room, and that the corner room (my bedroom) with the balcony had been a library, where tea was often served in the afternoon. I remembered with a start Nick's strange words about the "tearoom," as he had identified it that day in September, 1973. Perhaps, with questioning, I would learn more.

"Were you aware of any tragedies that occurred there?"

"Well, yes," she said, reluctantly.

"What?" I asked.

"Many divorces."

"Anything else?"

"Well, a maiden lady, who lived downstairs, committed suicide," she said in a low and hesitant voice.

"Do you remember her name?"

"No," she said.

I hung up, perplexed and troubled. Each call told me something, but little that was really tangible; yet, for all that, there continued to be disconcerting pointers that suggested a confirmation of what the psychic investigators had drawn—however they did so—out of the fingerprints of the past.

The first piece in the jigsaw puzzle I was able to identify came from the name "Fanny." I discovered that a "Fanny Taylor," along with her husband "Leonard," owned the building from September, 1950, to April, 1956. I telephoned Mrs. Taylor and asked her whether she could tell me anything about it. She said emphatically that it was a beautiful building—there had never been any problem there. She explained she was a Christian Scientist and spoke for awhile about her belief. I learned that her late husband, who had died in the upstairs apartment, had had a beautiful smile on his face at the moment of his death. She firmly discouraged me from investigating further concerning the house, as, in her view, anything negative related to it would have been caused by my own hyperactive imaginings.

She did, nevertheless, supply the names of three of her former tenants. One with whom I spoke had lived in the house in the 1950's, and had been divorced. This was the second divorce I learned of relating to Apartment 2 —mine from a marriage early in my tenancy being the first. Later, as my researches continued, I discovered that five of the couples who had lived there had been divorced, and in the building as a whole there had been five known alcoholics. This struck me immediately as confounding the law of averages.

The only exception to the list of divorces were the "James Hubles." I learned about them from one of my sources, a former tenant who had been extremely reluctant to talk until I'd assured her that I would not reveal the couple's true identity. The conversation I had with this source was unexpectedly revealing.

After the usual civilities, I'd mentioned that I had found that all the couples who had lived in Apartment 2 had divorced.

"There was one couple who didn't."

"Oh? Who?"

"The 'James Hubles.' But their story is so bad and so sad, I don't want to tell you about it."

"Please, I must have all the information I can, to be sure my investigation is as thorough as I can make it."

"They were such good people to have so many horrendous things happen to them."

"What do you mean?"

"Well, they lived very comfortably in that house— actually in great style. She never took a bus anywhere, always a cab—and then, his accident—that awful accident."

"What accident?"

"Well, he fell, you know, and was gravely injured."

"And then what happened?"

"After that he couldn't work anymore. They had to move. They had mountains of bills—they were about to be evicted. . . . But they were such nice, good people, and we gladly lent them some money."

"Can you tell me where they are now?"

"No, they've disappeared. I can't tell you any more. . . . I shouldn't have even told you that . . . You mustn't use their names . . . They were such nice people. They can't even afford a telephone now"

And with that, she hung up.

There were so many more questions I wanted to ask. Where did he fall? What were the circumstances? But I knew it would be useless, and none of the other tenants I interviewed knew anything about the couple. I had no reason to doubt what she had told me; she had been a reliable witness to other pieces of information that I had been able to confirm. And on checking the phone book for the fifties I was able to find out that the "James Hubles" had indeed been listed at my old address.

The house had certainly been an unhappy place for many more besides myself, and I began to experience a return of that creeping of the flesh I'd felt when I last went there. There were moments when the thought of the miasma of horror emanating from my old rooms assailed me. Only the determination growing in me to get to the heart of the mystery still drove me on.

More and more details came to light. I gleaned from one source, another previous tenant, confirmation that in the ground floor apartment there had been a woman, an alcoholic, who had killed herself. She added some details: The woman had kept two Pekinese dogs and had come from a prominent and wealthy family. A record player constantly played "Mocking Bird Hill," the very tune that so disturbed Carolyn and me, and which we had tried vainly to trace to its source.

Next I spoke to a woman whom I had known as an acquaintance for some years. I'd quite forgotten she had lived in the apartment at one time and been divorced after moving out. Her name was Emily Livingston. I began what were becoming routine questions: Could she tell me anything about the apartment or the house?

Once again there was a discouraging negative. But she had never liked it there, and had almost been electrocuted by a portable dishwasher. And, oh yes, the woman who'd had the apartment before her had been an alcoholic: all the ice trays had been perforated, obviously in her frantic effort to extract ice cubes for her drinks. This was the second alcoholic I recorded.

I now tried reading her the list of names the psychics had compiled.

"And does the name Angela, or Angelina, mean anything to you, Emily?"

"No," she said.

"Then what about De Lucci or De Lucca?"

An audible gasp of amazement.

"Why, that was the name of the maid we had when we lived there! I remember quite clearly, because that was the year of a fairly big earthquake, and this Mrs. De Lucca was frightened out of her wits and left!"

Another name had struck home. Elated, but a little apprehensive, I continued my questions.

"What about the name Ralph?"

"That's funny," she said. "That's my son's name. I was pregnant with him at the time."

After this promising start, I expected more, but none of the other names yielded anything.

Perhaps the most perplexing coincidence—if coincidence is after all the right word—developed when I learned of a "Joanna Drew," who had lived in the apartment prior to my time there. The name was totally unfamiliar to me, because the only name I knew of earlier tenants, when I lived there, had been a foreign one. When I reached "Joanna Drew" on the telephone, she seemed reluctant to talk to me, but gradually warmed a little.

I asked her how she'd liked the apartment.

"I loved it," she said. "It was the only happy time of my marriage."

Once again I pricked up my ears: an unhappy marriage. These unhappy marriages began to assume a meaning, like a symptom of an illness.

"Did anything strange ever happen to you there?"

"No," she said, "as a matter of fact, I probably got married in order to live in that apartment—it was so beautiful. Yet that decision proved to be the most disastrous of my life." I was dying of curiosity to ask her why, but she hurried on. "But I really did like the apartment," she said, "only I got sick there . . . I lost five to ten pounds in one week, and was desperately ill—an illness that was never diagnosed, and one from which I have never fully recovered."

As I listened, I could detect a deep, underlying melancholy in the woman, and little by little she uncovered a few details of a dreadful marriage that had terminated in divorce. She couldn't get over the fact that I had obtained her name through a psychic or that I had found her name at all. And I finally discovered that her name concealed the identity of the tenant I knew under a foreign one. Few people knew her by her first name, and she explained this in some detail. She had been called Jo as a child and Anna when she was an adult, so that almost nobody knew her whole given name. Ultimately she poured her heart out and admitted that she had had a sense of unrelieved oppression since she had lived in that house. As I read off the few names left on Gerri's list, she stopped me at Angelina. "That was my grandmother's name," she said, "but she's been dead for years."

I added her information to my growing store, and as I continued my research, my memory was jogged of a man who had lived in the downstairs apartment, a widower who'd died shortly after I had moved in, and further searching brought to light two more persons who had been alcoholics and had been terribly sick in the apartment.

As more and more information about the building swelled my files, I went back and back again to the names. Two more hit the mark. First, "Lemaire." This eventually explained itself clearly enough. It was the name of a man closely associated with the law firm of the original owner, Vernon Cranston; and someone named Jack had lived in the upstairs apartment at one time.

Another possible identification, that of Peter B., would be Peter Baker, a next-door neighbor. In earlier years he had been a frequent visitor to the Lombard Street house.

After a while I felt it was time to take stock of the information I'd been able to obtain. It hadn't been easy. Most of the people were reluctant to talk or were apprehensive about my putting what they told me into a book; some were adamant their names should not be mentioned. This had not made my task any simpler. On top of that, it was difficult at first to select, to know what might later prove to be important or significant.

What, after all, had I found out? A certain pattern of misfortune seemed to have dogged many of the house's residents. The recurring references to the "many divorces," and "alcoholics," appeared to point to an unusually high proportion of unhappy or ill-adjusted persons. And the misfortunes seemed to be cumulative, witness the suicides of which I had discovered three, and the final tragedy of Mary Lou's death.

Even stranger was the gradual confirmation of so much of the apparently disconnected and obscure report by Gerri Patton and Nick Nocerino. Much of what I might have dismissed as irrelevant had been shown to be confirmed by my investigations: the names, the nature of the rooms in the house, the references to violent death. Quite enough had now been established to convince me of the authority of their findings, especially as they could not possibly have known in advance of the data they produced. After all, I knew the difficulty I'd had in getting it myself.

I kept in touch with Gerri and Nick, who both warned me earnestly to keep away from the apartment or at least never to go there alone. And Nick said he felt there was something of value upstairs and that the house was being watched. Was there still more to come, something that would link some vital facts to make an unbreakable chain?

Of all the names I knew, independently of those given me by the psychics, I had until this time avoided the most obvious—the couple who had lived in the upstairs apartment at the time of Mary Lou's death. I discovered they were still living not far away. They'd moved out after the fire.

The wife told me she had had several conversations with Mary Lou in the few days before the tragedy, and she had seemed concerned about me; she also appeared to be extremely nervous. On the night of the fire they'd been awakened by a neighbor from a nearby apartment house, beating on their door and yelling, "There's a fire!" She remembered quite distinctly looking out of their upstairs apartment window, down at my living room windows—and the east window on the north wall was wide open and smoke was billowing out.

I felt myself whitening with shock. Here, at last, I was brought face to face with horror. All my old doubts and suspicions rose again to torment me. I remembered that in the report of the coroner's inquest it had been stated that the house had been securely locked, and of course, this could not have been so, if a window on the north side—away from my bedroom—was open, as was stated.

"Are you certain the window was open?"

"Oh, yes," she said, "I'll never forget it."

Then something more was revealed, a crucial fact, that made me start wondering again about the possibility of murder.

They both said that on the day after the fire they went

back to their apartment to discover that someone had obviously been inside, as various objects had been disturbed and in some cases torn up.

A chair had been taken from the kitchen and placed in a closet; and they saw that a false ceiling, which they had not known to exist, had been moved. They called the Fire Department and Police. They said the Police arrived looking like the Mod Squad. They were told the false ceiling had concealed thousands of dollars' worth of drugs, and knowing this, the police had been keeping the place under surveillance. I could not help but wonder what the connection might be. Could the pushers have been keeping watch on the apartment all that time, as well? Could they have murdered Mary Lou, thinking she was me? Or not caring who she was, as long as they gained access to the apartment. Had they got out again unseen? I just did not know—did not know enough—and yet the ugly pieces of the jigsaw posed all these sinister questions.

It was the sum of all these things, nagging me into action, that finally determined me to take all the shreds of evidence to the district attorney.

I got in touch beforehand with my old friend Judge Alarcon, knowing he would have some influence, and on Friday, March 22, 1974, he accompanied me to the assistant district attorney's office. I did not expect much from the meeting, but I felt I had to present the facts.

The assistant district attorney, Walter H. Giubbini, had the file on Mary Lou before him. He listened politely as I told him about the open window and the upstairs burglary; and also the story I had been told by the landlord, of seeing an ashtray in the living room, overflowing with cigarette butts, the morning of the fire. Mary Lou did not smoke and it had been established that she had not entertained. And I pointed out that the television set was not plugged into the closet, as had been alleged at the inquest.

Mr. Giubbini had read the coroner's report, and had

also spoken to Inspector Toschi, he said, and his feeling was that the coroner, Dr. Turkel, now deceased, was noted for "not leaving a stone unturned," and was a stickler for detail. Therefore, if Dr. Turkel had ruled that the case was an insoluble mystery, I could be assured it was done only after agonizingly careful deliberation.

Judge Alcarcon kept pressing for a more thorough investigation, but Mr. Giubbini said, "Well, I'll check a bit more, but I don't expect to find anything."

I left his office unsatisfied, wishing there were some more stones I could overturn. Judge Alarcon had been a former prosecutor, and I asked him bluntly, "Arthur, if you had been presented with this additional evidence, when you were prosecutor, what would you have done?"

"I would have had to start over," he said, "not necessarily expecting to find anything at this late date, but to satisfy myself that I'd done all I could do."

His words reassured me that I, too, had been justified in reporting what I knew, to satisfy myself that the mystery, though unsolved, had more to it than had ever appeared in the police report or coroner's inquest. And furthermore, I was personally convinced that the psychics' information was incredibly accurate. Gerri had been 80 percent correct on the names alone. This went far beyond mere coincidence. And there had been at least four tragic, untimely deaths associated with the building:

1. Mary Lou
2. My cousin Carolyn
3. Vera Scott
4. The suicide downstairs.

All these had been unmarried females at the time of their deaths.

This information also goes far to corroborate Nick's psychic investigation. If, as the psychics suggested, Mary Lou was murdered, how was it done, and why did it not show up in the thorough autopsy at which all the vital organs were found to be intact? (It was suggested, it is true, by the arson inspector, George Lucas, at the inquest, that Mary Lou might have died of fright.) But of what? If she'd become frightened by the fire, there would have been smoke in her lungs.

Frightened of what?

During a later discussion with Inspector Lucas, he told me, "The fire had strangely burned a perfect V from the closet directly to the place where the 'victim' was found."

When I asked him if the bedroom door was locked, he wasn't sure, but didn't think so. If it had been, he felt sure the firemen would have reported it.

There was only one person left to talk to: Inspector David Toschi of the Homicide Detail. Inspector Toschi has an outstanding reputation as an investigator. He told me that the coroner, Dr. Henry Turkel, called him in expressly on the case, as he was so concerned about it.

"It was one of the most interesting and challenging cases in all my years as a member of the Homicide Detail," stated the inspector. "I went back to the house four or five times on my own to double-check."

"So many strange things took place in that house . . . it doesn't seem to be like any ordinary happenstance," I said.

"No, ma'am, I remember your telling me about your experiences at the time . . . it was an unusually strange case."

"But . . . do you know . . . was the bedroom door locked?"

"Yes, ma'am, she was secure, the bedroom door was locked. She died alone."

Here was confirmation—if indeed I needed further confirmation—of the obscurities surrounding Mary Lou's death, and from one of the most thorough and experienced of investigators. Yet, once again I was confronted with a curious conflict of testimony. For it is certainly most unusual for any bedroom to be so elaborately locked and bolted. That being so, why indeed hadn't the firemen reported it?

I believe I have now presented enough evidence to the reader to show that there is a mystery, a genuine, unsolved mystery in the house on Lombard Street. The mystery remains. What happened in that bedroom on the night of June 20, 1969, I still do not know. I pray Mary Lou did not suffer. I remember so many things about her; her quick, sunshine smile and great joy in living, her unique sense of humor, her warmth and sensitivity and her unselfish loyalty. She was the best friend I ever had. Often, in writing this book, I would find myself, in the midst of some early chapter, trying to remember a detail, and I would think, "Mary Lou will know," and then abruptly remember she was gone. I like to consider this book my gift to her.

My lawsuit against *TV Guide* came to trial in June, 1972, and after eight days of relentless cross-examination, I received a verdict in my favor and was awarded $151,000 in damages. All through it, I thought of Mary Lou. She was so much a part of that whole strange episode. And on the witness stand, when I was asked about her, I could not restrain the tears.

So many of the events experienced seemed at the time to be isolated incidents. I was trying to cope with each problem as it happened. Certainly I felt entrapped, puzzled, and bewildered by so many troubles and inexplicable manifestations. I did not see them, as I do now, from the security and happiness of my present life, as falling into an inevitable pattern. And I am convinced that something—some forces, some people, perhaps—loom in the background of those events. Whether they were paranormal forces, human agencies, or something I cannot even guess at, the reality of the evil has convinced me of the existence of such forces.

At this point in my life I would not dream of going

back into that house, but I am often impelled to look down—it is, after all, lying in full view of my present apartment—and look at it searchingly, as if, by looking, I could wrest from it an ultimate answer.

While I was writing, I began to feel many of the old pressures building in me. Reliving the past was a cruel, exhausting experience. To help me, Gerri Patton gave me a verse to repeat, a kind of charm, to exorcise the evil; she told me I was protected by it. Late one evening, I began to say the words aloud, while looking down at the house on the twisty street. It was brilliantly lit, even the garden. As I repeated the lines, the lights in the house on Lombard Street went out one by one, until all were extinguished. The building was no longer visible. A black void greeted my gaze. There was nothing there.

A. No, I am just showing you the other closet in the other room.

Q. May we keep this? We will see it comes back to you

Appendix: Documentation

The following represent only a fraction of the documents I have in my possession supporting the facts appearing in the main body of the book. Only the most significant items in this mass of material have been included.

Chapter 2
Letter Concerning the Astrology-Party Curse

I, Olympia Martyn, heard the curse given by the Tarot card reader at Pat Montandon's horoscope party. It was a peculiar incident and seemed embarrassing to Pat.

Later, I also met "Earl Raymond" and was shocked when Pat called and told me how he had held her in the rain and tried to choke her.

During her recovery from that episode, I visited Pat and was aware that a damp chill pervaded the house. I had never noticed it before. Pat was frightened of the strange noises and the "feeling" in the house and mentioned it to me several times.

I was also present at the maharishi party when a fire broke out from the awning. We were mystified as to the cause of the fire; and it left a feeling of depression on me and others with whom I spoke.

The last time I was in that house at [. . .] Lombard Street was for a small birthday party Pat gave for Mary Lou Ward. I felt uncomfortable in that house and preferred not to go there again.

(signed)
OLYMPIA MARTYN
San Francisco, CA

Statement from the Landlord

I, [. . .], residing at [. . .] Vallejo Street, San Francisco, California, owned the building located at [. . .] Lombard Street, from 1957 to 1973.

Pat Montandon was the tenant in Apartment [. . .] from 1960 to 1969. During the last two years of her residency there, she often complained to me about the house being cold, and I had the heaters and the boiler checked and found them to be in perfect working order.

That building [. . .] surely was a voodoo for me. I had nothing but trouble with that property and was glad when I finally sold it in 1973.

(signed) [. . .]

State of California, City & County of San Francisco

On this 15th day of January in the year one thousand nine hundred and seventy four before me, William A. Dixon, a Notary Public, State of California, duly commissioned and sworn, personally appeared [. . .] known to me to be the person whose name subscribed to the within instrument, and acknowledged to me that he executed the same.

IN WITNESS WHEREOF I have hereunto set my hand

and affixed my official seal in the City & County of San Francisco the day and year in this certificate first above written.

William A. Dixon
Notary Public, State of California. My Commission Expires November 6, 1974.

Chapter 3
Letter from Merla Zellerbach Concerning the Apartment

San Francisco Chronicle
THE VOICE OF THE WEST

Dec. 21, 1973

Dear Patsy Lou,

I'm happy to put in writing what I've expressed to you verbally many times.

Being the World's Greatest Skeptic, I have little faith in ghosts, spirits, and the like—nor do I believe your apartment is in any way "haunted."

I will say, however, that it always gave me the creeps for reasons I don't understand.

Maybe I was reacting to your reaction—or any number of other factors. I don't know.

I do know that I never felt comfortable or at ease there. If you'll recall, I once tried to convince you to move into "cheerier" quarters—even though you hadn't mentioned a desire to move.

Perhaps it's the architecture, the eery sound of the wind through the trees, the cold aloofness of its location—or a combination of all three that give it such strong negative vibrations.

Whatever it is—you couldn't pay me to live there!

Love,
(signed)
Merla Zellerbach

Letter from Judge Alarcon
Concerning the Apartment

CHAMBERS OF
The Superior Court
LOS ANGELES, CALIFORNIA 90012
ARTHUR L. ALARCON, JUDGE
March 19, 1974

Ms. Pat Montandon
San Francisco
California
Dear Pat:

Recently we discussed your tragic experience connected with your residence at [. . .] Lombard Street. Since our conversation I have reflected back to 1967 when I first you, to sort out my own memory of that apartment and your reaction to it. I have very good cause to have vivid memories concerning [. . .] Lombard Street.

I first met you in late June 1967 when we were both guests at a dinner party given by mutual friends. After the party I escorted you to your apartment. We agreed to meet for cocktails at your residence the following week. As I left your doorstep you told me not to drive to the Bay Area from my home in Los Angeles because of the long distance and the dangers of highway travel. I told you that I had a greater fear of air travel than of highway traffic.

The following Saturday on my way to see you at your apartment I was involved in a head-on collision in Monterey County which smashed all the bones in my right arm, bruised my heart muscle, collapsed my right lung and broke all my ribs. I had never been in a hospital nor suffered a broken bone prior to this accident. During the next six months I spent a large percentage of my time in San Francisco for hospitalization, convalescence and medical check-ups. I was fortunate to spend part of this time as your escort to various functions.

On many occasions while with you as escort during my convalescence I observed that you appeared to be frightened. When I inquired you stated that you were quite afraid that something would happen to you. I noted that your front door had extra bolts and locks. You also told me that at night you closed yourself off in your bedroom, locking all doors and windows because of your fears.

I also recall that you frequently appeared to be physically exhausted and had to take time off from your work to regain your strength to be able to continue at a job you seemed to enjoy immensely.

I also noticed that you were a very happy and vivacious person away from your home, but upon arrival at your doorstep your mood changed rapidly.

I am so delighted that all of this is now behind you, and that you now seem to enjoy beautiful good health.

Sincerely,
(signed)
Arthur L. Alarcon,
Judge

ALA:MVM

Chapter 6
Newspaper Account of TV Guide Libel

San Francisco, Calif.
The Chronicle
(Cir. D. 486,330—Sat. 462,105)
SEP 19 1968

Pat Montandon

A 'Party Girl'
Who's in a Snit

It's getting so a nice girl can't hold her head up in public anymore.

This was, in essence, the complaint made in a lawsuit filed in Superior Court yesterday by the star-kissed queen of the Jet Set, Miss Pat Montandon.

It all began with a book Miss Montandon wrote, entitled "How to Be a Party Girl." Only an evil-minded cad could misinterpret such a title. . . .

TV GUIDE

Enter Pat Michaels, the resident intellectual of KTVU Channel 2, and *TV Guide* magazine. In a recent issue of the magazine appeared a program note for Michaels' show, reading: "(Color) 'From Party Girl to Call Girl.' Scheduled Guest: TV personality Pat Montandon and author of 'How to Be a Party Girl.'"

"By the publication of such words," Miss Montandon's suit complained yesterday, "the readers of said publication understood said words to mean that the plaintiff (Miss Montandon), the only person referred to in said article, had gone from a party girl to a call girl, to wit: a prostitute who may be called by telephone to visit male customers and said defendants, and each of them, intended that such words be understood in such a defamatory manner."

'FALSE'

Furthermore, she said, the statement is false, and the defendants—the station and the magazine—knew it was false.

Miss Montandon's attorney, Charles O. Morgan Jr., said yesterday that the program never took place: Miss

Montandon refused to take part after she saw *TV Guide*.

Officials of *TV Guide* were unavailable for comment. At the station, general manager Roger Rice said, "I know nothing about it," and reserved comment until he could look into the matter further.

Chapter 8
Newspaper Report Concerning Mayor Cavanagh

The Party Girl
Who Dated Our
Mayor Cavanagh
BY JENNIFER JARRATT
Free Press Staff Writer

On a date, Mayor Jerome P. Cavanagh is "charming, considerate, gentlemanly." He is a man of "great character and sensitivity," reports Pat Montandon, who had dinner with him in San Francisco a few weeks ago.

Miss Montandon is in Detroit to publicize her book, "How to Be a Party Girl." She doesn't expect to see Jerry, however.

"There is no romance," she said Friday. "He is a friend." Mayor Cavanagh, she said, is the kind of man who will help you on and off with your coat and pull a chair out for you. She also found him a good listener.

"I was impressed with his brilliance. I got the impression that his office here as mayor weighs heavily on his shoulders."

They discussed the difficulties of being in the public eye, she recalled. One of those difficulties was being noticed by columnists, one of whom—Herb Caen— said Cavanagh was very impressed with the lovely Miss Montandon.

The mayor admitted he saw her once—but briefly— and claimed that talk of a romance was just part of a publicity campaign for "How to Be a Party Girl."

Miss Montandon's book, published by McGraw Hill, is her first. It's about how to give a good party. There are positive reasons for having a bash, one of which is that it spreads joy.

Miss Montandon walked into the middle of the biggest party she'd ever seen when she arrived in Detroit at 2 a.m. Friday after the Tigers won the World Series. "I was completely caught up in it," she said. "I'd never seen so many people celebrating."

Divorced six years ago, Miss Montandon spent her childhood in a small town in Oklahoma before she went to San Francisco as an executive trainee in a department store. She still lives in the apartment she found then, although now she is hostess of a morning TV show and probably the best-known and most successful party-giver in San Francisco.

Chapter 9
Letter Concerning TV Request For a Place to Move

I, Esther Goodman, vividly recall hearing Pat Montandon announce on her television show, approximately in December of 1968, that she was looking for a place to move because her own apartment frightened her. She requested anyone knowing of a quiet secure place for rent, to please let her know.

I remember this very well because I thought it was such an unusual request, especially over television.

(signed)
Esther Goodman
Mark Hopkins Hotel
San Francisco, CA

Chapter 10
Letter from Doris Cherin Concerning "Dog"

San Francisco, CA
February 11, 1974

I, Doris Cherin, am the current owner of Pat's white
Lhasa Apso "Dog." Pat gave him to me the first of April,
1969. At the time, she told me he was nervous and
fearful and seemed to hate her apartment. She felt he
might be better in a home where he could receive more
attention.

"Dog" had a bad sore on his hip and although Pat had
taken him to the vet, he did not seem to be recovering.
She particularly emphasized the fact that he seemed
happier away from the apartment than in it. I agreed
to take him for a month and if we were happy with him,
he would become our "Dog."

When the time was up, Pat arrived at our home to see
what our intentions were. "Dog" greeted her like a long
lost friend. We wanted to keep him but we were afraid
he would be upset when Pat left without him. When the
time came for her to leave, I found it quite strange, that
when Pat went to the door and called "Dog" to say good-
bye, he turned and ran away from the door, backed himself into the kitchen and started trembling. He remained
there until she drove away.

However, a year later when Pat no longer lived at [. . .]
Lombard, she kept "Dog" for me over a long weekend
and he was very happy to go with her and returned in
perfectly good health.

(signed)
Doris M. Cherin

Acknowledgment—General

STATE OF CALIFORNIA,
County of San Francisco
S.S.

On February 11, 1974, before me, James Henry Quinn,
a Notary Public whose principal place of business is in
the County of San Francisco, State of California, personally appeared Doris M. Cherin, known to me to be
the person named in the within instrument, and whose
name is subscribed thereto, and acknowledged to me
that she executed the same.

IN WITNESS WHEREOF, I have hereunto set my
hand and affixed my official seal the day and year in this
certificate first above written.

(signed)
James Henry Quinn

Chapter 13
Newspaper Account of Fire

From SAN FRANCISCO EXAMINER—Saturday,
June 21, 1969

Apartment Fire
PAT MONTANDON'S SECRETARY KILLED
By Baron Muller

Pat Montandon's private secretary was burned to death
early today in a fire which swept through the TV personality's luxurious Russian Hill apartment.

Mrs. Mary Louise Ward, 45, was found dead in bed,
burned almost beyond recognition.

The two alarm fire caused more than $25,000 damage
to the [. . .] apartment at [. . .] Lombard Street.

Miss Montandon—married since May to financier
Alfred Wilsey but still using her maiden name—now
lives with her husband on Green Street.

She had loaned the Lombard apartment to Mrs. Ward, who in turn had loaned her own apartment to her recently married daughter. Mrs. Ward is a widow . . .

Neighbors reported the fire at 2:31 a.m. when they saw flames and smoke pouring from the apartment. Firemen were delayed in getting into the burning apartment because the front door was chained and barred from the inside.

Chapter 14
Necropsy Report
CITY AND COUNTY OF SAN FRANCISCO
CORONER'S OFFICE   NECROPSY DEPARTMENT
CASE NO. [. . .]

JANE DOE # 23
MARY LOUISE WARD Date and Hour of Necropsy
21 JUNE 1969 9:39 AM Age 47 Height 5'2" Weight 110

The body is that of a small white female appearing about the stated age of 45 years showing evidence of 3rd and 4th degree charring of the body, particularly of the head, neck, extremities, left side and back and left extremities. The charring has extended down to the bone in many areas. A large part of the scalp is completely charred down to the bone. The facial features are partially destroyed by the intense burns of the face. The skin of the hands is thick, and black. The bones of the upper extremities and the muscles are exposed by the charring similar on the entire left side of the body including the feet. The bones are exposed as well as muscle and other soft tissues. There is pinkish red skin on the surface of the thorax and abdomen on the right side. The mouth has natural teeth and the tongue protrudes from the mouth. The abdomen is tense and firm.

BODY CAVITIES: There are small amounts of thin pink fluid in each of the pleural pericardial and peritoneal cavities.

The HEART is within normal limits of size. The epicardium is smooth and glistening. The myocardium is red brown and uniform throughout. The endocardium is normal. The valves are unremarkable. The coronary vessels display mild atherosclerosis and the lumens are patent throughout.

The LUNGS are moderately severely congested and contain thin hemorrhagic fluid throughout. The vessels are congested. The bronchi contains thin frothy dark blood.

The STOMACH contains a small amount of dark brown fluid and large quantity of gas. The intestinal tract is distended with gas.

The LIVER is of normal size, reddish brown, smooth and glistening and shows the usual markings, on section. The liver is slightly pale.

The GALLBLADDER, BILE DUCTS, and PANCREAS are normal.

The KIDNEYS are of the usual size. The capsule strips with ease. On section they show the usual architecture. The urinary bladder contains a small quantity of thin yellow urine.

The UTERUS and OVARIES reveal the surgical absence of the uterus excluding the cervix. The cervix is still present, the ovaries are still present. The fallopian tubes are surgically absent.

The SPLEEN is of normal size, soft reddish purple and the markings are indistinct on section.

The ADRENAL GLANDS show partial autolysis, and the cortices are pale yellow.

BRAIN: The brain shows evidence of heat coagulation and is moderately firm. The brain is pale. A small amount of coagulated blood is present in the posterior fossae bilaterally. The skull shows no evidence of fracture and the scalp reveals severe thermal burns with charring down to the bone, particularly on the right side.

DIAGNOSIS:1) THERMAL BURNS OF APPROXI-
MATELY 95% of BODY SURFACE, 3rd and 4th
DEGREE 2) CARBON MONOXIDE POISONING

Spec. to Path.: (Liver and lung)

Spec. to Tox.: (Heart blood, stomach and contents, portions of liver and kidney)

WRIGHT:km

cc:O

ADDENDUM:

NECK ORGANS: The larynx is intact. The cartilage is
unremarkable. The glottis is patent. The hyoid bone shows
no evidence of trauma. No hemorrhages are evident.
There is granular discoloration to the musculature due to
the intense heat coagulation of the soft tissues.

> (signed)
> M. Alluson, DEPUTY
> R. Wright
> Necropsy Surgeon to the Coroner.

Pathology Report

**CITY AND COUNTY OF SAN FRANCISCO
CORONER'S OFFICE
PATHOLOGY DEPARTMENT**

JANE DOE #23

Case No. [. . .]

This report based on the examination of the following
specimens from the body of the aforesaid: 21 June 1969
Received are the left lung and a portion of liver.

GROSS DESCRIPTION

LUNG: The left lung weighs 580 gms. It is covered by
smooth glistening pleura. Cross section into the lung
shows large accumulations of white frothy edema fluid.
The bronchi contain edema fluid. The blood vessels are
within normal limits.

LIVER: The piece of liver has a sharp anterior edge. It

is covered by a smooth glistening capsule. Cross section into the liver shows a well defined lobular architecture. There is a slight pallor. There is no increase in fibrous tissue.

MICROSCOPIC DESCRIPTION

LUNG: Sections show distended alveoli. In areas the alveoli are filled with edema fluid. In some areas intact erythrocytes are present in the alveolar spaces. The vessels of the alveolar walls show marked congestion. The larger pulmonary vessels are within normal limits. The bronchi show sloughing of the epithelium. The basal layer that is present shows a normal architecture. There is no increase in inflammatory cells. The cartilage is within normal limits. The hilar lymph nodes show accumulations of anthracotic pigment.

LIVER: The liver has a normal lobular architecture. The capsule is thin and uniform. The portal areas and central veins show a normal ratio. The portal areas are thin and uniform and show no increase in inflammatory cells. The central veins are thin walled. The intervening liver cells are arranged in a single cord plate and show a normal architecture. There is no increase in fat. The sinusoids are within normal limits.

DIAGNOSIS: PULMONARY EDEMA AND CONGESTION

CAUSE OF DEATH: UNDETERMINED

OTHER FINDINGS: EXTENSIVE BURNS OF BODY

JOT:O'R
cc-O

(signed)
M. Alluson, DEPUTY
J. O. Trowbridge, MD, Pathologist to the Coroner.

Toxicology Report
CITY AND COUNTY OF SAN FRANCISCO
CORONER'S OFFICE
TOXICOLOGY DEPARTMENT

CASE no. [...]

1–July 1969
BLOOD, KIDNEY, STOMACH & CONTENTS
Jane Doe #23
Toxicological laboratory 23–June–69 I have made an analysis of same and have found 1.5% saturation of carbon monoxide in the blood. Trace of secobarbital in liver. No barbiturate in stomach contents. Negative for other common drugs and poisons.

ALCOHOL blood level: 0.04%
BARBITURATE Pos
HEAVY METAL Neg

> (signed)
> M. Alluson, DEPUTY

> (signed)
> Cisisine, M.D., Toxicologist to the Coroner.

CORONER'S REGISTER
CITY AND COUNTY OF SAN FRANCISCO
RECORD OF DEATH
Jane Doe #23
Poss Mary Louise Ward
NAME Mary Louise Ward
RESIDENCE [...] Webster
Place of Death Or Where Found [...] Lombard [...]
Date of Death Or Date Found 6-21-69, Time of Death Or Time Found 2:57 AM
Time Reported 6/21/69, 2:57 A.M., By Police Comm

Police Notified Thru Officer Spinner, Central Station
Homicide Notified
Relatives Notified 6/23/69, Via phone By rgm
Ht., (approx) 5'1", Wt. 110, Eyes?, Hair?, Amputations
Scars, Moles, Tattoos, Etc.,
Identif. By Dental comparison
Age 47 Yrs.
Birthdate Oct/14/21, Birthplace Seattle, Wn
Sex Female, Race White, Religion Prot
Marital Status Widowed
Usual Occupation secretary (part time)
Employer Pat Montandon
Remains Received at Coroner's Office 6/21/69, 5:10 AM
Remains Released from Coroner's Office 6/26/69, 2:20
PM
Received for N. Gray, Funeral Director, S.F.
By B. Bartram, Assistant Funeral Director. Clothing Received No
Order Signed By Jean Rose, Relationship Daug
Remains Released By E. Ravare, Deputy or Attendant
(RAF)
Fingerprints to be Taken If Poss
Photos to be Taken Yes
IN CASE OF ACCIDENT, SUICIDE, ETC.
Date and Time 6-21-69 abt 2:30 AM, Place [. . .]
Lombard
Nature Fire

HISTORY OF CASE (Supposed facts to be verified)
According to information received from Police Officer
Spinner, on 6-21-69, at about 2:55 AM, [. . .], who
resides at [. . .] Lombard Street, apartment [. . .] was
returning home, when he noticed flames coming from
apartment [. . .], at the above address. Mr. [. . .]
notified San Francisco Police Department. The fire department
responded with Chief Gautier in charge. According
to Arson Inspector Lucas, the fire apparently origi-

nated in the master bedroom of apartment [. . .], where the deceased was found in bed. Examination at the scene revealed the deceased to be lying in a prone position, on the sidewalk, in front of [. . .] Lombard Street, where she had been placed by San Francisco Police Department. The body was covered with 3rd degree burns, and there was extreme charring of the lower extremities, below the knee. There was some black and white print material found on the lower back region of the deceased. GD

10:30
Driver S. Hortin, Deputy G. Davis

WITNESSES
Jean Eileen Rose, [. . .] Webster, Daughter; Mrs. Frank Rose Jr, [. . .] Webster, ? Daughter; Pat Montandon [. . .], [. . .] Green, dec's employer; Bronson Bronson, [. . .] Calif, notify only John Rubens, atty for est; Insp Lucas or McDonough, Arson Sq, 260 Golden Gate Ave., Invest.; [. . .], [. . .] Lombard [. . .], resided in same building, called fire dept.; Evelyn Walker, [. . .], Friend; Pauline Kendall, [. . .] Walnut, Friend; Police Officer at Scene, yes, Name [. . .].

AUTOPSY SURGEON'S REPORT
Having Performed an Autopsy on 6/21/69, at 9:32 AM, Upon the Remains of Jane Doe #23
I Hereby Certify the Apparent Medical Cause of Death to be Spec to P & T
R. Wright, M.D.
Autopsy Surgeon

PATHOLOGIST'S REPORT
Cause of Death as Shown on the Pathologist's Report on Specimens Submitted is: UNDETERMINED
OTHER FINDINGS: EXTENSIVE BURNS OF THE BODY.

TOXICOLOGIST'S REPORT

Findings of Examination of Specimens and Tissues Submitted are:

Alcohol Blood level: 0.04%

1.5 Saturation of Carbon Monoxide in the blood—
trace of secobarbital in liver. No barbiturate in stomach contents. Negative for other common drugs and poisons.

Death Certificate Completed 8/21/69

RESULT OF INQUEST

Date of Inquest 8/21/69

Verdict of Jury/Coroner. We, the jury, are unable to determine the cause or actual circumstance of death of Mary Louise Ward.

Property

Receipt No. 1232

PROPERTY

Body Searched By Davis At [. . .] Lombard

Premises Searched By Davis & SFFD At [. . .] Lombard

Premises Sealed By no

The Following Property was Taken with 1 Witness(es) Present.

And Receipt Issued To Off Spinner

Watch

P.S. Jewelry ym band

P.S. ym a w stones & clear stone

PAPERS

P.S. misc papers, To be probated

OTHER PROPERTY HELD

Clothing Yes (parts of only)

Property Found on Research at C.O. two rings see above

G. Davis, Deputy

Above Items Received by Property Custodian M O'Malley, 6-23-69

Placed in S.D. Box No. 593 By M. O'Malley, Property Custodian

DISPOSITION OF PROPERTY

The Items of Property Initialed Above Were Received

By: Phillip L. Straus, for attorney of estate, July 25, 1969
Delivered by M O'Malley, Deputy
PUBLIC ADMINISTRATOR
To Be Notified no
M. Alluson, DEPUTY

Coroner's Inquest Report

IN THE CORONER'S COURT OF THE STATE OF CALIFORNIA, IN AND FOR THE CITY AND COUNTY OF SAN FRANCISCO, HENRY W. TURKEL, CORONER
CORONER'S INQUEST UPON THE BODY OF JANE DOE #23 identified as MARY LOUISE WARD [. . .]
TRANSCRIPT OF TESTIMONY, DATE OF INQUEST, AUGUST 21, 1969

INDEX OF WITNESSES

FREDERIC R. TOOKER, CERTIFIED SHORTHAND REPORTER
IN THE CORONER'S COURT OF THE STATE OF CALIFORNIA, IN AND FOR THE CITY AND COUNTY OF SAN FRANCISCO, DR. HARRY W. TURKEL, CORONER
CORONER'S INQUEST UPON THE BODY OF JANE DOE #23 identified as MARY LOUISE WARD, Register No. [. . .], Deputy Gerald Davis

TRANSCRIPT OF TESTIMONY of witnesses produced, sworn and examined on August 21, 1969, by said Coroner and a jury of good and lawful men of said City and County duly summoned and sworn by said Coroner to inquire who the above named deceased person was, and when, where and by what means said person came to his or her death, and into the circumstances attending said death, and to render a true verdict thereon, according to the evidence offered.

The following history, taken from the Coroner's Register, was submitted to the jury:

According to information received from Police Officer Spinner, on 6-21-69, at about 2:55 A.M., [. . .], who resides at [. . .] Lombard Street, [. . .] was returning home, when he noticed flames coming from apartment [. . .] at the above address. [. . .] notified San Francisco Police Department. The fire department responded, with Chief Gautier in charge. According to Arson Inspector Lucas, the fire apparently originated in the master bedroom of apartment [. . .], where the deceased was found in bed. Examination at the scene revealed the deceased to be lying in a prone position, on the sidewalk in front of [. . .] Lombard Street, where she had been placed by San Francisco Police Department. The body was covered with 3rd degree burns, and there was extreme charring of the lower extremities, below the knee. There was some black and white print material found on the lower back region of the deceased.

THE CORONER: We have one more case to consider, and that is the matter of the death of Mary Louise Ward.

We will go to the matter of the death of Mary Louise Ward and first we will call Ms. Montandon. Would you come forward, please?

PAT MONTANDON,

having been duly sworn, testified as follows:

THE CORONER:

Q. You are Ms. Montandon of [. . .] Green Street?

A. Yes, sir.

Q. And you were acquainted with Mary Louise Ward?

A. Yes.

Q. What was your relationship to her?

A. She was my friend-secretary.

Q. I see. I understand that she had occasion to be occupying your apartment or an apartment you had.

A. Yes.

Q. This was with your permission and understanding?

A. That's right.

Q. You know now that she died as a consequence of a fire on the premises on the 21st of June?

A. Yes.

Q. When did you last see her before this fire occurred?

A. The day before.

Q. When did you last talk with her? Was that the same day?

A. The afternoon of the day before, which was the 20th.

Q. That was the last time you spoke with her?

A. Yes.

Q. What was her mood then? Was she her usual self?

A. Yes. She was happy.

Q. Did she indicate what her plans were for that day or evening?

A. She said she was going to a movie with her son, or she thought she would, but she was so tired she didn't really want to go.

Q. That was which night, Friday night?

A. Yes. Friday afternoon about 4:30.

Q. You have learned since, I presume, she did not go to the movie?

A. Yes, sir.

Q. Her son visited with some people and decided to ask permission to stay there, which was granted?

A. Yes.

Q. Do you know these people?

A. No, I do not.

Q. Had you lived in this apartment sometime yourself?

A. Eight and a half years.

Q. In that time, had you had any difficulty of any kind

with fire or concern over fire?

A. No concern whatever over fire.

Q. You never had a fire?

A. No.

Q. Some question arises as to whether Mary Ward did or did not smoke. Would you know?

A. She did not smoke.

Q. You knew her well enough to say with certainty she did not smoke?

A. Yes, sir. She did not smoke.

Q. Would you have any knowledge as to whether anyone visited in the apartment that night?

A. I don't think so.

Q. To your best knowledge, no one did?

A. To my best knowledge, no one visited.

Q. Did she sometimes have callers, people who might come and visit with her, men or women?

A. Yes.

Q. Have you known any to stay through an evening on occasion?

A. No.

Q. I don't mean through the night, through the evening, perhaps spend some hours there.

A. Well, in her own home, I am sure she had visitors who did.

Q. How long had she lived in this apartment?

A. In my apartment?

Q. Yes.

A. She had been there one week.

Q. One week. Then you really wouldn't know what her practices were?

A. No.

Q. I see. All right.

I should explain to you, and particularly to the jurors, that we have examined Mary Louise Ward as carefully as we know how and at great length and we cannot establish any reason for her death. She did suffer severe burns and we believe she was apparently dead when these burns did occur, but we don't know why she died.

Q. Did you know of any illnesses she might have had?

A. No, sir.

Q. She had no serious illness, that you know?

A. No, she didn't.

Q. Had she been going to any doctor?

A. I don't think so.

Q. None that you know, at least?

A. None that I know of.

Q. We find a trace of sleeping medicine in her body tissues. Would you know, did she tend to use these?

A. Occasionally.

Q. Not regularly?

A. I don't think so, to the best of my knowledge.

Q. Yes. Well, if you knew her rather well, you might know that she needed sleeping pills every night.

A. Occasionally.

Q. Only occasionally, not every night?

A. As far as I know.

THE CORONER: Very good. All right. Thank you. You may step down.

THE WITNESS: Sure.

[Witness excused.]

THE CORONER: Jean Rose.

JEAN EILEEN ROSE,

having been duly sworn, testified as follows:

THE CORONER:

Q. You are Jean Eileen Rose and the daughter of Mary Ward?

A. Uh-huh (affirmative).

Q. Had you been staying with her?

A. No. She did—The reason she was staying at Ms. Montandon's apartment is that she was planning to go up north to Seattle, and so I just recently got married, and she let her house to us as a wedding present, so just in the interim she was staying at Ms. Montandon's, while she was getting ready to leave.

Q. I see. Very good.

Had you been in that apartment on previous occasions?

A. Oh, yes.

Q. Over some period of time?

A. No. I just have been there, you know, like for dinner or something, before my mother started staying there.

Q. Would you know of any illness that your mother had any disease or disorder?

A. She had encephalitis I'd say about 10 years ago something; so she still had, you know, the aftereffects headaches from that.

Q. She had headaches?

A. Yes.

Q. Did she ever have any seizures or convulsions?

A. No seizures or convulsions, just painful headaches.

Q. Had she ever collapsed or fallen down as a consequence of it?

A. Not that I know of. I know she would feel faint at times.

Q. Did she ever actually faint in front of you or pass out?

A. No. Not in front of me. I just know she'd feel it coming on or something.

Q. She'd feel faintness?

A. Yes.

Q. But you have never actually seen her faint before?

A. No.

Q. Apart from this, was she being treated for anything like diabetes, or heart trouble, or epilepsy, anything like this?

A. No.

Q. Nothing you know?

A. She just had pills for headaches.

Q. Do you know what pills they were? Do you know what was in them?

A. No. They were complicated names.

Q. Would you know what doctor she was going to?

A. Yes.

Q. What was his name?

A. Dr. Gamble.

Q. Dr. Gamble?

A. Uh-huh (affirmative).

THE CORONER: Inspector Toschi, did you check with him at all?

INSPECTOR TOSCHI: I did, sir.

THE CORONER: Okay. Thank you. Pointless to ask. You always do.

Q. You have heard me say we have not found any reason for your mother's death, that she apparently died or collapsed and then suffered burns that some fire developed.

Can you help us understand the sequence of events? You probably can't, but we wonder, maybe you have some ideas.

A. Well, it was my understanding that she never woke up and that she probably suffocated before she suffered any pain.

Q. Well, that is not quite what we find.

A. Oh. I didn't know.

Q. We thought that initially would likely be the case, but our tests and so on do not demonstrate this. Do you have any reason to be suspicious that there's anything wrong with your mother's death or it's just an unfortunate accident?

A. Well, it's just terribly freaky, but that is all I can think.

THE CORONER: Sure. All right. Thank you. You may step down. That's all.

[Witness excused.]

THE CORONER: Pauline Kendall.

PAULINE KENDALL,

having been duly sworn, testified as follows:

THE CORONER:

Q. You are Pauline Kendall?

A. Yes.

Q. Your address, please?

A. [. . .] Walnut Street.

Q. In the city here?

A. Yes.

Q. And the record here says that you were Mrs. Ward's best friend. Did you consider yourself such?

A. I considered myself very close to her.

Q. I see. Well, all right. That is a relative term, but you were close to her?

A. Yes.

Q. Did you talk with her on a confidential basis when you did?

A. Yes.

Q. I understand that the evening before this fire you spoke with her on the phone for some time.

A. That's correct.

Q. For how long, roughly?

A. Perhaps an hour.

Q. Now, any two women who get together and talk for an hour at a stretch generally talk about things very close to one another.

A. Yes.

Q. Did she confide to you she was having any problems of any kind?

A. No.

Q. Would you know, was she a chronic user of sleeping pills?

A. I don't know what you mean by "chronic."

Q. Well, if you take as many as two a day, you are addicted, two sleeping pills a day.

A. I wouldn't say she was.

Q. Did she take one a day regularly?

A. She took sleeping pills, but she tried not to take them unless they were necessary.

Q. Right. The criterion is if a person can skip a few days, she is not addicted.

A. She tried to do that.

Q. Did she, though?

A. I heard her mention at times she did get along without them.

Q. This is what we need now. Do you know of any illnesses she suffered which might have caused her to collapse?

A. She had encephalitis, like Jean said. She also had low blood pressure.

Q. Was she being treated for this?

A. She took pills for it. I know when it got very low, she would get very weak.

Q. Did you ever go to Dr. Gamble's office with her?

A. I never went with her. I have been in the office with her and I did go to Dr. Gamble, because of Mary Louise.

Q. Then apparently you did know her rather well?

A. Yes.

Q. Would you know, did she smoke?

A. No.

Q. Let me ask, did she have callers who would spend the evening at the home?

A. I am certain that she did not, because she was very tired that evening.

Q. That particular night. Did she sometimes have callers? I don't mean to be prying—

A. No.

Q. —but we are trying to establish—

A. She didn't have any privacy, really.

Q. I see. This particular night she had expected her son to be home, is that not right, until it was decided that he was going to stay elsewhere?

A. Well, there were kind of plans in the air. Like Pat said, she was planning to go to the movie with Jimmy, then I had tentative plans with her. Nothing firmed up, so . . .

Q. You would have no reason to think that someone might have spent the evening who did, in fact, smoke and left a cigarette in the premises?

A. No.

Q. You have no knowledge of this and you have no reason to think that that did happen?

A. Well, from what I know of Mary Louise, I don't think she would have allowed anyone to come over at that time of the night at the last minute.

Q. Very good. When did you finish your conversation with her?

A. About 9:30.

Q. Well, it would seem improbable anyone would be coming, but they might have. We just don't know. You don't think they did?

A. I doubt very much.

Q. Very good. Do you have any information which would help us explain this event in any way?

A. (Witness shrugs shoulders.)

Q. You don't know. We don't either, so we all have to shrug, as it were, and we are hunting for what we can find. This is a very unusual case. In my 16 years I have run into something like this only very rarely.

All right. Thank you very much. You may step down.

[Witness excused.]

THE CORONER: ["Evelyn Walker,"]

["EVELYN WALKER,"]

having been duly sworn, testified as follows:

THE CORONER:

Q. ["Mrs. Walker"], you live [. . .] from where Mary Louise Ward died?

A. That's right.

Q. I understand that your apartment is such that if people walk about above you you can hear it.

A. Well, occasionally.

Q. Did you know Mrs. Ward?

A. Not well. Just an acquaintance.

Q. You know she was living there, though?

A. Yes.

Q. Did you know her son was living with her?

A. Yes. She had told me.

Q. I am given to understand you at times could tell whether there was one person or two persons above, depending on the movements, is this correct?

A. Well, I couldn't answer that exactly, except that evening I just remembered that I heard footsteps earlier in the evening. I had gone to bed early and watched television, but I just remembered I had heard these footsteps earlier in the evening, which didn't bother me at all. I just recalled. I thought, "Mary Lou is home."

That was all. But there was nothing out of the ordinary.

Q. There were no unusual sounds?

A. No.

Q. No sounds of a struggle?

A. Oh, no.

Q. Nothing of an undue stomping about?

A. Not a bit.

Q. Anything to suggest more than one person?

A. Not at all.

Q. Do you think there was just one person home, from what you heard?

A. Yes, as far as I would know.

Q. Of course it would be entirely possible for one person to walk and then the other.

A. That's right.

Q. But you didn't hear two walking at one time?

A. No. No. No.

Q. You have no reason to think then anyone else was on the premises through the evening?

A. No. Not a bit.

THE CORONER: All right. Thank you. That is all. You may step down.

[Witness excused.]

THE CORONER: Inspector Lucas.

INSPECTOR LUCAS,

having been duly sworn, testified as follows:

Q. Inspector Lucas, you investigated this matter for the Arson Squad of the Fire Department?

A. Yes, Doctor.

Q. And you were at the scene of the fire?

A. Yes, Doctor. In fact, I was with two of the firemen when we discovered the body.

Q. It's your practice in the Arson Squad to go out always when there is a death?

A. Well, this happened to be a second alarm and we responded automatically.

Q. I see. That was the reason you were there?

A. So we were there a lot sooner than— At a normal fire, if there is a death, there might be a delay of 20 minutes or half an hour before they would call us.

Q. I was coming to that and the reason you were there was because of the intensity of the fire?

A. The heavy smoke. The fire itself was not too intense. It was just that the apartment was so, as we say, buttoned up that there was no place for the smoke to go until the two windows on the [. . .] side broke, and that allowed more air, oxygen, to get in and then everything burst into flame.

Q. This suggests that it was a smoldering fire?

A. It was a long, smoldering fire, Doctor.

Q. Have you been able to establish the source of the fire?

A. Yes. The fire started in the closet, which would be on the north side of the bed, and burned out through the closet and up into the attic, the attic space, across the room, and then into the main—into the bedroom, where

Mrs. Ward was found, throughout that room completely.

Q. I understood you to say the closet was next to the bed.

A. It was about four or five feet from the bed, in the same room.

Q. It went up through the attic?

A. Went up through the attic and also out into the bedroom at the same time.

Q. From the closet?

A. From the closet. Now, Ms. Montandon, when I talked to her, she told me that when she had lived there she was in the habit of sleeping late some mornings, and she had heavy drapes on the windows, which would explain the fact that the fire wasn't discovered for so long, that the fire had to burn through those drapes, and nobody on the outside could see in, and that when the window burst, that was the first sign of anybody having any knowledge of the fire.

Q. You say it started in the closet. What started the fire? Can you say?

A. It was most likely the wiring, Doctor, because there was a television set in the bedroom, and the outlet was in the closet itself. I went through the debris looking for the outlet. I could not find the outlet. I even looked downstairs in "Mrs. Walker's" place in the debris and I couldn't find the outlet, and we have to presume in a case like this, and I presume that Mrs. Ward had gone to bed, she had taken a sleeping pill and gone to bed and fallen asleep, leaving the television on, and that the wiring in the place, a lot of it was illegal. That wouldn't necessarily mean it was defective, but there were places in the ceiling where the wiring had been illegally spliced before and I presume that the wire became overheated and it traveled back from the television right into the closet, where all of the wires were, and those wires started burning, and they burnt, and a fuse was found to be blown in the closet out in the hall, where there was a small fuse box. One of the fuse stats

was blown and that would show there had been a fire,
because that is all that would blow a fuse like that, is a
fire.

Q. You think if there [were] enough heat being generated
to start a fire it would have blown the fuse. That is what
they are for, I understand.

A. Yes, they are, but if it's a slow rise in heat. For a fuse
to blow, it has to be a rapid, sudden thing, but a slow
rise in the heat, the fuse would hold it for quite a while
until something in the closet ignited. The closet had a
shelf on it and according to Ms. Montandon there had
been a fluorescent light in there that did not work, and
there is a similar closet in the other room, the other bedroom, and I have a picture of that, if you'd like to see
it, Doctor.

Q. All right.

A. I checked everything, I mean as you know I have
been in this business for quite a while, and I was so
concerned that I called you up and told you about that,
if you remember.

Q. Right. I do.

A. Because the position of the body for one thing, Doctor—

Q. Let me interrupt. What you are showing is—

A. This is the other closet, Doctor.

Q. The other closet with the wire coiled up to demonstrate?

A. No.

Q. What does this demonstrate for us?

A. It just shows the shelf. There was a shelf in the main
bedroom, similar to that in the closet, but it wasn't
quite as big a closet.

Q. But this doesn't demonstrate anything in relation to
why a fire would start?

A. No. I am just showing you the other closet in the other
room.

Q. May we keep this? We will see it comes back to you.

I will leave this for the jurors.

A. Yes.

Q. All right. Anything else you would add before I ask a few questions?

A. No. Go ahead.

Q. In this case, the carbon monoxide level in the blood was 1.5 percent, which is nothing. We get two or three times that from a cigarette.

A. I was very amazed when I called up and found that out from Mr. Scannell.

Q. That is why we are still amazed.

To the jurors, whenever there is a fire of the type described here and the person is alive while the fire is in progress, they will wind up with high levels of carbon monoxide, since that is always produced in fire, and the level in a case might be 30, 40, 60 percent saturation. This is less carbon monoxide than you get from standing on a street corner from traffic fumes, so this suggests to us that at the time of the fire the person was dead.

Secondly, examining the body, even though extensively burned about the lower extremities, the internal organs were all in good order, and we find no way to account for why this person would be dead when the fire started.

The sleeping pills that are said to have been taken, that sometimes prevent a person from responding to the smoke, really don't enter here because the level is so small in the body that she may not even have taken a sleeping pill that night. That could be a little bit left from the day before.

There was only a trace of secobarbital.

Inspector, you suggest the most unbelievable coincidence, that this would be an electrical fire occurring by chance after somebody is dead for no apparent reason.

A. Well . . .

Q. You see what I am saying?

A. I see what you mean.

Q. This raises [a] question in my mind.

A. I don't know whether— Well, that is one of the reasons why I called you, Doctor. I have seen so many bodies, I mean after 21 years in here I have seen so many bodies burned at fires, and this one just didn't strike me right for the simple reason [of] the position of the body. She was face down on the bed. Well, that doesn't mean anything, but it looked like her legs were over the end of the bed, as if maybe she had gotten up and then just fallen back on the bed. That is the thing that I . . .

Q. This is true. She may have, but why she collapsed, we can't say.

The whole thing is unusual, and I didn't expect we'd come up with an answer, but I wanted to air it and let everyone have their say and see where the difficulty lies.

A. In regard to anybody else being in the place, definitely, in my opinion, no. The front door had a sliding bolt on it, which was a very big bolt, and it took the Fire Department quite awhile to break in that door to get in.

Q. No other entrance?

A. No other entrance. I mean there was a back door that was locked, that was opened by the Fire Department.

Q. Deadbolt?

A. No. One of those round knobs and you screw it. You turn it in and it goes into the other part of the door. It's a bolt.

Q. It's a bolt?

A. Yes.

Q. Nothing you could slam shut and leave?

A. No.

Q. So the apartment was indeed secure?

A. (Nodding affirmatively.)

Nobody could have been in there and gone out.

Q. My first concern was that someone might have left a cigarette or she in fact might have been smoking, but we learn she was not a smoker.

A. Definitely not a cigarette, Doctor.

Q. She would have had no callers who would have left a cigarette?

A. Definitely not.

Q. Well, I must confess for the jurors and whoever is listening that we cannot give a suitable explanation. We can only tell you we made a very determined effort to solve the case, as to what caused the death and so on, and we simply cannot with our best effort.

You apparently are unable to tell us how it is she came to be in this position?

A. That is the only thing that bothers me.

Q. You are indeed satisfied it was an electrical fire?

A. Definitely, Doctor. I had the electrical inspector up there with me several days after.

Q. Was he of the same opinion?

A. He was of the same opinion, yes.

THE CORONER: All right. That is all I ask. Thank you.

[Witness excused.]

THE CORONER: Inspector Toschi.

INSPECTOR DAVID TOSCHI,

having been duly sworn, testified as follows:

THE CORONER:

Q. Inspector Toschi, you investigated this matter for the Homicide Detail in response to our request?

A. Yes, Doctor.

Q. And the jurors should understand this is because of the irregularities in the case and not because we have any immediate suspicion, but we felt it would be wise to let the Homicide Detail know of this case and let them study it.

Inspector, you did carry out an extensive investigation along with Inspector Lucas?

A. I did, Doctor.

Q. Or at least paralleling his in part?

A. Yes, sir.

Q. In essence, do you find the same things he had related, apart from his official opinion?

A. Everything that has been said today from all the witnesses, including Inspector Lucas, who was at the scene, is consistent with information that I have. I have contacted all these people, spoken to them, gone into background on the deceased, spoken several times with Inspector Lucas. I can find no one who can say that Mary Ward smoked. I have spoken to quite a few people that have known her for several years. She did not smoke. She was a moderate drinker.

According to Mrs. Kendall, as she stated, Mrs. Ward was home for the night, that Friday night, June the 20th. Her son had gone out to spend the night with friends in the area. She did take sleeping pills. There is evidence of it in your autopsy. However, I did talk to Dr. John Gamble, who has known her for about 12 years, and he said that he has prescribed only nembutal for her these last few years, and he couldn't understand why there was seconal, but it's very possible she had gone to another doctor to obtain this.

THE CORONER: Let me explain to the jury that we are talking about two types of sleeping pills, and this doctor didn't prescribe the particular type that we found, but you can get them from friends or another doctor. There is no problem here.

Q. Go ahead.

A. Her last prescription for the nembutal was on April 17th of this year and apparently she had asked for some more nembutal in May, but it was turned down by one of his associates, a Dr. Smith, because they didn't want her to have too many over such a close period of time.

According to Dr. Gamble, she was in good health. He hadn't seen her for several months. She was a very hypertensive person.

Q. Hypertensive?

A. She was something—

Q. High blood pressure?

A. Yes.

Q. She had high blood pressure?

A. No. No.

Q. "Hypertonic"? She was keyed up?

A. Yes. She was a very nervous type person. But as far as he knew, her health was good and he couldn't give any specific reason as to what might have been wrong with her recently.

We know she had encephalitis approximately 12 years ago and occasionally did get headaches from this and as a result of this took sleeping pills when she felt she would probably have a bad night.

Lately I learned from the family and friends that she was in the habit of taking a small glass of wine before retiring to calm her down.

Now, as Inspector Lucas says, the apartment was quite secure that evening. The front door and back door. She apparently was alone. "Mrs. Walker" said that she thought she heard only the one set of footsteps, which was about 9:30 or so.

At this time I don't find any evidence of any criminality coming out of that apartment, Doctor.

Q. All right. Then you are entirely satisfied there is no crime in relation to this death?

A. I am, sir, at this time. Yes, sir.

THE CORONER: Very well. That is all we would ask you to establish. You may step down.

THE WITNESS: Thank you, Doctor.

[Witness excused.]

THE CORONER: Are there any questions from the jurors? Any comments?

(No response.)

THE CORONER: If not, I would point out that the cause of death in this case must remain undetermined. We have made an exhaustive study to find something which would account for the death. We cannot relate it to the encephalitis, either. This doesn't appear to be the cause of death.

We did find extensive burns of the body. The carbon monoxide in the blood is not consistent with one being alive in the presence of a fire. The amount of sleeping medicine in the body was infinitesimal and there was none in the stomach to suggest she had recently taken a dose.

The blood alcohol level was .04 percent, which in the average person is consistent with having had one drink. It can only remain for you to conclude, as we cannot account as to the cause of death properly or the circumstances of the death, you could not say she died as a consequence of the faulty wiring because we don't know why she died, and it would appear she was dead already when the fire occurred.

While we leave the case in doubt, I felt obliged to hold the hearing. We wanted to make a permanent record under oath and see what others might offer, and sometimes we learn things in the course of the inquest we don't learn otherwise.

Is there anyone who would like to make comment in this case?

If not, we thank you for coming and this is as far as we can go in this matter.

Thank you again.

[Testimony closed.]

IN THE CORONER'S COURT OF THE STATE OF CALIFORNIA IN AND FOR THE CITY AND COUNTY OF SAN FRANCISCO HENRY W. TURKEL, M.D., CORONER CORONERS INQUEST UPON THE BODY OF Jane Doe #23, identified as MARY LOUISE WARD No. [. . .] VERDICT OF THE JURY

INQUISITION taken at the above entitled court on August 21, 1969, before said Coroner and 7 qualified jurors who, being duly summoned and sworn to inquire who said deceased person was, and when, where and by what means said person came to his or her death, and into the circumstances attending said death, do say upon their oaths aforesaid that the said deceased was the person above named, and do further say:

That the said Jane Doe #23, identified as MARY LOUISE WARD, female, white, widowed, age: 47 years; residence: [. . .] Webster St., San Francisco, California; nativity: Seattle, Washington; occupation: secretary; came to her death on June 21, 1969 at 2:57 a.m. at [. . .] Lombard St., [. . .] San Francisco, California. CAUSE OF DEATH: Undetermined.

Other findings: Extensive burns of body. 1.5% saturation of carbon monoxide in the blood. Trace of secobarbital in liver. Alcohol blood level: 0.04%.

AND WE FURTHER FIND: We, the jury, are unable to determine the cause or actual circumstance of death of Mary Louise Ward.

IN WITNESS WHEREOF, the said Coroner and the Jurors aforesaid have to this Inquisition set their hands and seals on the dates thereof.

EARL E. PRIGMORE	Foreman, (L.S.)	
ARDSON SHEGOIAN	(L.S.)	(L.S.)
JOHN B. PEARCE	(L.S.)	(L.S.)
SYLVIA M. SANCHEZ	(L.S.)	(L.S.)
ARLENE SPLINTER	(L.S.)	(L.S.)
BONNIE M. PORTER	(L.S.)	(L.S.)
JUDITH A. BOYD	(L.S.)	(L.S.)
HENRY W. TURKEL, M.D.	Coroner, (L.S.)	

CITY AND COUNTY OF SAN FRANCISCO STATE OF CALIFORNIA S.S.: REPORTER'S CERTIFICATE INQUEST UPON THE BODY OF: JANE DOE #23 IDENTIFIED AS MARY LOUISE WARD REGISTER NO. [. . .]

I hereby certify that I am the duly appointed qualified and acting Phonographic Reporter of the Coroner's Court of the City and County of San Francisco, and that the testimony in the matter of the aforementioned inquest was taken down by me in shorthand, and that the foregoing is a full, true and complete transcript of my shorthand notes taken at said inquest, and a full, true and complete record of the testimony taken therein.

FREDRIC R. TOOKER
CERTIFIED SHORTHAND REPORTER

DECLARATION OF JEAN EILEEN ROSE

I, JEAN EILEEN ROSE, am the eldest child of Mary Louise Ward. I was first informed of my mother's death at approximately 5:00 a.m. the morning of June 21, 1969 by two members of the San Francisco Coroner's Office.

Following investigations by the Homicide Bureau of the Police Department, a Coroner's Inquest was held to establish the exact cause of death. At the inquest, which was held in front of a jury, various witnesses were called to testify. I had gone thinking it was a mere formality and was quite taken back by the extensive nature of the proceedings. I had been told by the person who served the Subpoena on me that hearings such as this were held when there is a question as to the precise cause of death.

Among the witnesses called were Kelly Kendall and Pat Montandon who were asked about my mother's mood and condition the last time they had seen her. The questions seemed strange to me since I had assumed that my mother was asphyxiated in the fire. The line of questioning seemed to indicate that the Coroner's Office had serious doubts as to the cause of death. However, the answers provided no clues that there was any wrongdoing. When they examined the lady who lived in the downstairs apartment, they inquired into any unexplained noises she may have heard that night or any signs of struggle. Her responses were negative. My mother's personal physician testified as to her good health up to the date of the accident.

The inquest concluded with the Coroner's statements that the autopsy report showed that she had taken one sleeping pill and a glass of wine. Her heart showed no signs of trauma or cardiac arrest. Most importantly, her lungs had a minimal amount of carbon monoxide, less than that which one gets from smoking one cigarette. Had she died as a result of the fire her lungs should have contained 80% carbon monoxide.

The Coroner concluded by saying that this is one of the strangest cases he had ever seen. He shook his head in frustration and said nothing points to the cause of her death. It's a total mystery.

I hereby declare that the foregoing is true and correct to the best of knowledge and belief.

DATED: January 23, 1974

Jean Eileen Rose
JEAN EILEEN ROSE

STATE OF CALIFORNIA,

(SEAL)

County of SAN MATEO]ss

On this 23rd day of January, 1974, before me, SHIRLEY BUCHIGNANI, a Notary Public State of California, duly commissioned and sworn, personally appeared JEAN EILEEN ROSE, known to me to be the person whose name is subscribed to the within instrument, and acknowledged to me and in my presence that she subscribed the same.

IN WITNESS WHEREOF I have hereunto set my hand and affixed my official seal in the City of San Mateo County of San Mateo the day and year in this certificate first above written.

(signed)
Shirley Buchignani
Notary Public, State of California

Letter from Homicide Inspector David Toschi
POLICE DEPARTMENT
City and County of San Francisco Hall of Justice 850
Bryant Street San Francisco, California 94103

Office of the CHIEF OF POLICE

31 May 1974 In reply, please refer to our file: [...]

Ms. Pat Montandon
[...]
San Francisco, California
Dear Ms. Montandon:

As per our telephone conversation of May 30, 1974 regarding the fire death of Mary Louise Ward on June 21, 1969, following is some information you requested which may be of some help to you in your book.

Initially the San Francisco Fire Department Arson Squad investigated the case; however, Coroner Henry Turkel requested that a Homicide Investigator look into the matter for more detailed investigation, which is how I came into the picture.

After discussing the details with Dr. Turkel he stated that he would inquest the death, and requested that I locate and question any and all persons that might have pertinent information.

I began my investigation at the scene with Arson Squad Investigators so that I could personally view the room where Miss Ward expired.

On another occasion I returned to the building and the landlord let me gain entry so that I could pursue my investigation further.

I did what I thought was an extensive background on the deceased, her habits, her friends, and her family. I spoke to people who were present when the fire broke out and canvassed the area for any possible witnesses.

Throughout the investigation and up to the inquest I was in close contact with the then Coroner, Dr. Henry Turkel, regarding my findings.

This proved to be one of the most interesting and challenging cases in my seven years as a member of the Homicide Detail. After completing my work on the case and discussing it in detail with the Coroner, I felt in my mind that there was no known evidence of criminality.

Hoping this information will be of some assistance, and wishing you much success on your book, I am

Sincerely yours,
(signed)
DAVID R. TOSCHI
Inspector of Police
Homicide Detail

4498 Crestwood Circle
Concord, CA
March 17, 1975

Ms. Pat Montandon
[. . .]
San Francisco, CA
Dear Pat:

I distinctly remember the fire which gutted your home in June 1969, in which Mrs. Ward died.

There was something so unusual about it all, that after many hours of investigation, we were unable to ascertain why the victim could not or did not get out of the bed, and I asked the coroner to make an extensive investigation as to the cause of death.

I personally went back to that apartment on my own several times to try to solve the mystery there. In my 22 years as a member of the Fire Department, I have had lots of experiences of death by fire. There was something about this one that just wasn't right. I do hope that you are able to get to the bottom of the matter.

Sincerely,
(signed)
George Lucas
Inspector George Lucas, Retired
San Francisco Fire Department

Chapter 15
Letter from Allan Carr

582 Market Street
San Francisco, California
June 18th, 1974

Dear Pat,

I have a very clear recollection of accompanying you to the apartment where you used to live on the "crooked street" in the sixties, and particularly the moment when we both noticed a smell of acrid smoke in the living room. Afterwards, as we were taking leave of the then tenant's wife, I smelled it again in the foyer, and thought you had not noticed, until I mentioned it to you as you got into your car, and found you had had the same reaction. At both times it was quite strong and unmistakable, although our hostess apparently did not notice it at all. It was a most peculiar experience.

I also went along later, as you know, when Gerri Patton and Nick Nocerino conducted their psychic investigation at the apartment, and saw and heard all they did. It was all very business-like, and undramatic. The photographic prints they produced, which you showed me, were particularly interesting, especially the one of a woman bending over a drawer in the bedroom, as there was no one at all like the figure at the time the pictures were taken who could have posed for it.

There certainly seems to be something mysterious about the house. I hope you will be able to discover what it is.

Kindest regards,
(signed)
Allan Carr

Chapter 16
Newspaper Article Concerning Gerri Patton
One can't be skeptical about Gerri

Sunday Scene
S.F. Sunday Examiner
& Chronicle
September 22, 1974

By Bea Pixa

WHEN PSYCHIC Gerri Patton says, shortly after you've met her for the first time, "You are innovative, sensitive and creative," it's hard not to stifle a yawn and easy to play the skeptic.

But when she tunes in on your "vibrations," mentions the name of a friend, the place he has just spent a vacation, goes on to state diseases that run in your family and follows up with at least a dozen other personal remarks that are right on target, skepticism wanes.

Then, when she turns to your associate and tells him what brand of car he drives at home, that he sustained bad knee injuries, and proceeds to draw an accurate personality picture with specific details (such as the number of his college football jersey), another skeptic is won over.

(At one point in the reading, she lets out a whoop and bellows, "Now this is the damnedest thing! What's this about a plate of spaghetti? A huge plate—lots of it!" The photographer ponders, then chuckles as he recalls that a few days before he was assigned to photograph a 500-pound pan of lasagne at a convention. He decided she deserves full points, despite the mixup in pasta.)

Wed to an industrial engineer who uncomplainingly provides the money for his wife's unusual avocation, Mrs. Patton lives comfortably, and not at all spookily in a modern and probably expensive condominium. She is a slim, youngish 53, daughter of a concert pianist mother, and graduate of the University of Utah. Before deciding to concentrate on psychic research, seven years ago, she sang professionally as a lyric soprano. The show-biz style lingers on.

Irrepressibly, Carol Burnettishly zany, she mugs, makes charming moues, strikes poses that are all arms and legs, and slips into different accents as the telling of a tale demands them. Between rattling on about life, people and esoterica, she also manages to toss in her recipes for a special salad dressing and instructions on how to grow alfalfa sprouts at home.

Mrs. Patton considers herself on the side of science. She does not do private readings, and accepts money only for her lectures, which are often given before the scientific community.

Much of her research involves checking the skills of other psychics, "sleuthing around to see if they're in a charlatan's game," with a tape recorder concealed in her purse and a pseudonym taking care of her identification. Over the years, she has accumulated thousands of tapes.

Dr. Ken L. Evensen, ex-clinical director of research for Cutter Laboratories, now leader of inner growth workshops, describes her as "one of the few psychics in the area who is quite consciously concerned with what she's doing, rather than trying to make a buck." He knows personally of one woman whose depression was traced back to specifically identified childhood traumas with Mrs. Patton's assistance.

A Bay Area professor of psychology, who asked to remain anonymous, has had Mrs. Patton address some of his classes. "She's definitely on the level and she keeps wonderful records. I have seen her do some diagnoses on people that she'd never met before which were quite accurate. She's quite good at identifying predominant diseases in people she has just met. I have seen her identify the major disease problems in families, without knowing any of the people involved."

Mrs. Patton describes her gift as clairvoyance. To get the "messages" she may hold something metal belonging to her subject—a watch, a ring, a camera—or else she combines psychic vision with what she calls "analytical palmistry."

"I wasn't really aware till I was in my 20s that I was psychic," she says, adding coquettishly, "I always thought I was just a brilliant, intuitive woman."

To her, it's all a matter of "energy input and output," something anyone can develop. For instance, she maintains anybody can see his own aura—a halo of light energy said to surround the body. "Just stand in front of a plate glass mirror in a darkened room. After you try it a few times, when your eyes get used to the dark, you'll see your own energy fields."

Ultimately, she hopes to get to the how-and-why of phenomena. One of the mistakes most researchers make, she says, "is that they put a psychic in a laboratory and ask him to perform. A psychic is like a ball player. They're not 'on' all the time. He should be in his natural habitat. Some, for example, work well near water."

She prizes her status as a researcher. "Don't use the word magic around me," she chides. For neophytes interested in the subject she counsels, "Do a little study about it beforehand. Then you can be the judge of whether a reading is good or not."

Parapsychology, she notes, is a burgeoning department on many campuses, and she suggests the university or college setting as a reputable place to begin.

She is unable to do readings for herself, she says, and only recently got around to doing one for her husband.

"After living with him over 30 years," she marvels, "I found I didn't really know him at all."

Chapter 17
Newspaper Account of the Lawsuit

Pat Montandon Wins $151,000 in Libel Suit

Former TV personality Pat Montandon won a $151,000 libel suit yesterday against TV Guide on grounds it had insinuated four years ago that she had been a call girl.

Miss Montandon was tearful but obviously overjoyed when a jury of seven men and five women returned the verdict after a full day of deliberation.

The first trial of her libel suit ended in a hung jury last December. She was represented both times by Attorney Charles Morgan.

"Naturally I'm very pleased," she said. "Mr. Morgan did an outstanding job. We won because we had all the evidence."

Her husband, Alfred Wilsey, took her arm and said, "Honey, let's go home and get back to living."

Yesterday's jury awarded the 42-year-old Miss Montandon $150,000 in damages. She had accused the magazine of blighting her KGO television career. She also won $1000 in punitive damages.

The sole defendant in this trial was TV Guide, which in 1968 ran a listing of her guest shot on the Pat Michaels Show on Channel 2 which said:

"From Party-Girl to Call-Girl. Scheduled guest: TV personality Pat Montandon and author of 'How to Be a Party Girl.' "

Attorney James Brosnahan, representing TV Guide, said he would appeal the verdict.

San Francisco *Chronicle* 1972